Existential Hope

To my parents
Susanne and Andrew
Who gave me this precious life

And to my friends
Who danced it out of me

Existential Hope

Facing Our Future When the Signs Look Bad

SJ Beard

polity

First published in 2025 by Polity Press Ltd.

Polity Press Ltd.
65 Bridge Street
Cambridge CB2 1UR, UK

Polity Press Ltd.
111 River Street
Hoboken, NJ 07030, USA

ISBN-13: 978-1-5095-6304-3

A catalogue record for this book is available from the British Library.

Library of Congress Control Number: 2025932169

Typeset in 11.5 on 14 Adobe Garamond
by Fakenham Prepress Solutions, Fakenham, Norfolk NR21 8NL
Printed and bound in Great Britain by CPI Group (UK) Ltd, Croydon

For further information on Polity, visit our website:
politybooks.com

Contents

A note on notes.*

*I grew up reading Terry Pratchett. Indeed, given the significant challenges I faced as a blind dyslexic person learning how to read, I am not sure how I would have ever found the motivation to become a truly proficient reader without his fierce and unrelenting humour. Pratchett taught me that notes were often the very best part of a book, adding tangential remarks that made you see the text in new and exciting ways. Then, when I started doing more serious reading, I found that they were often used quite differently, and an exciting-looking * would merely lead to a dry citation I couldn't even make sense of at first. Needless to say, I eventually reached a point in my academic development where these citations became just as exciting and insightful as Pratchett's footnotes, if I took the trouble to follow them up. Nevertheless, I would rather spare my reader such disappointments. So, in this book I will include two types of note. First, those marked with an asterisk, like this one, which can be found in the Notes section at the very end of the book, listed by page number and the last few words leading up to the asterisk. These try to say things or make suggestions for further reading that I hope could be at least as accessible as this book. Second, those marked with a superscript numeral appear in the References section and contain academic citations.

Introduction: Beyond Risk and Anxiety

> There once was a man who encountered a tiger. He fled, the tiger after him. Coming to a precipice, he caught hold of the root of a wild vine and swung himself down over the edge. The tiger sniffed at him from above. Trembling, the man looked down to where, far below, another tiger was waiting to eat him. Only the vine sustained him. Two mice, one white and one black, started to gnaw away at the vine. The man saw a luscious strawberry near him. Grasping the vine with one hand, he plucked the strawberry with the other. How sweet it tasted![1]

This little parable, associated with the Japanese Zen tradition, captures something important about the human condition. According to a modern Buddhist interpretation,* we are, since birth, driven forward by our desires and needs and our fear of not getting them met, until we notice that ahead of us lies an inescapable death. Tigers above, tigers below, we desperately cling on to anything we think might preserve us, but know that inevitably this will not last long. However, the universe does offer us one alternative to this duality of fears. To face each moment exactly as it is, take ourselves just as we are, and accept it all without judgement. An opportunity of genuine sweetness to free ourselves from the suffering of life.[2]

Right now, however, this parable reminds me of the extinction event taking place in my kitchen. A short while ago, I mixed together water, salt, sugar, oil, flour, and a little dried yeast and put it in my breadmaker. The delicious smell of baking tells me that the breadmaker's warmth has reactivated the yeast, which is currently feasting on some of the sugars in the dough and producing carbon dioxide, which causes it to rise into a light fluffy loaf. However, as the number of yeast organisms quickly grows, they will soon run into a problem. When the sugars run out and the carbon dioxide levels increase, the yeast will struggle and die. Victims of their own success.

It would be easy to apply the parable of the tiger and the strawberry to this yeast. Driven by its need to feed and reproduce, the yeast runs quickly over a cliff and gets caught by the tigers of famine and poison. Perhaps when we tell this story we feel that the yeast is being industrious and helpful and regret its demise, or perhaps we see it as greedy and profligate. However, these are human judgements and do not really belong in the yeast's story. Yeasts are not aware of their fate and they do not entertain a desire to avoid it. Nor do yeasts appreciate their situation, or take joy in the bread they are making.

However, humans can and will do both these things. Right now, we are in a real mess. My breadmaker is not merely the cause of a very local extinction event, but a symptom of a much larger one. In its own small way, it speaks directly to my species' desire to reshape and repurpose life on our planet, to consume and to own far more than we need, and to automate basic human tasks and activities. These desires are another kind of tiger, pushing humanity, as a whole, to a point of real danger.

However, in this respect we are really just like bigger versions of yeast. What differentiates us is that we also have an understanding of this crisis and a belief that we may have the power to avert it. That is a truly exceptional situation. The dinosaurs never knew anything about the asteroid that wiped them out and, even if they had, they would not have been able to formulate a planetary defence strategy to save themselves. We are the first species in the history of our planet to have this power; it's not impossible that we are the first in our universe.

This power may yet turn out to be a wild vine, a hubristic belief that we can transcend the inevitable rise and fall of species that will only lead us into making things worse. Yet, it could be a genuine strawberry. A realization that the underlying reality of our existential predicament points the way to a deeper fulfilment of our human potential. That's the possibility I want to explore.

Existential risk and anxiety

Existential is not an inherently scary word; it just means 'relating to existence'. Yet, over the last two centuries, it has come to describe two of the most complex and off-putting subjects of human enquiry. In my experience, introducing the term existential into conversations is seriously off putting. Yet, it seems increasingly hard to avoid.

The first existential problem is Existential Risk, the risk that human existence, as a species, may be coming to an end.* Historically, this has generally been thought to be impossible; the world might end but humanity will surely either survive, if only in heaven, or remerge at some point in the future. Perhaps the first popular presentation of the idea that humanity could just go extinct, in a secular and naturalistic context, was in Mary Shelley's 1826 novel *The Last Man*,[3] in which she imagines a global catastrophe at the end of the twenty-first century, combining a great plague and series of extreme weather events (including heatwaves, floods, and storms), that gradually wipe out every human but one, who is left to roam an empty world. More recently, researchers have discovered many possible pathways to such a global catastrophe, and this risk has moved from the realm of speculative fiction to the forefront of scientific research and global policy.

Our second problem is Existential Anxiety. First developed by the Danish philosopher Søren Kierkegaard in his 1844 treatise *The Concept of Anxiety*,[4] this relates to the unnerving feeling many people have from the state of existing as a human being, with apparent freedom to make their own decisions. While this freedom can be exhilarating, but it is also unsettling. As an example, Kierkegaard describes the disturbing realization many of us have when standing at the edge of a cliff, that there is nothing to stop us from jumping off except our continuing to choose not to do so. To make matters worse, it is often hard to determine the right thing to do, or to do what we believe is right even once we have worked that out. The consequences of our actions cannot be known in advance and yet, regardless of our intentions, we must face these consequences whatever they may be. While we long for an ultimate source of meaning or purpose to guide us, many feel that either there is no such metaphysical answer to the riddle of our lives or that, if there is, then we will never fully understand it.* This does not mean we are absolutely alone. We can and do connect with other people and things that bring us reassurance in life. However, every one of these is just as existentially precarious as we are, and trusting too heavily in them only serves to obscure our authentic freedom. So, ultimately, there is nothing for us to fall back on but ourselves.

Both these ideas rocketed into widespread consciousness in the aftermath of the Second World War, when people all over the world were forced to come to terms with both humanity's incredible moral capacity to do terrible things and our accelerating technological capacity to cause death and destruction on a global scale. These ideas speak to the profound social, cultural, technological, and environmental challenges of our age, yet they are quite different in origin and meaning. People, like me, who work on dealing with one of these problems can end up spending a lot of time explaining the difference between them. However, I have started thinking that this may be a mistake.

Existential hope

The differences between existential anxiety and existential risk become blurry when we ask ourselves about their opposite, about what kinds of lives and futures we actually want – in short, about Existential Hope. To be sure, existential hope is a term that has been used in many ways: to assert our ability to express our authentic nature beyond culture and context,[5] our capacity to find meaning and purpose in even the bleakest of situations,[6] and our potential to make our collective futures substantially better.[7] It is my contention that these various uses of the term end up describing the same thing.

As an existential risk researcher, I do not think that this hope is to be found in technocratic solutions to scientific or political problems, although both technological and social innovation are certainly needed. Solutions to the pressing global challenges that threaten our species, from climate change to transformative AI, will not simply come fully formed from clever people in elite positions of authority working out what everybody else ought to do. A complex system of 8,200,000,000 humans simply does not work like that!

Achieving existential security and sustainability for our species requires systemic solutions that are adaptable and long-lasting and so must involve all of us. Even if we manage to halt climate change and safely navigate the development of beneficial AI, I believe the ultimate causes of our problems lie far deeper in the human condition.

Homo sapiens emerged perhaps 300,000 years ago. The average mammalian species can expect to last for ten times as long.[8] Yet, we have been living with industrial technologies, secular philosophies, massive populations, and globe-spanning institutions for only around 300 years; 0.1 per cent of our history. It is no wonder that we feel lost and confused and struggle not to harm ourselves with these new and powerful playthings. We still have a lot of growing up to do, a lot of learning about ourselves and our environment, understanding our capabilities and weaknesses, establishing sensible boundaries, and making wise choices.

I believe in the possibility of existential hope; that there are things human beings can do now that, collectively, will move us towards safe, joyous, and inclusive futures, and I believe that finding our place in this collective project is precisely the kind of authentic expression that can help us come to terms with our place in this beautiful and dangerous universe.

However, I sometimes feel that when I talk about hope I mean something slightly different from many other people. Emily Dickinson once wrote a poem about hope as a 'thing with feathers' that always keeps singing and never asks even a crumb from us in return.[9] Perhaps that kind of hope does exist. However, when I talk about existential hope, I mean more than just feeling good about ourselves and our futures. When I say that I believe in hope, I do not mean that I think everything will necessarily be OK in the end. In my experience, one can be almost certain that something will go well and yet terrified that it might not. Similarly, one can be up against immense odds and yet motivated by the hope that things just might work out.

A formative experience behind this thinking occurred when I was aged eleven and my house tutor, Mr Young, told us about a book he was reading, in which the author explained that human beings do not simply run away from things because they are afraid; we are also afraid *because* we run away. In my experience, this is spot on, and I think the same is true about hope. Hope is born inside us, when we decide not to turn away from our problems but begin taking ownership of them and how we can respond to them. We do not feel hope because we think things are going to work out. Rather it is only when we really face up to our problems and try to resolve them that we find hope, or at least existential hope. In this sense, my understanding of hope is similar to Joanna Macy's in her book *Active Hope*[10] and Rebecca Solnit's in her book *Hope in the Dark*,[11] although this book is not like either of those.

In this book, I want to take you on a journey to where and how I find my existential hope. In that sense, it feels like a very personal book, not just to myself but to myself right now, and the discoveries and insights that have led me to this point. For me, now, existential hope has some important qualities:

1. It is engaged and non-judgemental: resisting the urge to externalize risk, while not rushing to judge humans as inherently bad or deserving of punishment.
2. It is counter-utopian: seeking to understand how we got where we are and what that tells us about where we are going, and focusing on how we can make our futures better without postulating some perfect 'end goal' for humanity.
3. It is communal: understanding that behind talk about 'technologies', 'institutions', and 'systems' there are always real human beings working together to achieve shared goals.
4. It is reasonably demanding: requiring substantial commitments from us to maintain it, while still allowing that we are imperfect and limited in our capacities and abilities.

The four sections of this book will each explore one of these themes, while building up towards a fuller understanding of the many difficult problems facing humanity. I understand that for many people the idea of having hope in our future, or hope in humanity, can sound unrealistic or even unfair. There is a lot of pain and injustice in the world. I do not think that existential hope is something we instinctively feel, and it doesn't say anything about you if it isn't something to which you can relate. However, hope is something we can all cultivate if we face our existential predicament with genuine courage (to acknowledge these problems), curiosity (to understand them) and compassion (to work on solving them together).

Arthur – Is that all it's got to say? One word? 'Harmless?' What the hell's that supposed to mean?
Ford – Well, there are a hundred billion stars in the galaxy and only a limited amount of space in the book. And no one knew much about the Earth of course.
Arthur – Well, I hope you've managed to rectify that a little?
Ford – Yes, I transmitted a new entry off to the editor. He had to trim it a bit but it's still an improvement.
Arthur – What does it say now?
Ford – 'Mostly harmless.'

Douglas Adams, *The Hitchhiker's Guide to the Galaxy, Fit the First* (1978).[12]

PART I

The Ends of the World

Once upon a time, most people knew how the world would end. Sure, they might disagree with one another on the exact details, but all things come to an end and why should our world be any different? To people living in an uncertain, and often cruel, world, speculating about its eventual destruction has been a source of both horror and comfort . So, it is only natural that we have told so many stories about it.

In Hinduism there is the prophesy that the great god Vishnu will appear in his tenth, and final, incarnation, Kalki, riding a white horse and wielding a flaming sword. He will bring to a close the Kali Yuga, the Great Age in which we live, and which is marked by misery and unrighteousness. In doing so, however, the cosmic cycle will return to Satya Yuga, the first and most virtuous age.[13]

For the Aztecs, the world had already been destroyed and recreated four times, under the protection of five different suns. According to this story, the most recent apocalypse, caused by a world spanning flood, was supposed to be final, but Quetzalcoatl was unwilling to accept the destruction of his beloved humans, so he stole back our bones from the underworld to repopulate the Earth. However, our current age is vulnerable, because our sun Tezcatlipoca must share the sky with many stars who are jealous of his light and wage war on him every night. The Aztecs believed they had to offer human sacrifices to ensure he prevailed each dawn; but, should these cease, then our sun will go dark and the world will be destroyed by earthquakes.[14]

For the ancient Zoroastrian religion of Persia, the end of the world would be marked by a great battle between good and evil, which would end with the final triumph of Ahura Mazda, the god of the sky, over his adversary Angra Mainyu, leading to the final renovation of the universe. This myth had a profound effect on subsequent religious thinking in the area, including that of Judaism, Christianity, and Islam.[15]

These are but a few of the many stories people have told about the end of the world. They clearly have many differences, but they also have some important similarities. Firstly, in all these stories the end is never really understood to be The End. Just as night follows day, day also follows night, and we instinctively believe that there will be a 'time after' in which some version of humanity might continue, in an eternal heaven or a rejuvenated Earth. Secondly, it is not humanity that brings about its destruction but an external force, usually either God or a god, who decides to end things. However, thirdly, even though we lack the power to bring about the end of the world, these stories often conclude that we deserve it. In cultures all over the world, the end is a result of humanity's flaws, and only through this final act of destruction can we be redeemed. Ultimately, stories about the end of the world exist as morality tales that help people relate their own ethical situation in a grand cosmic narrative, with the promise that if we get things right then either the world will not end in our times, or at least that we will be among the favoured ones when it does.

People working on existential risk often get told that we are simply providing a new genre of apocalyptic visions to make up for the fact that some people no longer believe these older ones. However, in these core respects, I think the kinds of stories we have to tell are very different from these ancient myths. We really are talking about the possibility of a final end for the human species, in which none will be favoured and there will be no coming back. The reality is that human beings really are causing most of the things that could lead to our extinction, but the reality is also that there is no cosmic narrative making us deserve that fate.

1

Scanning the Trees

Do you ever find yourself worrying about the worst things that could happen? If so, it's not your fault and you are not alone. Our brains feature a Default Mode Network that is activated whenever we don't have much else to focus on. This web of tightly connected neurones, across the medial prefrontal cortex, posterior cingulate cortex and angular gyrus, is responsible for many of the unbidden thoughts that come to us in such times. It is there to help us make use of our brains when they would otherwise be underoccupied, by guiding us to reflect on our goals, review our relationships, and scan our environment for possible threats, like tigers lurking in the trees. In our ancestral environment, humans used this part of our brains less often, because we had so much to keep us occupied, and, when we did, it helped us take action to stay safe, develop ourselves, and strengthen our relationships. However, in our present environment we are often understimulated, meaning it engages more often, but we also lack clear opportunities to improve our situation. This is why our minds gravitate chronically towards personal inadequacies and everything that could possibly go wrong.*

Right now, there is a lot that could go wrong. In one hundred years' time there might be no humans still alive. Or it could be that while some of us survive we do so in conditions of squalor, conflict, and isolation, which many reading this book would struggle to imagine. Neither of these outcomes is guaranteed, far from it, but they are certainly possible.

I work in the emerging field of Existential Risk Studies; I spend my days thinking about these possibilities and how to avoid them. It would be nice to say, 'I spend my days thinking about this, so you don't have to.' However, I don't think that would be very helpful. For one thing, my thoughts may not be the right ones. For another, I certainly wouldn't want to say that I could do this by myself. And, for a third; well, I suspect a lot of you may be thinking about these possibilities anyway. So, I would rather say 'I spend my days thinking about these possibilities so that, when you do so, your thoughts might go beyond worry and doubt and be constructive and hopeful.' That is why I am writing this book.

A question that I am often asked is 'what should I be most afraid of?' And my answer is always the same. I don't want you to be afraid of anything, so in the pages that follow I will do my best to talk honestly and candidly about humanity's existential predicament with as little alarmism and as few triggers as I can. I don't want you to be afraid, because fear is not a very motivating emotion. Fear, for me, is something that makes me pull the duvet over my head. For our ancestors, fear was something that made them scan the trees, stay still, or find shelter, even if that meant putting off food gathering, camp building, or other essential activities. However, I don't think you should do that. I think that, by now, most of us have a pretty good idea where the danger lies, and we increasingly understand what to do about it. We gained this knowledge from hundreds of years of work by scientists and visionaries, authors and activists standing on each other's shoulders. What we lack are 8,200,000,000 humans who all feel empowered to go out and use it!

Still, it's helpful to briefly scan the trees and remind ourselves where those tigers are before proceeding.

Deadly diseases

A fear that has dogged humanity since the dawn of civilization is disease.[16] We live in a complex and flourishing microbiome: every breath of air you take, every sip of water you drink, and every patch of earth you stand upon is literally teeming with microscopic life. All but a tiny, tiny fraction of these organisms are no threat to us whatsoever. For instance, there are more cells in your body that belong to microorganisms than there are human cells; most of them are helpful and without them you would be very unwell. Some microorganisms are helpful if they are in some parts of our bodies (such as our gut) but can be harmful in others. Only a few have evolved to have purely pathological relationships with us, making us sick. However, even these pathogens will normally harm us only to the extent that this is helpful to them (such as by hijacking our cells to replicate themselves). If they harm us too much, then that is likely to harm them as well (the death of a host often means death for their pathogens too). It is a fundamental law that whatever reproduces the most will spread, and this is generally not the most harmful form a pathogen could take. Evolution works by harnessing this simple fact to power processes of variation, in which possibilities are created, and selection, in which those that spread will tend to replace those that do not.*

However, as we know, a few pathogens can and do make us very sick and even kill us in large numbers. Sometimes this is because facts about us (such as age, malnutrition, or multiple infections) make us especially vulnerable to them. Poverty, population ageing, urbanization, and global travel all serve to increase these vulnerabilities.[17] However, pathogens can also be deadly because evolution sometimes works in unusual ways. For instance, it is generally the case that when people get slightly sick, they carry on moving about, infecting others as they go, but when they get very sick, they stay put and don't see others.* This tends to give an evolutionary advantage to milder pathogens, leading them to outcompete their more deadly peers. However, in certain extreme conditions, like disasters and wars, the opposite can happen. People who are slightly ill may stay put and only the sickest are evacuated for treatment elsewhere. This helps deadlier strains of diseases to spread, giving them the evolutionary advantage. It is thought to be one reason why the 1918 influenza pandemic at the end of the First World War was the deadliest of the century – killing more than twenty million people, many of whom were young and fit.[18]

The other way that pathogens become very harmful is when they are (relatively) new and evolution hasn't had time to work yet. Deadly pathogens often emerge when a disease is transmitted from one animal (in which it may only cause a mild illness) to another (in which it may be, accidentally, far more lethal). This is called zoonosis, and it is the origin story for many of our most feared plagues – from smallpox (originating from gerbils about 4,000 years ago) to HIV (from chimpanzees in the early twentieth century) to Ebola (from fruit bats in the 1970s). Other pathogens, like influenza, experience relatively frequent retransmission between species, occasionally causing new flare-ups of significantly more dangerous disease. To be clear, most zoonotic diseases are neither deadly nor transmissible between humans.* However, due to their unpredictability, zoonotic diseases can be far more dangerous than those endemic to our species.

Yet, these are unlikely to remain the most dangerous of diseases humanity will ever face. This is because, even though zoonosis can circumvent evolutionary pressures that tend to make diseases less dangerous, at least they are not designed to be as dangerous as possible. At some point, we are going to have to contend with pathogens that *have* been so designed, by scientists working in laboratories. In fact, such pathogens are already being developed both for important medical research, to investigate how new pathogens might emerge and what we can do about them,[19] and (probably) to develop bioweapons.[20] This work is carried out under strict safety protocols. However, as these kinds of dangerous research become cheaper and easier, the number and diversity of people working on them is growing, increasing the risk that pathogens will either be released accidentally, because of unforeseen escape routes or simple human error, or intentionally used to cause harm.[21] Estimating this risk is very challenging. Rival studies in 2014 and 2015 put the expected number of deaths from one laboratory working on this kind of research for one year between 0.00002[22] and 1,400,000.[23] This has not been made any easier by the significant controversy surrounding the idea that COVID-19 may have originated from such experiments – my own view is that it almost certainly did not.

However, we will not have to face those threats empty-handed. While much of human history has seen a rising tide of deadly diseases, caused by urbanization, agricultural intensification, global trade, colonialism, and war, the last 250 years have seen us turn that tide, at least to some extent. The greatest advances came from the discovery of vaccines in the eighteenth century (using weakened or altered forms of pathogens to train our immune systems to fight them more effectively),* improvements in sanitation during the nineteenth century (especially clean drinking water, widespread hand washing, pasteurization, and refrigeration), and the development of antibiotics in the twentieth century (harnessing the natural tools moulds develop to fight bacteria). Meanwhile, the same biotechnologies that create the possibility of engineered pathogens are also paving the way for further developments that may be even more significant than these in the fight against disease. We are also starting to better understand social responses to disease (both positive and negative) and how these can be used to buy crucial time in the early stages of an outbreak.

Many of the problems we face in using these tools are ethical and policy-based. How can we ensure antibiotics are available for all who need their assistance to fight off bacterial infections without them being overused in ways that encourage the development of antibiotic-resistant bacteria?[24] How can we ensure adequate uptake of vaccinations to prevent future disease outbreaks, while respecting individual autonomy?[25] How can we ensure adequate healthcare in places where new diseases are most likely to emerge and create responsible early warning systems that serve the interests of the communities they monitor?[26] There is still a lot of work to be done but, in general, the threat of disease looks to be more under control now than at any point in the last 12,000 years.

Planetary disasters

Another threat that humanity has lived with for thousands of years is that of explosive disasters that could be triggered by asteroids, volcanoes, or solar flares. Certainly our ancestors experienced the awesome power of such planetary events, such as the eruption of Mount Toba 75,000 years ago (that may have cooled the climates of Asia and North America by four degrees),[27] or the asteroids that struck Kalli (in Estonia), Campo del Cielo (in Argentina) and Henderson (in Australia) between 1,000 and 3,000 BCE, causing explosions, comparable to those of an atomic bomb, that are still remembered in traditional folklore of these areas.[28]

However, people only became concerned about the planetary risk of such disasters towards the end of the seventeenth century, when the development of infinitesimal calculus and Newton's theory of gravity made it possible, for the first time, to reliably predict the trajectories of objects through space. One of the earliest applications of these tools was by the astronomer Edmond Halley, who was able accurately to predict the return of a comet he had observed in 1682, which now bears his name. Halley was spurred to conjecture that some of these comets could have collided with Earth in the past, and even that this might be the reality behind the biblical story of Noah's flood. He also thought it was possible that Earth might be struck again in the future.[29]

This idea gained scientific support over the years but was also a topic of ridicule. In his 1726 satirical novel *Gulliver's Travels*, Jonathan Swift writes of the scientists of Laputa who 'are under continual disquietudes, never enjoying a minute's peace of mind' out of fear of cosmic catastrophes, for instance that 'the Earth, very narrowly escaped a brush from the tail of the last comet, which would have infallibly reduced it to ashes; and that the next, which they have calculated for one and thirty years hence, will probably destroy us'.[30]

However, other authors were more sympathetic with these concerns and began speculating about how to alleviate them. For instance, Lord Byron, the radical poet and close friend of Mary Shelley, not only worried deeply about the risk posed by comets and other celestial bodies but proposed to his friend Thomas Medwin that 'when a comet shall approach this globe to destroy it, as it often has been and will be destroyed' we might 'hurl mountains, as the giants are said to have done, against the flaming mass'.[31]

As with diseases, both our understanding of the risk posed by asteroids and comets and our ability to mitigate it have come a long way. Nowadays NASA runs a Near Earth Object Observation Programme, to detect, track, and evaluate any large object with the potential to collide with our planet, and a Planetary Defence Coordination Office, to assess and respond to the risk they pose.*[32] Contrary to popular belief, the best response to an asteroid or comet that may impact Earth isn't to try to blow it up – large objects may well reform under their own gravity and even many smaller impacts could still pose significant risk to humanity (with a greater chance of one of them hitting a large city or other vulnerable target). It is far safer to change their trajectories so that they are less likely to cause damage, such as the impact deflection method demonstrated by NASA's DART mission in 2022. Still, as with biotechnology, these methods are dual use, in that any technique that would allow states to deflect asteroids away from our planet could also be used to deflect them towards it or to influence which part of the planet they strike.[33]

For other planetary natural disasters, such as large volcanic eruptions, we have made far less progress. Both predicting and preventing large volcanic eruptions presents significant challenges and are not seen as realistic possibilities any time soon. However, that does not mean we are powerless against them. Decades of disaster research has taught us that there is no such thing as a 'natural' disaster and that in reality all disasters take place because of the interface between the natural world and human societies.* For instance, volcanic eruptions are most likely to have global impacts when they occur in areas with globally important infrastructure, such as the 2010 eruption of the Eyjafjallajökull in Iceland that temporarily closed much of Europe's airspace.[34] By studying these infrastructure vulnerabilities, we can greatly increase our collective resilience to future eruptions. Even in the worst case, such as a volcanic eruption large enough to block sunlight and cool Earth's climate, the greatest disaster would be a failure of food supplies caused by loss of agricultural production. However, researchers are working on strategies that could significantly reduce this risk, even if the resulting global calamity would still be terrible.* We will consider this further in Chapter 8.

Artificial Intelligence

It was Lord Byron's daughter, Ada, Countess of Lovelace, who helped to introduce humanity to our next potential threat. Lovelace's mission in life was to combine the imagination and creativity of her father with the analytical reasoning of her mother, the mathematician Anabella Millbank, to help shape the future. Her first project, taken up at age twelve, was to devise a method for humans to fly. However, when she was eighteen her mother took Lovelace to meet her fellow mathematician Charles Babbage, and she learned of his work to develop a machine to solve complex polynomial equations and his still more ambitious plans to produce one capable of any mathematical operation. Lovelace was instantly captivated by the possibilities of this machine and was the first person to see that such computing machines might not only be used for mathematics but also 'other things besides number, were objects found whose mutual fundamental relations could be expressed by those of the abstract science of operations' such as composing music.[35]

However, Lovelace was not only interested in the potential of this new technology but also its wider social implications. Byron had been one of the few prominent people of his day to support the Luddites, who smashed newfangled industrial machines to preserve their traditional livelihoods, and this was a cause dear to his daughter as well. In thinking about all the potentialities inherent in a computing machine like Babbage's, it therefore made sense for Lovelace to ask whether it could ever replace human beings. Her answer was a definite no, having 'no pretensions whatsoever to originate anything … Its province is to assist us in making available what we are already acquainted with.'[36] That didn't mean computers would not transform society, but their transformative power would be indirect: by augmenting people's reasoning capacity, they could enhance our ability to understand and change the world.*

However, other developers of computers have not shared this conviction. In the subsequent history of computing, there have broadly speaking been three responses to Lovelace's initial assessment that raise the prospect that computers might come to possess an artificial intelligence with the capacity to replace or eliminate humanity.

The first of these responses broadly accepts that computers are merely servants of human creativity but argues that this does not mean they cannot have disastrous consequences for us, via their transformative impact on our society alone. For instance, in his 1863 essay *Darwin Among the Machines* and his 1872 utopian novel *Erewhon*,[37] Samuel Butler considered the development of technology from the (then newly discovered) perspective of evolutionary theory. He argued that technological developments were following the same evolutionary forces as living organisms (such as those affecting pathogens that we described above). However, in this case the key selection pressure would be for machines to be more and more useful to the humans who created them – since any development that improved usability was likely to replicated and thus become more prevalent and be further developed in future. That might sound great at first, but the result, he concluded, would be that 'day by day we are becoming more subservient to [machines]'. Even if we remain responsible for their development, instruction, and supervision, Butler feared our role would gradually become that of servants, tending to the needs of masters we had lost the ability to live without. Thus, he claimed, we were developing our own successors as the dominant species on Earth.*

The other two responses rely on the notion that, contrary to Lady Lovelace's belief, computers are capable of original thought and action, or perhaps we should say that 'thinking' is not as metaphysically creative as Lovelace implies (this is a rather knotty philosophical question we shall consider in Chapter 3 and Chapter 11). The first, and far less interesting of these, is the idea that thinking computers may develop malevolent intentions towards humanity; think of the Terminator or the Matrix. Yes, this makes good screenplays and click bait, but it is little more than a modern retelling of the tales of Frankenstein and Faust. As the science-fiction author Isaac Asimov noted:

> I was an ardent science-fiction reader in the 1930s and I became tired of the ever-repeated robot plot. I didn't see robots that way. I saw them as machines – advanced machines – but machines. They might be dangerous but surely safety factors would be built in. The safety factors might be faulty or inadequate or might fail under unexpected types of stresses, but such failures could always yield experience that could be used to improve the models.[38]

While it may tell us something about our own subconscious fears, this idea of malicious robots is not what concerns people working on AI today.

The final, and most interesting, response is something of an extension of Butler's concerns, that in developing Artificial Intelligence we may unwittingly become victims of our own success. The key concern here is that, assuming AI does benevolently serve our intentions, how do we know what we should tell it to do, or even how it will respond to our instructions? Humanity has a long history of trying to do things that seemed very clever at the time (like controlling an invasive pest by introducing another species we hope will act as its predator) but turned out to be very stupid in the end (as the little old lady who swallowed a fly could have told them).*

We might hope that machines more intelligent than us would do a better job, but that will only work if we don't give them instructions so tightly specified that they cannot avoid repeating our mistakes. However, the more open and general the instructions we give to a machine, the harder to it is to predict how it will respond, or if it will interpret these instructions in the way we intended. Maybe you would think that we just tell the AI to make people happy and let it figure out the details for itself? However, humans have never been able to agree about what happiness really means or how to achieve it; and we should probably hope that any future AI given such an instruction didn't chose to side with the ancient Greek philosopher statesman Solon, who argued that one should 'call no man happy until he is dead'.*

Working out how to manage AIs that are more intelligent than we are is the task of researchers in AI safety and AI ethics. While we are making progress in these fields,* there are few who believe this is anywhere near sufficient to match the phenomenal pace of breakthroughs in the development of AI, such as the emergence of Large Language Models (LLMs) able to produce compelling answers to any question or game-playing engines able to outperform human players at just about any contest. As one prominent researcher in the field, Eliezer Yudkowsky, puts it 'The AI does not hate you, nor does it love you, but you are made out of atoms which it can use for something else.'[39]

Environmental breakdown

While surprisingly longstanding, fears about the threat posed by automation and AI are hardly the only concerns arising from technological progress. People have long feared that the growth of cities, agriculture, and industry were doing irreparable damage to our environment and the complex web of life on which we depend, including air and water pollution, biodiversity loss, and soil erosion.[40] In recent years one environmental change, heating Earth's climate, has become especially prevalent but it never has been, and never will be, the only environmental issue of concern.

The underlying mechanics of climate change deserve a brief explanation. While they may appear transparent to us, most gases absorb a certain amount of light as it passes through them, which they turn into heat; it's just that many of them only absorb light at wavelengths that the human eye cannot see. They do this because they are made of asymmetrical molecules, with atoms revolving in irregular orbits. These atoms' charges thus create tiny electromagnetic fields that interfere with light waves. Only a few gases, either consisting of single atoms (like argon) or molecules of two identical atoms (like oxygen) lack this property and allow light to pass freely through without heating up at all. More than 99 per cent of the Earth's atmosphere is made up of these, unusual fully transparent gases, with only a small proportion of the others, known as greenhouse gases. However, if you take a molecule of one of these non-greenhouse gases, oxygen, break it apart, and combine its individual atoms with atoms of a different kind, such as carbon or hydrogen, this will usually release a lot of energy. That is why burning carbon in oxygen creates heat, and also how living organisms power themselves through respiration. It is also the reason so many other chemical and industrial processes, from creating fertilizers to setting concrete, are so likely to produce greenhouse gases.

However, that likelihood does not mean that global heating is inevitable. Life on Earth has evolved into many different forms while still maintaining, for the most part, this delicate balance of gases in our atmosphere. However, this has certainly been a long and complicated process, with many bumps along the way. For instance, beginning in the late Devonian period, about 375 million years ago, the emergence of large plants across the Earth's land surface saw the level of carbon dioxide in the atmosphere decrease, as more and more of it was photosynthesized into oxygen. This in turn triggered a prolonged period of global cooling, known as the Late Palaeozoic Ice Age. The following fifty million years would witness three of the most severe mass extinction events in Earth's history.* However, the huge amount of carbon now stored within these abundant plants, combined with climatic conditions that slowed the rate of decomposition, made the resulting Carboniferous period one in which ninety per cent of all Earth's coal was deposited. Eventually carbon dioxide and temperature levels bottomed out around 305 million years ago, due to the 'Carboniferous Rainforest Collapse'. Still, the long-term success of our biosphere shows the possibility of life flourishing within the physical constraints of atmospheric chemistry; something we will explore further in Chapter 8.

The challenge we now face is how to replicate this success. That is a technical challenge of gargantuan proportions (although it is perhaps the subject of more coordinated scientific effort than anything else in history). However, simply knowing what needs to be done (for instance, transitioning all energy-consuming domestic and industrial processes to electrical power, while simultaneously transitioning all electricity production to low emission sources) does not mean knowing how to achieve this, let alone how to do so fairly and fast. Like many other problems we have mentioned in this chapter, it is a technical challenge that is wrapped inside an economic quandary, political predicament, and social catastrophe. In part, this is because of how invested we (and especially the economic and political institutions we have created) are in doing things the way we currently do them – damaging or not!

Nuclear war

The last major threat to emerge historically is also perhaps the one that first springs to mind for many today: nuclear weapons. These work by harnessing the forces within atomic nuclei. Put simply, nuclei consist of protons and neutrons that are held together by the 'strong nuclear force', while simultaneously being pushed apart by electromagnetic repulsion between positively charged protons. The balance of these two forces means that if a large atom is split into two smaller ones (fission), or if two small atoms join together (fusion), then this can produce a very large amount of energy, which can be put to explosive effect.

Scientists began to unravel this physics at the end of the nineteenth century. However, to begin with, the only forms of atomic energy release they could observe were gradual and long lasting. For instance, in 1909 the pioneering nuclear physicist Frederick Soddy described how the newly discovered element of radon undertook a continuous and prolonged process of gradual nuclear fission to give out heat and light 'like an Aladdin's Lamp'.[41] Once again, however, it was speculative fiction authors who first really got to grips with the implications of this discovery. The idea that nuclear physics might one day be used in weapons of mass destruction was first explored by the pioneering science-fiction author H. G. Wells in his 1914 novel *The World Set Free* (which came out just a few months before the start of the First World War), in which he invented the concept of atomic bombs.* Consistent with Soddy's discovery, Wells's bombs were long-lasting weapons that continued emitting destructive power for years, not the ferocious explosives we know today (indeed, our understanding of the risks posed by nuclear weapons continues developing as we become more aware of their wider health and environmental impacts). Nevertheless, Wells predicted that harnessing the power of the atomic nucleus for military purposes might pose an existential threat to humanity. He proposed that the only way of responding to this was to establish a world government to prevent their future use, as I discuss in Chapter 9.

Initially, nuclear physicists were highly sceptical of Wells's ideas. The only ways they had found to actively split atomic nuclei to release energy on demand required more energy be spent splitting atoms than could be released from them. Most were thus convinced that their discoveries were largely of theoretical importance and would not have practical applications, let alone military ones. This all changed in 1933 when, after the eminent nuclear scientist Ernest Rutherford had once again publicly stated their practical impossibility, a young Hungarian physicist named Leo Szilard suddenly realized how one might harness the energy released by one atom's fission to induce another to split, setting off a self-powering chain reaction that might be put to use – over several years for energy production, or amplified to explode in an instant. That this discovery was made just before the outbreak of the Second World War, and that it was based on research from scientists working across Europe and America, created a unique set of conditions in which scientists on both sides of the Atlantic worked on developing this new technology with a speed and dedication never before seen in human history.

For many of the scientists working on developing the first nuclear weapons in the UK and USA, the aim was to ensure that they could defend themselves against the hostile intentions of Nazi Germany. However, for the political and military leaders who resourced their efforts, this was only the beginning. That the weapons were first used in an aggressive action against civilians in Japan was shocking, even to those who developed them, and many (though by no means all) of these scientists went on to commit themselves to ensuring that nuclear weapons would never be used again, through initiatives like the *Bulletin of the Atomic Scientists*, the Pugwash Conferences on Science and World Affairs, and the Union of Concerned Scientists.[42]

It was these concerned scientists and their advocates across media, politics, and civil society, who forged the first major global conversation around humanity's existential predicament and how we could improve it. They taught us both that human annihilation was dangerously close but also that our fate was in our own hands. No longer passive victims to external threats, like plagues or asteroids, humanity was a powerful species able both to save and destroy itself. As one of the most famous statements of this predicament, the 1955 *Russell–Einstein Manifesto*, put it:

> There lies before us, if we choose, continual progress in happiness, knowledge, and wisdom. Shall we, instead, choose death because we cannot forget our quarrels? We appeal, as human beings, to human beings: Remember your

humanity, and forget the rest. If you can do so, the way lies open to a new Paradise; if you cannot, there lies before you the risk of universal death.*

Confronting the tiger king

And yet, this statement reminds us that, as well as these five tigers hidden in the trees, there is also a sixth, the king of the tigers; but they will not be found with the rest. It is tempting, when we consider the fate of our species, to imagine these threats as distinct problems that we just need to solve one at a time. However, their deep history reveals a deeper truth: they may have more in common than separates them.

Ultimately, existential risk is not something that exists out there in the world, like a vicious god playing dice with their creation. Rather it exists because of the decisions that human beings take and those that we refuse to take: our ability to imagine nightmares in our future and the irresistible compulsion we feel to carry on regardless; our connection into a global community of competition and conflict and our inability to understand or control where this will lead. For just about every case of possible existential catastrophe, there are things that we could do that would make that outcome a lot more, or less, likely. However, knowing what to do is not the same as doing it. What makes our world dangerous are the things that stop us from making wise choices: conflict and distrust, pride and greed, uncertainty and ignorance, obsession with the past and fear for the future, a reluctance to change and a failure to learn.

Sometimes these factors are described as great human weaknesses that should make us despise ourselves and, if you feel like that, then I do understand and sympathize. However, for myself, I think that is too simplistic a reaction to our situation. The truth is that you are also a tiger, fierce and loyal, beautiful, and dangerous. We did not evolve to live in a world where our choices might threaten the lives of every human, maybe every living thing, on this planet; yet here we are, dancing in the rumbling dark: so, come a little closer and let us begin.*

2

Who Would Destroy the World?

Sometimes when I start talking to people about human extinction a rather strange thing happens. People who give every appearance of being compassionate, kind, and lovely have the unnerving ability to start saying things like 'but would that really be so bad?' and 'don't we kind of deserve it?' My standard protocol for these conversations is to ask people how they would feel about the death of a friend or neighbour. Naturally they say this would be terrible. So, would it be more or less terrible if all their friends and neighbours died, or everyone in their hometown, country, or continent? Or, I ask them if it would be bad if a cultural group were to vanish from our planet or a language to die out, and whether it would then be better or worse if all the other groups were to vanish along with it? Is there really some point at which the accumulation of death and destruction is supposed to stop making a situation worse and start making it better?

However, this is simply a rhetorical protocol, not a philosophical argument. Everyone I have tried it on has concluded that, yes, human extinction would be very bad and that their initial reaction, that it might not be, was mistaken. However, there is no hiding the fact that some people have thought differently. In particular, some have concluded that human death can be a good thing and the more of it the better. Millions were killed in genocides during the twentieth century, in which people were organized to carry out mass murder at unimaginable scales. At least five genocides (against, predominantly, Jews, Ukrainians, Cambodians, Armenians, and Tutsi) killed at least 500,000 people. Twice in that century, the world descended into globe-spanning conflicts that killed tens of millions, but millions also died in civil wars in Russia, China, Nigeria, Korea, Ethiopia, Mexico, Afghanistan, Vietnam, and Sudan. Individuals and groups have gone even further in the levels of destruction they wish to cause. For instance, Ted Kaczynski, known as the Unabomber, carried out a series of terror attacks in the US from the 1970s to the 1990s in the hope of overthrowing 'the economic and technological basis of the present society.' Similarly, the Japanese doomsday cult Aum Shinrikyo carried out a terror attack using the nerve agent sarin with the aim of taking over Japan to initiate a nuclear Third World War that would trigger Armageddon.[43]

As these examples show, at the extreme end of humanity's ability to harm itself lies the painful truth: we might do it on purpose.

Omnicidal actors

But are there people who would really bring about the extinction of humanity? The most obvious answer to this question is to start thinking of real-world equivalents to cinematic supervillains, people who simply desire to destroy, to watch the world burn, or at least to perform actions that could lead to that happening. Within the study of existential risk, we call such people 'omnicidal agents' (omnicide being a Latin word that means 'killing all'). Of course, these aren't the only people we should worry about; people who 'only' wish to cause genocide, civilization collapse, or global war are almost certainly risking the possibility of even worse outcomes. However, omnicidal agents are still an important place to start.

The philosopher Emile Torres has suggested that such people are likely to fall into one of four categories, according to their particular omnicidal motive. The first three groups consist of people who see the destruction of humanity as a moral act: because they believe it is the will of God (apocalyptic terrorists); because they believe it is necessary to prevent suffering (radical pessimists); or because they believe it is necessary to save the biosphere (ecoterrorists). The fourth group consists of idiosyncratic actors, who don't see destroying humanity as moral but nevertheless desire it, often because they desire to do as much harm as possible before ending their own lives.[44]

With all these possibilities, we might think that it is an urgent priority that such people should be identified and controlled, to protect the rest of us. However, in reality, this is likely to be both difficult and ineffective.

Recent research in cognitive psychology suggests that around ten per cent of the adult population believe themselves to be omnicidal agents.[45] Dr Rana Qarooni and Professor Rob Jenkins at the University of York conducted experiments in which participants were presented with a metaphorical 'doomsday button' that they were told would kill all human beings and asked if they would push it. Around ten per cent of participants said that they would push the button and sixty per cent said they could imagine situations in which they might. They also ran a series of similar experiments in which participants were told the button would cause unimaginable suffering leading to extinction or that it would destroy all life on Earth. Reframing the decision in this way changed the proportion of people who said they would push the button, but not by much; it was never lower than nine per cent. Nor did this appear to be the result of participants not taking the question seriously: when offered a chance to explain their decision, the vast majority of those who said they would push the button provided one, often in terms that the researchers found harrowing to read. When people who said they would not push the button now, but could imagine a situation in which they might, were asked to describe what that situation could be, the most common answers were protecting humanity from a worse fate, punishing us for some collective crime, or a deterioration in the participant's own mental stability.

While they may sound shocking, these results actually support, rather than refute, other psychological evidence. For instance, successive US General Social Surveys have found that over twenty per cent of people show very high levels of misanthropy (i.e. negative attitudes towards humanity),[46] while decades of experimental research has shown that ten per cent of people, or more, choose to inflict harm on other research participants in experiments, even when this doesn't benefit them (or makes them worse off).[47]

Indeed, starting with Sabina Spielrein in 1912, psychologists have explored the possibility that humans possess an innate drive for death and destruction (sometimes called Thanatos), although most attribute our destructive inclinations to social, cultural, and environmental factors.[48] Spielrein hypothesized that a death drive may have served evolutionary functions: since there are often inconsistencies between a person's own good and their reproductive successfulness, she thought life might require us to accept, and even value, the destruction of one of these in service of the other.[49] This idea was adopted and popularized by Sigmund Freud, who had previously thought humans were solely motivated by a desire for pleasure. However, Freud viewed the death instinct in more fundamental terms, arguing simply that 'besides the instinct to preserve living substance and to join it into ever larger units' (which he called eros) 'there must exist another, contrary instinct seeking to dissolve those units and to bring them back to their primeval, inorganic state'.[50]

Of course, even if people did possess such an innate drive, that would not make us all omnicidal actors; just as the fact that many of us feel an urge to jump when standing over a sheer drop (as Kierkegaard noted) does not make us all suicidal. However, that is not the point. The point is simply that these desires are common, and it would be impossible, not to mention undesirable, to keep track of everybody who showed signs of feeling this way.

Understanding evil

So, having omnicidal thoughts certainly isn't sufficient to make someone bring about the end of the world. However, is it necessary? Almost certainly not.

A phrase often used to describe people's capacity to do great harm without intending is 'the banality of evil'. This idea owes its popularity, and its name, to Hannah Arendt's 1963 book *Eichmann in Jerusalem*, but also to a series of psychological experiments conducted by Stanley Milgram in 1961. In her book, Arendt gives an account of the trial of Rudolph Eichmann, one of the chief architects of the Nazi-orchestrated holocaust that killed six million Jewish people, alongside many others. Eichmann had been captured by Israeli intelligence agents from his home in Argentina and brought to Jerusalem to answer for his crimes before a Jewish court. Arendt argued that, far from being a monster, Eichmann showed every sign of being both sane and, in his own way, moral. She thought that he fervently believed people have a strong moral duty to obey the law and sought to find a place as a good citizen in society by joining organizations he saw as promoting the common good. He acted callously, she claimed, not because he wanted to harm but because he had been convinced by these very organizations that this was his duty. The psychologists who examined Eichmann had found that his most pronounced psychological characteristic was that he was excessively normal; '[t]he trouble with Eichmann' she concluded 'was precisely that so many were like him, and that the many were neither perverted nor sadistic, that they were, and still are, terribly and terrifyingly normal'.[51] That didn't mean we should not condemn Eichmann. Others had acted differently and some, such as many people in Denmark who actively frustrated Nazi efforts to deport Jews and successfully persuaded German officials to do the same, had shown the possibility of resistance. Totalitarianism doesn't remove our humanity or our capacity for moral decision-making. However, it does lead people into performing evil acts like Eichmann's as failures of omission, to think and resist, not commission, to intentionally pursue harm.

Similar conclusions were reached by the psychologist Stanley Milgram, who conducted a series of experiments in which participants were asked to press buttons they were told would inflict a series of progressively more powerful electric shocks to another 'participant' (really an actor) in a separate room. They were told that this was to see if the shocks would improve the other participant's memory recall. Although participants were informed that they would not harm their subject, as the 'shocks' got progressively higher they heard the other person scream in pain, declare they had a heart condition, and then fall silent. The experiments, which began in the same week as Eichmann's trial, were intended to study people's willingness to obey orders to do harm and to investigate the psychology behind totalitarian atrocities like the Holocaust. Milgram found that almost all participants were willing to inflict some electric shocks and that 65 per cent of them went all the way to the maximum level of shock (450 volts). He concluded that 'ordinary people, simply doing their jobs, and without any particular hostility on their part, can become agents in a terrible destructive process.'[52]

Both studies were, in their own ways, ground-breaking, and they have had a profound impact on our understanding of totalitarianism and people's willingness to do harm. However, despite, or perhaps because of, that, they have also faced considerable criticism. For instance, it has been pointed out that, while Eichmann showed many moral inclinations towards his family and friends, his hatred of Jewish people was rampant and persistent, although this was most pronounced during parts of his trial for which Arendt was not present, and he did appear to both take initiative in his murderous work and draw pride from its results.[53]

Milgram's experiments have similarly been criticized for many aspects of their method and analysis: for instance, participants were repeatedly told that their actions were not actually harming the other person and may well have noticed (even if subconsciously) that, although the experiment was intended to study of effects of electric shocks on the learner, the experimenter stayed in the room with them and showed no interest in their fellow participant. Indeed, 35 per cent of participants chose to withdraw from the experiment prior to its completion, at least one of whom did so because they correctly guessed its purpose and didn't wish to be part of it. Furthermore, Milgram's data showed that, as the instructor's orders became more insistent, people's obedience to them dropped off, and that participants seemed most motivated to act when politely requested to do so as a contribution to science, not an order demanding blind obedience from authority.*

Another interpretation of the apparent banality of evil is that people psychologically separate themselves from the consequences of their actions where these involve significant harm. This may be a matter of choice, but is also a consequence of 'psychic numbing', the human inability to imagine fully or engage with the very worst things in life.[54] On this view, it is not that technocrats like Eichmann cause genocides, but rather that the presence of large-scale violence or the possibility of worst-case outcomes turns people away from their natural human response to situations and towards a less compassionate, more technocratic, mindset that simply refuses to acknowledge the harm they are causing.

Yet, even if we accept that the banality of evil can lead ordinary people into doing great harm, it clearly is not the only way this can happen. In the case of existential risk, it may also be less significant than other forces at work in our world today. Take, for instance, the case of Winston Churchill. Churchill was an avid reader and fan of H. G. Wells, including *The World Set Free*, with its predictions about atomic bombs and the devastation they would pose. This greatly worried Churchill. In a prominent 1924 essay, *Shall We All Commit Suicide?*, he clearly had this in mind when he warned of the possibility that scientists might one day invent 'a bomb no bigger than an orange' possessing 'a secret power to destroy a whole block of buildings – nay to concentrate the force of a thousand tons of cordite and blast a township at a stroke'.[55] A few years later, in December 1931, he went further and raised concerns specifically about the prospects of nuclear research:

> Nuclear energy is incomparably greater than the molecular energy which we use today. … There is no question among scientists that this gigantic source of energy exists. What is lacking is the match to set the bonfire alight, or it may be the detonator to cause the dynamite to explode.[56]

Such was Churchill's concern that he argued it 'would be much better to call a halt in material progress and discovery rather than to be mastered by our own apparatus and the forces which it directs'. He thus became the first politician in the world to oppose nuclear weapons research (albeit one who, at the time, was largely seen as past his prime and unlikely to play a significant role in future politics). Yet, less than ten years later, in August 1941, then Prime Minister Churchill became the first world leader to approve the creation of a government-sponsored nuclear weapons programme; several months before the United States' Manhattan Project and a direct inspiration for it. By June 1944, Churchill was so convinced of the need for nuclear weapons that he poured scorn on the concerns brought to him by the physicist Nils Bohr that atomic bombs should only be developed with great caution, given their potential destabilizing effects on the post-war world, arguing that it was 'just a bigger bomb' that 'made no difference to the principles of war'.[57] The following year Churchill gave his consent to the use of nuclear weapons against Japan.*

What prompted this significant change of heart is hard to say. Almost certainly the horrors of the Second World War played their part, but that cannot be the whole story. While the initial development of nuclear weapons took place at a time when people were actively worried about the intentions of Nazi Germany, by the time that they were in the final stages of development, it had become clear that the German's nuclear research had gotten nowhere and the country was no longer seen as posing a significant threat to the UK or USA (although it took a great effort to defeat and was still killing millions across Europe). By this point, Churchill and others were already most interested in the potential for Russia to develop an atomic bomb and felt the need to ensure that they did not do so first. However, this kind of international brinkmanship seems like exactly the sort of irresponsible development Churchill had previously warned the world against.

For myself, I find it hard to resist the sense that Churchill may have been motivated throughout his adult life by a desire to be the hero of the hour and save his country, or the world.* If he could do so by standing up against the development of dangerous future technologies, then he felt called to do that. However, if conditions shifted so that he felt it would be more heroic to be the political leader who brought these weapons into existence for his own side, then that was the course he would follow.

One can see similar patterns of behaviour among people most involved in developing Artificial Intelligence, some of whom, like Elon Musk, have been both early warners of the potential risks inherent in its reckless development but also great leaders in developing it as rapidly as possible.[58] This is not doing evil for evil's sake, but nor is it very banal either. It is doing evil because we convince ourselves that it is the great and right thing to do. Perhaps we might call it the Nobility of Evil.

Accidental and latent risk

While very different in form, intentional, banal, and noble evils all have something in common: they originate in the character and desires of people themselves. Within existential risk studies we refer to these as malicious, or type-1, harms.* However, there are also two other ways in which people could bring about a global catastrophe.

The first of these is accidental, or type-0, harm. One way this can happen is if risk is totally unseen, the 'unknown unknowns' and 'black swans' that keep scientists and politicians awake at night. Another is if risk is latent, something we think we understand or have controlled, but do not and have not.

A lot of attention gets paid to unseen risk and it is a scary topic; however, it has historically been much less of a big deal than one might think. The prospect of an 'unknown unknown' was popularized by US Secretary of Defense Donald Rumsfeld in the run up to the US invasion of Iraq in 2003,* with Rumsfeld arguing that we should not give too much weight to intelligence reports and UN inspections that indicated that Iraqi President Saddam Hussein did not pose a significant threat to other countries, because we simply did not know what we did not know about him. As it turned out, this was a disastrously bad argument that led to an illegal war and ongoing regional instability, which killed hundreds of thousands of people for little if any international gain, a likely outcome that very many people had foreseen and sought to avoid.

On the other hand, as we saw in the previous chapter, of all the significant threats to humanity that currently most concern us, people had foreseen their possibility decades or even centuries before it was fully realized and they had already started thinking of ways to mitigate the risk. I do not dismiss the possibility of genuinely unseen risks occurring; however, compared to many of the challenges I discuss in this book, humanity has a reasonably good track record of basic foresight and I am not convinced that total and utter ignorance is very often the real reason that people cause significant harm, even if actively ignoring the available evidence often is.

Still, our track record of risk foresight only exists because curious and courageous people did the work to think about the possible impacts of technological developments well in advance, while further scientific work has greatly increased our understanding of that risk and our ability to reduce it. For instance, the greenhouse effect was first discovered in 1856. Eunice Foot, who discovered it, speculated that 'An atmosphere [entirely composed of carbon dioxide] would give to our Earth a high temperature; and if, as some suppose, at one period of its history, the air had mixed with it a larger proportion than at present, an increased temperature … must have necessarily resulted.'[59] In 1908, the Swedish physicist Svante Arrhenius improved on this understanding both by calculating that 'any doubling of the percentage of carbon dioxide in the air would raise the temperature of the Earth's surface by 4°'* and realizing that this was a problem we could have to deal with, since 'the slight percentage of [carbon dioxide] in the atmosphere may, by the advances of industry, be changed by a noticeable degree in the course of a few centuries'.*[60] By the middle of the twentieth century, some ecologists had started to think that humanity's negative impact on our biosphere could also be endangering humanity;[61] however, in general people did not see climate change as a significant part of this. As the influential Limits to Growth report of the Club of Rome in 1972 put it, resource scarcity might force humanity to limit our emission of resource gases 'one hopes before it has had any measurable ecological or climatological effect'.[62]

However, history certainly has not borne this out! Within ten years, a high-profile study in the journal *Nature* concluded that:

> the anthropogenic carbon dioxide warming should emerge from the noise level of natural climate variability by the end of the century, and there is a high probability of warming in the 1980s. Potential effects on climate in the twenty-first century include the creation of drought-prone regions in North America and central Asia as part of a shifting of climatic zones, erosion of the West Antarctic ice sheet with a consequent worldwide rise in sea level, and opening of the fabled Northwest Passage.[63]

Similar conclusions were reached in an internal report for the Exxon oil company in 1982, which correctly predicted a one-degree average global temperature rise by 2022. Of course, like the tobacco companies before it, Exxon decided to bury this research and not let it influence their business model, but they knew exactly what they were doing.[64]

Latent risk involves situations in which a risk is theoretically known about, but its scale and severity are under-appreciated, often because we feel like we have it under control. Latent risks are not fully appreciated until they emerge in a disaster, or near disaster, often in an indirect or delayed way. For instance, many people fail to appreciate the full magnitude of the risk posed by nuclear weapons because they currently only cause small amounts of harm, in the extraction, processing and storage of their component resources or their tendency to destabilize international politics. People thus only wake up to this risk when international incidents make nuclear wars feel like a realistic possibility, but by this point attempts to reduce the risk, such as by getting rid of nuclear weapons, are particularly difficult and unlikely to succeed.

Indeed, for many who study nuclear war, the greatest cause for concern is that nuclear weapons will be used by mistake.[65] There are many instances in the past of misunderstandings and accidents around nuclear weapons use; from atomic bombs being accidentally dropped from aeroplanes and nuclear submarines colliding in mid ocean, to the North American Aerospace Defense Command (NORAD) mistakenly putting a pre-programmed training data tape, rather than a blank one, into their recording system, which prompted it to simulate a Russian nuclear attack.[66] Perhaps the closest the world has ever come to starting a nuclear war was when, during the height of the Cuban missile crisis, American bombers started dropping depth charges in the region of Russian nuclear submarine B-59. With a broken radio, and feeling that they should have been safe in international waters, the crew were left unsure whether this meant war had broken out. Russian orders were to retaliate to any attack with the submarine's nuclear torpedoes and the captain, Valentin Grigoryevich Savitsky, made the decision to do so. However, it happened that he was technically outranked by his second in command, Vasily Aleksandrovich Arkhipov, and could not fire without his consent. Arkhipov refused to second his captain's orders and insisted that the submarine instead surface and await further instructions – and the world was able to live another day. Yet it would be many years before this incredibly close brush with nuclear war became public knowledge.[67]

Similarly, people who talk about the background risk of global pandemics are often seen as incredibly pessimistic, until one strikes and they are seen as incredibly prescient instead (or even obviously complicit in some global conspiracy). Latent risks are especially dangerous when they involve kinds of disaster that have never happened before, such as the potential escape of a highly virulent pathogen from a laboratory (as described in Chapter 1) or the future environmental impacts of attempts to geoengineer Earth's climate.[68]

How institutions and systems create foreseeable harm

So much for accidental and latent 'type-0' harms and malicious 'type-1' harms. A final way in which people can contribute to existential risk is by foreseen, or 'type-2', harms. These involve situations in which people know that they are causing harm and choose to do so, but not for reasons of malice, obedience, or glory. Broadly speaking, there are two ways in which this can occur: flawed co-operation and unresolved conflict.

Let's start with the easy one. Conflict can lead to global catastrophes, because people's desire to win is often stronger than their objections to causing harm. This is easy to see in wars, which may start as localized conflicts that drag in more and more belligerents and worse and worse weapons. However, similar dynamics can also emerge in very different contexts. For instance, in developing new technologies like AI, the people who will have the greatest ability to shape the technology and benefit most from its creation will be those who develop it fastest and first. Even when developers intend to be careful and responsible, this may be of little value if they are outcompeted by irresponsible rivals, resulting in all their work, however well intentioned, going to waste.[69] Of course, responsible development does not have to be slow if responsible developers agree to pool their resources, but there are always likely to be at least some trade-offs between safety and speed. Competitive technological development, be that commercial (as in AI) or governmental (as in nuclear weapons) can cause even well-intentioned people to create foreseeable harms, because they see this as an acceptable risk of pursuing victory in service of a greater good. That makes competitive 'race mindsets' and rhetoric in these fields especially dangerous.[70]

However, we can also contribute to existential risk out of a desire to co-operate. This is because a powerful driver of human behaviour is the good opinion and trust of those close to us. Indeed, in our ancestral environment this was necessary for survival, as there were too many essential tasks (like building shelter or catching large animals) that people simply could not do on their own. However, for many people, the trust and admiration of their peers is directly linked to doing things that, upon reflection, they may find problematic. Executives at fossil-fuel companies and the large institutional investors that support them have probably spent their whole lives pursuing the good opinion of others, who admired them when they were successful and made profits for their companies, and criticized them when they were unproductive and got in the way. Financial success is also something these people can share with colleagues, family, and friends, by whom they want to do well and to help. These are pro-social and co-operative goals, but they can easily be corrupted by corporate systems that are heavily invested in damaging methods of energy extraction and do lack concern for human wellbeing. On top of this, these people are aware, as we all should be, of the huge reliance that society currently has upon their products and can take pride in fuelling global trade, industry and basic services like heating and lighting. That is not a misguided thing to be proud of; it is simply that the way we currently meet these needs is unsustainable. For what it's worth, I think that a lot of executives would, if their position were to shift drastically so that they could view their industry from the outside, agree that it had to change radically and quickly; and indeed, some will admit as much in private. However, in their public lives, their sense of self-worth makes it hard to accept and admit this, and even harder actively to work for change. That does not make people's choices any less harmful; sadly, intentions and motivations do not have any impact on this. However, it does mean that if we only view these choices as resulting from self-interest then we miss an important aspect of how we might change them.[71]

And, of course, these forces of flawed co-operation and unresolved conflict can combine in all sorts of ways. The same fossil-fuel executives who feel they owe it to close associates to stick with the corporate line on climate change may also fear that any resistance would only lead to their company losing ground to competitors, while the same political and military leaders who engage in dangerous brinkmanship and illegal wars are likely to be motivated by a desire to serve and protect their own national groups. These complex interpersonal webs of co-operation and conflict are foundational to the human condition and it is not always easy to tell where one ends and the other begins. It is sometimes claimed that if we could only bring an end to competition and conflict then we could live in peace and harmony, and existential risk would go away. However, as the philosopher Confucius argued, 'harmony' is very different from 'sameness';[72] an overreliance on blind co-operation can itself be dangerous, if people co-operate on the wrong projects and any dissent or attempts to change course get dismissed as unwanted aggression. We will need both to encourage co-operation and to accept conflict if we are to make the world safer. However, we also need to find ways of harnessing both forces in the service of that safety.

The possibility of goodness

So, what is to be done? Omnicidal intentions are common, and people can also do massive amounts of harm in many other ways, even without realizing what they are doing. Will it ever be possible for us to find ways of living in safety? I think so; however, I think that if we are to understand how, then we need to start thinking about this problem from the other end. It is indeed very easy to do bad things, but it is also perfectly possible to do good. As Hannah Arendt noted, the Second World War was not only characterized by bureaucrats, like Eichmann, easing the cogs of global destruction. There were others, in Germany and elsewhere, who reflected on what they saw happening and worked to resist the genocidal forces of war and oppression. Similarly, as the story of Arkhipov and submarine B-59 shows us, individuals who have had the opportunity to initiate world-ending disasters, even if they had orders to do so, have chosen to step back from the brink. Indeed, in every case thus far where there has been a clear decision about whether to launch nuclear weapons, and there have been more than a few, those with the power to do so have chosen not to use it.

Human beings are, at root, social animals.[73] In many ways, ant colonies and beehives have nothing on us in terms of the scale and complexity of co-operative behaviours that we have developed. It is easy to miss this when we are caught up in the existential anxiety of our own lives, the stark choices we appear to face, and the competing motives and values that are pulling us apart. However, the vast majority of decisions we take are determined by our social position and conditioning. We get on with our lives, study, work, play together, do things that cannot be explained by any evolutionary or psychological reason except that they fit with our understanding of what is expected of us and what will please those we care about. From Torres's classification of omnicidal agents and Jenkins and Qarooni's doomsday button experiments to the decisions of war-mongers and fossil-fuel executives, the most common reason that people do harm is because they believe it to be the right thing to do. Indeed, this seems to be part of a general trend of what some psychologists call 'virtuous violence'.[74]

We live in societies that have entrenched norms, practices, and institutions of dehumanization. Colonization, the carceral state, extractive capitalism, patriarchy, and so many other systems of oppression, are deeply baked into not just our societies and economies but our very sense of self, so that to many it seems impossible to imagine living without them. Despite this, compassion is still possible and it is a skill that we can develop, with significant benefits for ourselves and others.[75]

For as long as these evils have existed, people have come together to fight against them. Some of these people can appear like heroes; however, that doesn't have to mean they were 'great people' who changed history out of the force of their will. It is often truer to say that they were able to bring others together by creating shared identities and communicating common purposes to reclaim humanity from the dehumanizing forces of their age.

Ultimately, it is these dehumanizing forces and the world they are shaping that create the conditions under which human foibles and frailties threaten our continued existence. These forces have built a world in which it is no longer individual human beings who make each decision, but strange humanlike entities we have created. It has been large corporations and military establishments that have commissioned and resourced the creation of destructive technologies, successfully lobbied against safety regulations, prevented ordinary people from finding out what they have been up to, and stopped those who were worst affected by the harm they cause from effectively acting to stop it – for their own good and everyone else's. Out of these same institutions, yet another kind of non-human agent is also now emerging, Artificial Intelligences that increasingly make large numbers of decisions on our behalf and are being given more and more control over our lives.

The political-economist Luke Kemp powerfully refers to these as 'Agents of Doom'.[76] Yet that is a modern and cinematic name and the truth is that we have been aware for many centuries now of the powerful and dangerous role these entities play. We might also call them by a far older name, drawing on the sixteenth-century philosopher Thomas Hobbes – 'Leviathans', named after the biblical monster that was so fierce that it cast out all hope and, yet, which it was our doom to call up against ourselves.[77]

And yet humans still exist in this world and we still matter to it. The institutions we have created do rule over us in a sense, but they are also ruled by us. Imperfect as we are, we still are not to blame for everything that is going on in our world. Small as we are, we still are not (yet) powerless to do something about it.

PART II

How Did We Get Here?

I often feel that people's thinking about existential risk gets trapped in a 'crisis of the now'. At present, we seem to be living in a time of terrors that raise unprecedented questions and demand novel solutions. Maybe what lies ahead of us is utter disaster and ruin, or maybe it is a cosmic utopia? We stand at the shores of the unknown, facing a moment of decisive crisis. It is up to us – and us alone – to determine how things will turn out!

In many ways, that is the Hero's Journey, popularized by the American literary theorist Joseph Campbell and now a staple of Hollywood writing rooms and therapist consulting rooms alike. As Campbell summarized it: 'A hero ventures forth from the world of common day into a region of supernatural wonder: fabulous forces are there encountered, and a decisive victory is won: the hero comes back from this mysterious adventure with the power to bestow boons on his fellow man.'[78] It's good stuff, but there is a lot that it misses.

For instance, many of the problems we are urgently trying to solve, from 'can computers think?' to 'how can we achieve international co-operation?' are ones we have been working on for many centuries already. Also, the whole idea of a utopian 'happy ever after' is an inherently dangerous one, with a troubling legacy of its own. And, if we really want to go about changing our world, shouldn't we be looking carefully at previous examples of radical social and political transformation and how they turned out, before rushing headlong towards our own visions of a better future?

In the next four chapters, I want to take a brief look at how we developed our current ways of thinking about three things, firstly computers and AI, secondly corporations and internationalism, and thirdly utopias and utopian thinking. These aren't the only interesting ideas that are relevant to our understanding of what it means to be human in the twenty-first century, but I think they are important. Then, in Chapter 6 I will look at how these ideas combined into a genuine point of inflection, at least within the history of Europe, in which people started thinking about how they could change societies, the risk of globally catastrophic outcomes, and the need to bring the future into our decision-making in the present.

For me, what these stories reveal is the danger of thinking only about the future and never about how we got to our present. Our generation may or may not be the last, but it wasn't the first, and I think there is value in seeing ourselves as small players in a bigger story that has been going on for centuries and, hopefully, will continue for many more to come.

3

Thinking Machines

We are living in a period when Artificial Intelligence and the debates surrounding it are everywhere. It is easy to feel as though these have come out of nowhere and pose genuinely new and unprecedented questions about what it means to be human. Yet, the relationship between AI and human intelligence has been considered for a lot longer than you might think. To understand how, we should start with a curious relic of Boxley Abbey in Kent.

In the 1530s, Henry VIII of England set out to establish an unprecedented level of sovereignty over his realm. Medieval Europeans understood that there was a division of power between the Church and the state. Kings might claim to rule in the name of God, but they did not have exclusive power over spiritual and ecclesiastical matters and their authority could always be challenged and defied (with more or less success) by the Church. This had been the source of much conflict and bitterness over the years but, in general, rulers and priests saw it as necessary to make some kind of accommodation for one another. However, for Henry, this could not be allowed to continue; he must rule over all things in his own kingdom.

Henry's first move to achieve this was to separate the Church of England from the Roman Catholic dominion and place it under his personal authority. However, it wasn't long before he began to eye up the immense wealth and privilege that his ecclesiastical institutions possessed. To claim this for himself as well, he commanded that all the monasteries and shrines in his kingdom disband themselves in his favour and that they must do so voluntarily (a contradiction with which he was entirely comfortable!).

He appointed a team of commissioners to ensure that this was done completely and with nothing of value withheld. From one of these commissioners, Geoffrey Chamber, working at the Abbey of Boxley in Kent, he received a rather curious report. The Abbey was well known for hosting a powerful relic, the Roode of Grace, to which many miracles had been attributed. This took the form of an effigy of Christ on the cross that carried the power to move by itself. On removing the relic from the pillar on which it stood, however, Chambers found:

> certen ingynes and olde wyer, wyth olde roton stykkes in the backe of the same, that dyd cause the eyes of the same to move and stere in the hede thereof lyke unto a lyvelye thyng; and also the nether lippe in lyke wise to move as thoughe itt shulde speke; whiche, so famed, was not a little straunge to me[79]

Chambers had uncovered an early form of automaton, a mechanical device made to move like a living thing.

Chambers' account was clearly meant to persuade his master that this was an example of religious fraud, and just the kind of excess that justified the king in taking personal charge of the Church and its wealth. However, it doesn't seem as though the Monks of Boxley tried to hide the fact that their relic was an automaton. All the accounts we have of the Roode of Grace more or less assumed it was a mechanical contraption. In their official account of the relic, distributed on leaflets to attract more pilgrims to visit it, the monks said that it had been constructed by a carpenter, who was taken prisoner while taking part in a war with France, as a way of persuading his captors to release him. What they claimed to have been miraculous about the object was not its movement, but how it came to them. They stated that its creator had intended to sell it but that the horse that was carrying it had bolted, run straight to the abbey and planted itself at the base of a pillar, refusing to move until the Roode was removed and mounted there!

For most of the people who visited the Roode of Grace, questions about its operation were probably of only secondary importance. What mattered to them was whether it really could perform miracles; and its great popularity implies that many at the time were convinced that it could.

Mechanical marvels

One reason the Monks of Boxley may not have claimed that their statue was anything other than an automaton was that, already in the sixteenth century, people simply would not have believed them. The construction of automata has a long history, with examples going all the way back to Ancient Egypt, and the art of building increasingly complex machines powered by wind, water, and clockwork flourished across the Eastern Mediterranean, Middle East, and East and South Asia throughout the ninth to twelfth centuries CE.

Inspired by tales of these wondrous contraptions brought back by crusader knights, and probably built by multicultural and Islamic artisans from Iberia and Sicily, the earliest European automata were constructed in the gardens at Hesdin in northern France by Mahaut, Countess of Artois, around 1300. They included a moving boar's head, a self-playing organ, and six mechanical monkeys covered in beaver skins, which became famous across Europe until they were repeatedly sacked by English soldiers (perhaps including the Roode's carpenter) at the end of the fifteenth century.[80]

Fast forward another hundred years from when Henry VIII's men were investigating the Roode of Grace, and the craze for automata in Europe had neared its height. Most spectacular of all the marvels that engineers had created were the displays at the French royal palace of Saint-Germain-en-Laye. These included a lyre-playing Orpheus entertaining an audience of animals and trees that swayed and stretched their necks towards him; Perseus, confronted by a terrible beast rising out of the water and swinging his sword to behead it and send it back to the depths; and Neptune brandishing his trident on a chariot pulled by moving seahorses and accompanied by horn-blowing Tritons.[81]

An artificial life

One person who marvelled at these creations was the philosopher, René Descartes. Descartes had trained as a military engineer and was fascinated by the scientific progress of his age, with its ability to produce mathematically accurate descriptions of natural and artificial phenomena such as the movements of planets and the refraction of light. He wondered whether it might be possible to provide similarly precise descriptions of plants and animals and whether, if we did so, their behaviour would seem entirely predictable and automatic like those of these machines. Throughout his life, Descartes worked to develop such a theory; however, he never produced one that he was satisfied with. Nevertheless, he remained increasingly convinced that people would one day understand life in these terms. We should think of our bodies as simply 'like a machine which, having been made by the Hand of God, is incomparably better structured than any machine that could be invented by human beings and contains many more admirable movements'.[82]

However, Descartes saw an interesting implication in this argument. If it were true, then the operation of bodies, including human bodies, was entirely determined by their environment and could introduce nothing fundamentally new into the world. Yet human beings seemed capable of genuine novelty and free thought. The ways that we thought and acted were influenced by our environment, to be sure, but they also existed independently of that environment. For instance, even if the world were entirely different from how it is, we would still be able to engage in mathematical and logical reasoning that would take the same form (for instance that 1+1=2) and we could still arrive at logically necessary truths about ourselves (such as his famous inference 'I think, therefore I am.').[83] If this is so, however, and we are capable of thinking for ourselves, and not simply responding to our environment, then it would have to follow that human beings must be more than mechanical bodies; we must also be immaterial souls that are entirely different in nature from both automata and other animals.

Descartes' arguments have had a powerful influence on European philosophy and psychology in the nearly 500 years since he came up with them. However, even in his own day, not everyone was convinced that the human mind, or soul, had to be distinct from the body. For instance, the English philosopher Thomas Hobbes shared Descartes' conviction that scientific progress might uncover the secrets of physical bodies but also speculated about how it could do the same for our minds.

Hobbes, who corresponded with Descartes but was also greatly influenced by the English empiricism of Sir Francis Bacon (for whom he worked as a secretary between 1621 and 1626), believed that our nerves operated like a highly intricate hydraulic system. On his view, everything that comes into contact with our body, through physical touch, the sound waves we hear, or the light hitting our eyes, exerts pressure on our nerves, which is transmitted as tiny forces running down them and stored as literal 'impressions' somewhere in our brain (or heart). These impressions form the basis of our memory. However, human brains and hearts could also combine, modify, and compare these impressions, which is the basis for our imagination and reason. Hobbes believed that through these processes the mind could operate as a 'computer' – a word that had entered the English language just a couple of decades earlier to describe a (human) calculator or arithmetician. Such a physical computer turned these physical impressions into abstract thoughts, which we only seem to be creating out of nowhere. Thus, Hobbes argued:

> By reasoning, I understand computation. And to compute is to collect the sum of many things added together at the same time, or to know the remainder when one thing has been taken from another. To reason therefore is the same as to add or to subtract.[84]

The way that Hobbes thought this works is that, as we build up many impressions of a thing, our mind can sort these into different layers of abstraction. Thus, he suggests, when I see a friend from very far off, I may only know that there is 'something' there; when they get closer, I may see that they are moving and get the impression of a 'body' or 'animal'; when a bit closer I can see that they are 'human'; and only when closer still that they are my 'friend'. By both separating and combining these impressions, I build up a layered conception of what a human being is; and by combining this with impressions of other people and things I can produce many abstract ideas about them.

To be clear, Hobbes's account of how the mind works is as incomplete as the mechanical theory of the body was in his day, and it is not clear that his theory is even consistent.* However, his crucial insight, which allowed him to argue against Descartes' idea that mind and body had to be separate, was that reason and logic might not be something human minds arrive at independently of our environment but are rather baked in to universal laws of truth, such as mathematics, that enable our brains and bodies to function in the first place.

Hobbes also believed that the same might be true in the opposite direction, that not only could we explain the human mind in purely physical terms by understanding it as a computer, but also that even simple physical systems might have equivalent properties to human beings. As he put it 'why may we not say, that all Automata (Engines that move themselves by springs and wheeles as doth a watch) have an artificiall life?'[85] If that is so, then the idea of a purely mechanical mind becomes a lot easier to conceive, even if its actual operation was far beyond what engineers of Hobbes's time were able to achieve.

At the same time that Hobbes was developing his theory of mind, a demonstration took place in Paris (where Hobbes had fled to escape civil war in England) of the world's first practical mechanical calculator – the forerunner to all modern computing machines. This was developed by the philosopher-mathematician Blaise Pascal, aged eighteen, while working for his father, a French commissioner of taxes. This work involved doing many tedious sums. Whether to assist, or merely distract himself, Pascal started imagining how to create a machine to do the same work, using a system of cogs and gears. While others had attempted this project before him, Pascal was the first to devise a way for such a machine to carry over digits from one column to the next, so that when adding 2 to 9 it was able to return the answer as 11 rather than 1.

Pascal's first demonstration of his device in 1645 achieved considerable public notice and he was awarded an early form of patent by the King of France, to prevent others from copying it. However, Pascal, at least, was sceptical that his machine could be used as a model for the human mind. While he believed that his 'arithmetical machine produces effects which approach nearer to thought than all the actions of animals' he also believed that 'it does nothing which would enable us to attribute will to it, as to the animals'.[86]

Hobbes too, understood that computation could not be the whole story about how the mind worked. It might, perhaps, be able to explain how we reason and learn about the world, but our minds require something else to set them in motion. Hobbes thought this motivation came in two forms: the vital motions that occur in our body automatically, such as breathing and our heartbeat, and the animal motions, which came from our minds. These latter, he explained, originated simply with our desires, which were not part of the reasoning mind-as-computer but served to direct us towards some things and away from others. Some of these desires, such as the desire for food and to stay alive, are with us from birth, while others develop during our lives. Importantly, however, Hobbes saw these desires as immutably determining our actions and choices, like the springs that drive clockwork or the water that turns a wheel, only they are also entirely internal to us, rather than depending on our environment. Once we want something, we might be able to give up the belief that we will get it, but we cannot cease to want it and will try to get it if the opportunity arises. However, as with his theory of reason, Hobbes suggests that we can build up quite a sophisticated set of motivations but that everything is created from the process of addition and subtraction between our beliefs and desires. For instance, he offers the following list of definitions:

> For Appetite with an opinion of attaining, is called HOPE.
> The same, without such opinion, DESPAIRE.
> Aversion, with opinion of Hurt from the object, FEARE.
> The same, with hope of avoyding that Hurt by resistance, COURAGE.
> Sudden Courage, ANGER.
> Constant Hope, CONFIDENCE of our selves.
> Constant Despayre, DIFFIDENCE of our selves.[87]

before going on to produce still more convoluted definitions of benevolence, indignation, pusillanimity, and other more complex states of mind.

From this mechanical theory of the mind, Hobbes derived a powerfully influential, if extremely pessimistic, account of human society. Since the desires that drive us are constant and fixed, he believed that everyone who was able to do so, would seek to satisfy their desires in any way that they could in an entirely self-interested fashion. However, if everyone was free to act as they wished, what Hobbes calls the 'state of nature', then this would cause them to seize as much land and property as they could get their hands on and use it in whatever way would best satisfy their immediate wants. Worse still, knowing that other people were like themselves and thus would be similarly motivated, Hobbes believed that people in the state of nature would have to be on constant guard against one another and would thus be left in a 'condition of warre of every one against every one'.[88]

This is not to say that humans would not try to avoid this state. Hobbes still believed people are rational and capable of seeing that this state of war would be highly undesirable. However, since they are incapable of not acting on their desires (because that would leave them without the motivation to do anything at all) people cannot fix the problem directly. The only thing we can do to keep ourselves safe from this perpetual war would be to find somebody with enough strength to control us, and our neighbours, and then submit to that person's rule. This isn't because this person will be benevolent and good (since they will also be motivated solely by their own desires) but simply because their rulership will at least create some peace and security in which we can strive to do as well as we can, though that is unlikely to be very well for anyone but the ruler and their nearest and dearest. For instance, Hobbes approved of Henry VIII's efforts to bring the English Church under his personal authority.* Only a single strong ruler, Hobbes's Leviathan, could hold their country together; and if that ruler wanted to take your property or tell you how to worship, you were better off submitting to their will than resisting and risking something worse.

Mysteries of minds

In geopolitics, the Hobbesian vision that conflict is inevitable and can only be prevented by submission to a rigid hierarchy, however unjust, is so widely held that it claims for itself the name of 'realism',* with very few questioning the appropriateness of a title that would imply other means of achieving peace and security are unrealistic idealism. In the age of nuclear weapons, this view has become particularly widespread, with many arguing that the existence of one or two hegemonic states or even an all-powerful world government, to which other nations are expected to cling or submit, are the only viable way to keep the peace and thus prevent a nuclear annihilation.[89]

Similarly, In AI, Hobbes's concerns live on in many classic examples of how things might go wrong. Perhaps the most famous (though certainly not the most important) problem in AI safety research concerns a hypothetical AI given the task of maximizing the production of paperclips. To most people, that sounds like such an innocuous goal that it should hardly concern us. However, as Hobbes would have predicted, any simple desire pursued with single-minded determination can cause great harm. In this case, the AI that only wishes to manufacture paperclips might reason that if it could convert other parts of the global economy into paperclip production (say by hypnotizing or enslaving workers), or seize more paperclip-making resources for its own use (say by theft or war), this would only help it in its task. Furthermore, if it were really intelligent, then, like Hobbes, it could predict that people had their own desires, which might not be consistent with these activities and so might try to stop it or even turn it off. So, it might start by trying to neutralize such potential interference, by killing everyone say, so that it could go about converting the entire universe into paperclips in peace![90]

Yet, other views about the nature of mind and reason suggest important alternatives to this rather bleak vision. The next person to develop significantly both Pascal's mechanical calculator and Hobbes's computational theory of the mind was the German philosopher and diplomat Gottfried Leibniz. His calculator radically improved on Pascal's design. It could do multiplication and division as well as addition and subtraction and had separate components to store inputs and outputs, allowing for a basic form of memory that facilitated repetitive calculations. While hard to build using the technology of his own time, Leibniz's design formed the basis of mechanical calculators for the next three centuries.

Still more radical, however, was Leibniz's computational theory of mind. Rather than trying to develop Hobbes's mechanical theory of the computational brain, Leibniz believed that human thinking was a kind of logical software that we developed to run on this physical hardware.* His theory began by trying to work out the most basic logical principles that defined our thought processes, and then seeking to systematize these into a theory of reason. He believed that if we fully understood these principles, we would discover that that all human reasoning could be re-written in terms of purely logical manipulation of precisely defined symbols, in just the way we perform mathematical operations. He felt sure that this was ultimately how our minds worked, even if we didn't realize it.[91]

Or, at least, this is how they should work. However, in practice, our minds are only capable of reasoning in ways that we have either developed for ourselves or learned from other people. For most of us, this limits us to principles of thought that can be expressed in terms of everyday language. However, at present, this language is highly imperfect, imprecise, and sometimes downright meaningless, and this means that our capacity for reason is similarly impaired. Yet, that does not mean we are forever limited. This is because we also have access to other ways of thinking, other programmes that have been written using much better code, such as formal logic and mathematics. It is just that for now these programmes can only be used for a far more limited set of tasks.

Leibniz hoped that we would one day develop a better universal language that would make all forms of reasoning as clear and precise as mathematics, and that with this our minds would finally live up to their potential for rational thought. Parts of this optimistic thesis would go on to be developed and proved by the work of formal logicians in the nineteenth and twentieth centuries; culminating in the Church–Turing thesis, that any formally precise reasoning can, in fact, be written out in simple logical terms. This is the basis for how we are able to programme computers to perform such a wide range of tasks, even though they only think in 1s and 0s (a system Leibniz also developed). Indeed it would be possible for a device as simple as Leibniz's calculator to do the same if it were given enough time. However, whether this means that all human thought really comes down to the application of logical principles, as Leibniz believed, remains an open question.

Leibniz's optimism also carried over into his views about the nature of society and politics. He took seriously the concerns of Hobbes and others about the inevitability of conflict. As a working diplomat and political advisor, Leibniz was very aware of the reality and scale of these problems; and was not above political machinations of his own. However, ultimately, he believed that Hobbes was far too dismissive of the potential for human beings to find common solutions to our problems, at least once we had improved our reasoning with the help of philosophers. Leibniz was a champion of political reform and argued that judges and other government officers should be trained in the art of reasoning and use this to resolve disagreements and make everyone better off.

Somewhat unusually for the seventeenth century, Leibniz was also convinced that European thinkers and leaders were not always the best at solving problems, and he was keen to learn more about other cultures. He especially admired China, which he saw as offering a model for how a geographically widespread and culturally diverse people could live together in harmony; although he also thought that the Chinese could learn from Europeans.[92] Most ambitiously of all, Leibniz proposed that the nations of Europe should come together to establish institutions designed to identify and promote common interests, which would give them reasons not to compete, and provide a basis for reasoning together to resolve disagreements.[93] Recent history has shown that such institutions can exist (albeit imperfectly), even in tandem with conflicting hegemonies and global tensions, so perhaps these calls are no less realistic than those associated with Hobbes.

Possibilities foreclosed

At this point, however, Leibniz's internationalism should prompt us to pause and take stock. Together with Hobbes and Descartes, he has undoubtedly been one of the most influential philosophers of his or any age; and it is the ideas of men like these, perhaps more than any other, that shape contemporary thinking about human nature, the governance of societies and the prospects of artificial minds. This influence is a testament to the power of their insights and ideas. However, it is no accident that these were three *men* writing in Europe in the seventeenth century; a period in which Europeans were exerting unprecedented force on the rest of the world – not through the quality of reason but the power of guns.

We have already seen how the technology of automation was imported into Europe from elsewhere in Eurasia; even if European engineers developed it in new and powerful ways, like the mechanical calculator. The same is true for their ideas; these philosophers owed a huge intellectual debt to the work of their Jewish and Islamic counterparts such as Maimonides, Al-Ghazali and Ibn Sînâ (who developed the logical concepts of necessity, possibility, and impossibility, and first used them to explore the nature of human existence, reason, and morality).[94] However, it is men like Descartes, Leibniz and Hobbes who dominate our thinking for at least two reasons. Firstly, because theirs were the ideas that spoke to the cultures with the power and inclination to impose them onto other people and enshrine them for future generations. However, it was also because they lived in a time when their societies were encountering other cultures that were more interested in reason and debate than their superstitious and fractious European colonizers. In mimicking and learning from, these groups European society sparked a movement that has come to be known as the Enlightenment.[95]

When Thomas Hobbes describes a putative 'state of nature' in which human beings enjoyed total freedom but were thus condemned by their desires to a state of perpetual war, both he and many of his readers probably imagined this must be what it was like in the lands then being colonized by Europeans in the Americas and elsewhere. However, it is plain from historical and anthropological accounts that this was far from true. Almost invariably it was the greed and competitiveness of the colonizers that was the principal source of violence in colonized territories.

Meanwhile, Indigenous Peoples often sought, usually with little success, to find ways of mending bridges and rebuilding peace, while trying to show the Europeans the errors of their ways. These critiques and responses to colonization were as varied and diverse as the cultures that endured European colonization. Yet only a few such arguments ever found their way to European ears, and then mainly in reports of missionaries who were working to downplay or defeat them. Yet what did find its way back to colonial metropoles seemed to have a powerful effect on societies of the time and it became fashionable for European thinkers to start putting their own ideas into fictionalized reports of conversations with members of non-European cultures (even while dehumanizing these same groups in their descriptions and language).

The anthropologists David Graeber and David Wengrow have recently made a powerful case that at least some of these accounts may represent the actual views of colonized people. In particular, they draw attention to reports of the late seventeenth-century Wendat statesman Kandiaronk. In a series of debates Kandiaronk tried to persuade his European interlocutors that the problems of greed and conflict come not from human weakness, in need of legal or religious correction, but from their own society's structure, which effectively push people into harming one another.* Kandiaronk pointed out many imperfections in what he observed of European societies, not only from his interactions with European colonizers but also from his time as an ambassador of the Wendat to Paris.

> The more I reflect upon the life of the Europeans, the less wisdom and happiness I find among them. I have spent six years reflecting on the state

> of the Europeans but I still can't think of a single way they act that's not inhuman; and I genuinely think this cannot be otherwise, so long as you stick to your distinctions of 'mine' and 'thine'. I affirm that what you call silver is the devil of devils; the tyrant of the French, the source of all evils; the bane of souls and slaughterhouse of the living. To imagine one can live in the country of money and preserve one's soul is like imagining one could preserve one's life at the bottom of a lake.[96]

Furthermore, Graeber and Wengrow provide strong evidence that such views did not originate among the Wendat and other communities because they were primitive, naive, or ill-informed, or because these people had never had reason to pursue the material temptations of society. Rather, they show how hierarchical societies had emerged across North America from time to time but people had made a conscious effort to resist or escape them, due to the problems they created, then taught future generations the importance of not making the same mistakes again.[97]

Does this also have a bearing on how we should think about artificial intelligences? Again, Indigenous Cultures are diverse and resist the homogenizing influence of colonial mindsets that want to provide a simple answer to every question. However, at least some contemporary Indigenous thinkers believe that it does.

In one set of Indigenous protocols for AI, Angie Abdilla, Megan Kelleher, Rick Shaw, and Tyson Yunkaporta take issue with several of the ideas discussed above. Firstly, they raise concerns with the desire of Descartes, Hobbes, and their descendants to provide mathematical descriptions of things as mere objects and then treat these descriptions as standing for the thing itself. Instead, they argue that 'the quest by some in physics for a "Theory of Everything," a coherent set of rules that can describe all phenomena, is not achievable as a thing separate from the whole universe' because 'you can never stand outside a system and observe or intervene – you must embrace the fact that you are part of that system'. We should thus not be trying to understand ourselves and our existential predicament by viewing human minds as objects that can be studied independently, but begin by seeing how we exist in relation to one another, to our environment, and to the things that we create.

In this sense, the human element will never be absent from AI, and we should not think about AI as if it ever could be:

> to think that AI may or may not be 'ethical' is a folly. We don't consider toasters unethical if they burn toast. Automated systems are technologies which extend capabilities and may be given the spirit of their human users, as a child's spirit may be perceived as animating a teddy bear. Algorithms are not our kin – they are merely automated ways of expressing an opinion based on a simplified view of the world.[98]

Other Indigenous scholars have developed very different protocols based on local knowledge and understandings. Thus, another group of Indigenous researchers have warned that 'we are concerned that the Western rationalist epistemologies out of which AI is being developed are too limited in their range of imagination, frameworks, and language to effectively engage alone with the new ontologies created by future generations of computational systems'. For instance, 'most culturally critical approaches to AI call for prioritizing the flourishing of humans over all else' but:

> Many Indigenous epistemologies refuse to centre or elevate the human. These relational paradigms based on principles and practices of social and environmental sustainability have long informed technology development in our cultures, e.g. Hawaiian land tenure, ecology, and wayfinding. Approaching new machine entities from such frameworks opens up opportunities to develop relationships with them based on mutual respect and aid.[99]

These two Indigenous accounts of AI ethics certainly do not agree, with one arguing that we should view AI systems as simple tools that humans animate with our own spirit and the other suggesting that we should view them as potential equal partners in the greater web of existence. However, this only goes to show the diversity of views that can be found outside the mainstream Eurocentric thinking.

What these, and other, Indigenous perspectives firmly agree on, however, is that we should not seek to understand AI as a thing on its own but should study it as part of wider cosmic systems in which we, and other living things, are intricately enmeshed. As such, questions about

AI's supposed intelligence, and our own, cannot be answered once and for all, but must be considered in relational terms – where we evaluate AI as an element of this wider system and its impact on all other elements.

Let us then take this as, at least somewhat, representative of a third view about human nature and its relationship to the societies we live in and the technologies we create. While Hobbes saw us as having fixed desires leading inevitably to war and conflict, and Leibniz saw us as engaged in a perpetual project to perfect reason and work towards peace, this third view sees our reason and humanity as existing in systems of interdependence, which create the possibility of flourishing (both social and technological) but may be disrupted by colonial structures of alienation and control.

4

Unmasking the Powers

There is a common misconception that it took Christopher Columbus many years to obtain royal backing for his expedition across the Atlantic because he could not convince them of his radical belief that the Earth was round and not flat. This is patently untrue. Earth's roundness was a well-known fact among educated medieval and early modern Europeans,[100] especially as this was important for their understanding of astronomy and hence their ability to measure time. Indeed, the Earth's circumference had been almost exactly calculated by the Greek mathematician Eratosthenes around 250 BCE. Eratosthenes had heard that in a town in Southern Egypt the sun at noon on the summer solstice shone all the way down a well without leaving a shadow. Yet in Alexandria, where he lived in Northern Egypt, the sun did still cast shadows then. By measuring the length of these shadows and applying some very simple trigonometry, he was able to calculate the Earth's circumference (around 40,000km) to within 2.5 per cent of its true value.

The principal reason Columbus had such difficulty in persuading people to support his expedition was that he tried to argue that these calculations were inaccurate and that the Earth was only about two-thirds of the size they implied. He also believed that the length of the Eurasian continent was considerably greater than that reported by Marco Polo and other travellers and, as a result, that the Westward journey across the ocean to East Asia would be a distance feasible for ships to cross, rather than the suicidally long voyage across the trackless ocean that people assumed.

Whether Columbus really believed these geographical inaccuracies is hard to say, but it is worth noting that he had previously visited Iceland in 1477 and may have heard tales of the Danish colony of Greenland (which had recently collapsed). He also spent time on the Madeira islands in the mid-Atlantic between 1478 and 1482, and married the daughter of their Governor, Filipa Perestrelo.[101] There is also at least some evidence that sailors from across Europe were already aware of lands across the Atlantic, and maps of the fourteenth and fifteenth centuries sometimes marked a mysterious island named Brasil, or Bracile, lying far out in the Atlantic.

All of this makes it at least somewhat plausible that the reason Columbus was so committed to persuading people of his faulty geographical assumptions was not because he believed them but rather that he suspected, or at least hoped, that there was more to be found on the other side of the Atlantic than far-off Asia. Yet, if he or others were aware of the existence of America, why was it not already widely known?

The fact was that for most of the mariners who charted the Atlantic in this period, there simply was not much point in saying too much about what they found. Abundant fish stocks off the coast of Labrador would be a profitable draw, but only more so if knowledge about them could be restricted to a few trusted associates and supporters. Trade was important, but people were far more interested in finding ways to obtain more goods, at lower prices, from Africa and Asia than looking to open new markets with uncontacted peoples.

The idea of colonizing new lands was unlikely to have been on anyone's mind. Not that it had never been thought of. Viking colonies were established from Greenland and Iceland to Sicily and Ukraine, while European states had been trying, unsuccessfully, to settle the Eastern Mediterranean and Middle East as part of their crusading wars against Muslim and Orthodox peoples. However, the overwhelming experience of colonists was one of hardship and failure. With the notable exception of Iceland and Ireland, colonial experiments of medieval Europe either collapsed, were re-conquered, or became assimilated into their wider community.

Furthermore, Europe of the fourteenth and fifteenth centuries was reeling from a decades' long disaster. This was probably initiated by climatic changes during the late thirteenth century, known as the end of the Medieval Warm Period, which may have seen significant cooling of one degree or more across Europe and the North Atlantic. It was probably caused by changing ocean currents, although we still don't fully understand how.

It was not the direct effects of climate change, however, which caused the biggest trouble but the extreme weather that came with it. In the spring of 1315, it started raining heavily across Europe with unseasonably cold temperatures, and this weather continued for more than two years. These conditions made farming extremely difficult and harvest yields fell below fifty per cent of normal levels.[102] In these years, an average wheat seed that was planted may have yielded only two seeds come harvest, one to eat and one to replant, making it very hard for farmers even to feed themselves and almost impossible for them to recover when crops were wiped out by floods and pests. On the tail of these atrocious conditions, and probably in part because of them, a new disease, the Great Bovine Pestilence, started ravaging livestock, killing nearly two-thirds of cattle.[103] In the famine that ensued from these agricultural disasters, around one in ten Europeans died.[104]

Yet worse was to come a generation later when Bubonic Plague, known as the Black Death, spread across Asia and Europe. This was precipitated via a zoonotic spillover event in which new strains of the bacterium *Yersinia pestis*, from marmots, began infecting humans. However, this was also possibly caused by the pronounced climate changes of this period, which increased the viral load of *Yersinia pestis* in marmots as well as bringing them into closer contact with humans.[105] However it started, the plague rapidly became probably the deadliest disease outbreak of all time. More than half of the population of Europe died.[106] However, the plague was certainly not limited to Europe. The pioneering Arab social scientist Ibn Khaldun, whose parents both died in the plague, observed that 'Civilization both in the East and the West was visited by a destructive plague which devastated nations and caused populations to vanish.'[107] Together, famine, plague and climate change may have reduced the total human population on Earth by ten per cent (killing about 45 million of the 450 million people alive at the time), making this probably the second worst catastrophe to befall our species.

In the aftermath of such a calamity, Europeans hardly needed new lands to colonize and conquer. However, all that was about to change.

The dawn of colonialism

On 25 May 1420, King John I of Portugal made one of the most fateful decisions in human history – he granted his third son, Dom Henrique

Duke of Viseu, governorship of the Order of the Knights of Our Lord Jesus Christ.[108]

The Order had been established a century earlier when the Knights Templar, who had spearheaded European invasions of the Eastern Mediterranean, were dissolved by Pope Clement V. Across most of Europe, the Templar's property was seized and its knights arrested. However, in Portugal, King Denis created this successor order that swore personal loyalty to him. Medieval politics like this sounds inconsequential to today's world, and the idea that the Order's history might still be shaping our own sounds like the plot of a Dan Brown novel. Yet, in the hands of Dom Henrique, or Henry the Navigator as he is now known, this Order would become the pattern for much of our world.

Living at the Southwest corner of Europe, Henry had been fascinated by foreign lands since he was young. Aged 21 he distinguished himself as a commander in the Portuguese conquest of the port of Ceuta in Morocco, a centre for piracy and the African slave trade. In doing so he gained the Portuguese their first port on the south side of the strait of Gibraltar, allowing them greater control over entry and exit to the Mediterranean. Henry believed that the future of his kingdom lay in capitalizing on this early success by exploring and conquering lands to Portugal's south and west.[109]

The plan seems to have been simple. The wealth and networks of the Order could be harnessed to finance new expeditions to these lands and when they successfully brought back new riches these could be used to further bolster the Order and Henry's ambitious hopes. It appears to have worked, with Henry financing an increasingly daring succession of voyages down the African coast. In 1433 Henry's elder brother, King Duarte I, declared that the Order would henceforth have sovereignty over any new conquests or colonies it created, while his successor, Afonso V, granted it a five per cent levy on any trade to or from these lands. With these concessions, colonial expansion became more than a quest for land, influence, or personal glory. It became profitable.

A sign of the change brought about by this new endeavour can be seen in the fate of the islands of Madeira. These had already been discovered by European sailors in the fourteenth century but were apparently ignored as of little if any value.[110] However, when one of his earliest expeditions was blown off course sailing down the coast of Africa, and found itself in Madeira, Henry and his Order used them to found the first colony of Europe's expansion into the Atlantic. At first, the islands' forests were cleared to make farmland that could attract peasants from Portugal. However, when the volume of wheat they produced started declining, Henry demanded that they diversify their crops to ones that could be more profitably traded, most notably sugar. When there were insufficient peasants to cultivate the sugar, the Portuguese used their conquests in West Africa to bring enslaved persons to the islands instead. All of this could now be overseen and enabled by one person, sitting on top of a powerful organization that was able to finance his ideas and collect the profits, their power and influence at least as great as that of Leviathan kings.

It was an arrangement like this that Christopher Columbus wanted to establish when he approached, first the king of Portugal and then King Ferdinand and Queen Isabella of Aragon and Castile, with his ideas about sailing West over the Atlantic to Asia. Popular history remembers that he asked for ships and men but, in fact, he had money of his own to invest and what he really wanted was something only they could provide. In the agreement he finally made with Queen Isabella and King Ferdinand, he was granted not only ships and men but the official title Admiral of the Ocean, the position of Viceroy and Governor-General of any lands he conquered, and, perhaps most crucially, one-tenth of any riches that would be derived from them.[111] This secured, for him, the official protection of two of the most powerful monarchs in Europe for his profitable exploitation of any discoveries to which he could lay claim.

When Ferdinand and Isabella agreed to Columbus's terms, however, they believed that his primary goal was trade, and that he would be fulfilling a role similar to that of the Islamic merchants, through whom they currently imported goods from Asia, only more cheaply and with the profits staying in Christian hands. However, in a pattern that would repeat itself down the ages, European colonists arriving in the Americas very quickly gave up on ideas of trade and exchange, realizing that there was more money to be made in extracting resources and enslaving the local population. Columbus certainly wasn't going to stop them from doing so, when he had a Monarch's agreement to reward him with ten per cent of everything they made. Because of this, the Taíno people, whom Columbus first encountered, suffered terribly due to colonial violence, economic oppression and European diseases. Around two-thirds of the Taíno died within fifteen years of Columbus's first voyage.* Although genocidal atrocities against them continued, both Taíno-descended people and Taíno culture are still alive in the Caribbean. As a contemporary elder put it: 'Taíno are important people – you can't kill out a people like that. Columbus could not come here and kill out Taíno, too much Taínos for him.'[112]

When Ferdinand and Isabella began to hear about the consequences of their decision, they were personally appalled. Columbus was dismissed as Governor-General in 1500 and stripped of his ten per cent share of the profits from these new colonies, although this point would be contested in Spanish courts by his descendants. Others, like the Spanish theologian Francisco de Vitoria, saw more systemic problems with the colonizing project. In his 1539 lectures, *De Indis*, Vitoria argued that Indigenous Peoples had a clear right of dominion over the places they inhabited, as 'God given' as any right the Spanish had over their own territory. Denying this right by conquering and colonizing the Americas not only deprived Indigenous People of their rights and lands, it encouraged Europeans to violate the natural laws of justice.*

Nevertheless, similar agreements continued to be made with mercenaries and adventurers, who promised that they could do better, such as Hernán Cortés (over Mexico) and Francisco Pizarro (over Peru). These led to equally exploitative, if more immediately profitable, expeditions that ended in disappointment for both monarch and adventurer (Cortés was stripped of his governorship for abuse of power and Pizarro was censured for executing the Inca emperor) but especially for the colonized people.*

First disease, then guns, then whips and chains, laid waste not only to millions and millions of people but also to cultures, languages and ways of life that had developed over thousands of years of human habitation in the Americas. When local populations began to dwindle beyond Europe's desire for exploitable labour (as often happened just a few years after first contact), poor peasants from Europe and enslaved persons from Africa were forcibly relocated to fill the gap, often destabilizing and decimating their own regions and cultures as well. Meanwhile, the balance of European wealth shifted significantly as mined and looted precious metals and other highly valued commodities flowed out from the new world, making colonial exploitation more profitable than the small-scale emerging industries of the time, before flowing on to Asia and the Middle East, fundamentally shifting the balance of trade.[113]

While a few individuals were made wealthy from the profits of colonization, most actual colonists had their lives shortened by famine, disease, and violence (both among colonists and with Indigenous Peoples) and many were left worse off than they had been at home. Even the empires themselves would not prosper for long: the Portuguese, Spanish, Dutch, French, English, and American empires experienced no more than a century of global hegemony before turning into burdens that mired their metropolitan authorities in debt.

So profound was the shift caused by European colonization that there is hardly anywhere not affected by it, and for most places that impact was negative. As with the Black Death, we will never fully be able to count the costs of European colonization of the Americas, but it is estimated that, in the first hundred years of colonization, the population of Indigenous Americans fell by 56 million.[114] When we also factor in the economic and cultural losses and the impacts of the Atlantic Slave Trade, we find that this was almost certainly the worst global catastrophe to befall humanity to date; and, unlike the Black Death, its negative impacts for people and societies have continued to the present day.

The first modern corporation

European colonialism entered a new phase in 1551, with the establishment of the Mystery and Company of Merchant Adventurers for the Discovery of Regions, Dominions, Islands, and Places Unknown. The company brought together around 240 investors, contributing the regal sum of £6,000 (around £2.5 million today) to support the vision of its founders, Sir Hugh Willoughby, Richard Chancellor, and its first governor, the Italian born navigator, Sebastian Cabot, in their dream of finding a northeast passage to China.[115]

The company was born of a desperate need for England to find new partners in trade. Following Henry VIII's decision to separate from the Catholic Church, Tudor England had been cut off from many of its former trading partners in Europe and was rapidly losing its wealth and privilege. Unable to compete with Spain and Portugal, it needed to find new alliances quickly if it was to resist conquest from abroad. The company hoped to meet this need by combining two previously existing kinds of organization to form a new kind of enterprise that could rapidly create and exploit trading opportunities.

The first of these was the Company of Merchants. First pioneered by the Italian 'commenda' (or trust), medieval traders had long sought effective ways of pooling forces, capital, and, most importantly, risk, to help them produce, buy, transport, and sell their goods. It was understood that in such companies partners would share both the profits and the losses of their common endeavour and would work together to ensure its success. In much of Europe such companies existed only if there was a written partnership agreement between merchants but, under English common law, all merchants who were working together would be deemed to have formed a company for that purpose and could appeal to the courts if they felt their partners had treated them unjustly.

The second was the idea of a corporation. This was originally formalized under Roman law, in which a 'universitas' (literally 'association') was a distinct legal entity that could be created to own property, act in lawsuits, make contracts, and perform other actions in law. When Roman law was revived across Europe from the eleventh century, the idea of the universitas (also known as a corpus, or body) was reintroduced, and charters were issued to *incorporate* (i.e. form a corporation for) institutions such as churches, universities, and guilds. This gave them a legal identity, equivalent to that of a person, separate from the individual people who ran them. This had many benefits, including limiting the power of any one individual over these important institutions, giving them longer-term security, and allowing their terms of governance to be more easily overseen by the authority who had created them, such as a king or pope.

The first private corporation to involve itself in colonialism was the Society of Merchant Venturers in Bristol,* who controlled the city's harbour and served as a guild for its many merchants. From around 1480 they had started to sponsor small-scale expeditions into the Atlantic to search for the island of Brasil, following a belief that sailors from Bristol had already discovered it but that its location had then been forgotten.[116] Following the discoveries of Columbus in 1492, they redoubled their efforts with the backing of the English king, Henry VII. They hired John

Cabot, together with his son Sebastian, to make their own expedition and, in 1497, they sailed west to the shores of Canada, becoming the first Europeans to land in North America on St John's Day, 24 June.*

Yet John and Sebastian did not travel with anything like the authority and privileges of Christopher Columbus. While their voyage was paid for (if only a single small ship with just twenty men) and they were rewarded for their discoveries (with £10, equivalent to around £10,000 today), it would be the Merchant Venturers of Bristol who would reap the benefits: with the King's backing (in return for a promise of 25 per cent of the profits) they secured a monopoly on all trade to and from these newfound lands.

Perhaps it was the memory of this lop-sided deal that persuaded Sebastian, after fifty years of adventuring across the new world and the old, to seek to establish his own corporation. However, this time it would not be one for merchants who wished to profit from other's exploration, but a colonial entity of its own. This was a company of merchants, whose common endeavour would not cease with a single voyage or expedition but continue perpetually, and whose shares and wealth could be bought and sold, to ensure a constant supply of capital. With this, the joint stock company, the model for all modern business corporations, was born.

The value of this new kind of enterprise was quickly made apparent. The company's first voyage was a near disaster, with two out of its three ships lost in Arctic waters and its leader, Sir Hugh (who was chosen for his fame as a soldier but had no naval experience) dying. However, the one ship that did return home brought with it a letter from Tsar Ivan IV (Ivan the Terrible) permitting further trade between the company and Russia through its northern seaports.[117]

Had the expedition been a personal endeavour of its leader, then it would have perished with him. Had it been undertaken on behalf of a monarch, as previous endeavours had, then it is likely to have come under their control and these trading rights would have been dispersed across the entire kingdom. Had it even been a company of merchants bound in partnership on a common endeavour, then they would have struggled to capitalize on such an opportunity. However, as a joint stock company the Mystery, later renamed simply as the Muscovy Company, was able to secure a trading monopoly that lasted for the next 150 years. Indeed, the company continued trading until the 1917 Russian Revolution and it still legally exists today, albeit now as a charity run by the descendants of British merchants in Russia to support the Anglican Church.[118]

Where we went next

The success of the Muscovy Company inspired numerous imitators. In England, these included the Turkey Company (1581) and Venice Company (1583), which merged to form the Levant Company (1592), all seeking to trade with the Eastern Mediterranean. Meanwhile, in the Netherlands, the Compagnie van Verre (1594) and Brabant Company (1599) were among several established to challenge the Portuguese domination of trade in spices. However, these early endeavours were dwarfed by what was to come when the British East India Company (EIC) and Dutch Vereenigde Oostindische Compagnie (United East India Company, VOC) were established in 1600 and 1602 respectively.

These behemoths, and the others that would follow, such as the Virginia Company (established in 1606), the Royal African Company (1660, the world's largest trader in enslaved persons), the Compagnie française pour le commerce des Indes orientales (1664), or the Anglo-French Hudson Bay Company (1670),* not only reshaped the world but also our understanding of what a corporation could be. These companies, but especially the VOC and EIC, were by far the largest and most profitable commercial organizations the world had ever seen.* In their early days, both companies were able to return dividends to their investors in excess of one hundred per cent of their investment and, partly as a result, could raise capital investments that would be measured in billions of dollars today.

Initially, the VOC was more successful and dominated European trade, not only in spices but also other goods and enslaved persons. Interest in buying and selling stock in the VOC was so high that it led to the creation of most modern stock-trading practices,[119] while the practical difficulties in financing and administrating such a large organization forced it to pioneer much of what we now refer to as corporate governance and business administration.[120] While previous corporate entities were more or less understood to represent the people who made them up, both the British and Dutch East India Companies were so large that they could not be fully controlled from within, even by their leaders. Furthermore, their political influence, over both their home territories and the lands that they traded with (and later conquered), was immense, operating more like private governments than commercial enterprises. The VOC would conquer and administer the territories that make up modern-day Indonesia, while the EIC went on to establish the largest private empire in history, ruling over much of South Asia with over 200 million subjects, mostly obtained by paying South Asian people to fight one another on its behalf.[121] These corporations had become Leviathans in their own right, imposing powerful control not only over the states they controlled, but the countries that had created them and the individuals who made them up.

One instance in which this power to reshape the world around them first emerged took place in 1603, when Jacob van Heemskerk, working for the VOC, captured the Portuguese ship Santa Catarina in the Straits of Malacca off present-day Singapore. Van Heemskerk claimed that he had faced harassment from the Portuguese fleet and took the ship as compensation for this. However, at that time there was peace between the Dutch and Portuguese and he had no royal authority for such an act, making it potentially treasonous. The Portuguese demanded compensation from the Dutch and the company was put on trial for its actions. As part of its defence, the company hired van Heemskerk's cousin, a young lawyer by the name of Hugo Grotius. Grotius developed a novel argument, drawing upon the principles of Natural Law that had been developed by Francisco de Vitoria, he argued that the company was a natural person and had a right to defend itself, just as an individual human being might. This was a significant moment in the career of Grotius, who went on to build a reputation as one of Europe's principal legal authorities.[122] Today, he is widely seen as the father of international law and the principle he helped establish, that corporations can not only act as legal persons for the purpose of owning property or making contracts, but also claim the rights of persons according to natural justice, still stands as an important part of this.

These corporations also changed the world in ways that were less apparent at the time. The cyberneticist Buckminster Fuller pointed out that they were the first masters of our planet, in that they started engaging with Earth as a unified system, moving resources at will and using differences in climate, ocean currents, and even Earth's curvature to help them. That these corporations were also able to operate outside the social and communal laws and norms of any one country meant they, and their chief employees, started viewing their own interest as the only thing of any ethical importance. Fuller also noted how these corporations profoundly altered the way humans think of themselves – by requiring more and more specialization from their employees and no longer seeing value in well-rounded, self-sufficient individuals, they preferred dedicated buyers, sellers, accountants, navigators, administrators, and other specialists. This also meant that no single employee could ever understand how a corporation works. Each individual's partial and siloed understanding of their own role is only held together by the corporation itself, which provides structures for combining specialized expertise to produce collective decisions. Meanwhile, even a corporation's most treasured executives became expendable resources that are easily lost to disease, bad weather or political scandal.[123]

The scale of the VOC and EIC's wealth and power can invite triumphalist readings of their success. However, as trading companies they were profoundly flawed. They were generally run according to the philosophy of mercantilism, which held that wealth would be maximized if merchants exported as much as possible while minimizing their imports.* The idea makes intuitive sense; if you don't have to pay others to buy goods from them, but they pay you for what you sell, then you should get richer. Hence, for instance, once it started gaining influence over Bengal politics, the British East India Company worked systematically to dismantle textile production, which had once been the backbone of its economy, so that it would cease to be an exporter of fine calicos to England and instead be forced to import their mass-produced fabrics instead. Alternatively, where there were South Asian goods that the Company wished to acquire, such as gold, they used their influence to gain control of local tax revenues, which they could use to buy them with, effectively obtaining the goods for free. Meanwhile, in China, where the company could not find anything produced in England that local people wanted to import, they switched to selling opium. When the Chinese government, rightly, objected to this cruel practice the company sent in gunboats and forced their compliance, simultaneously taking the free port of Hong Kong as a British territory, to further facilitate the narcotics trade.*

While mercantilism might work for individuals, nevertheless, at the global scale it runs into serious problems. The whole premise of trade is that both parties value what they are getting more than what they are giving. Hence, whenever something is traded it becomes more valuable – not in a material sense of being physically improved but in the sense that it is transferred to someone who values it more. This should leave both sides better off, and thus in a position to make further trades in future. However, when one party tries to dominate trade via mercantilism, they starve this process of half of its worth. Forcing people to import more and export less means that they no longer have anything to offer for trade that you want to receive, so even if you do well in the short term, the trade is unsustainable and both parties will be left worse off in future. In fact, by the mid eighteenth century, this problem was already becoming very apparent. For instance, only a decade or so after it gained control of Bengal, the directors of the East India Company found that they had ruined its economy to such an extent that they were having trouble continuing to make a profit, even from their one-sided resource extraction, and were building up increasingly large debts, prompting them to seek a British government bailout.[124]

Extraordinary waste

One of the first people to fully understand the nature of this disaster was the Scottish philosopher, Adam Smith. Smith is often seen as the world's first economist, and as such he is associated with the economic mantra that 'greed is good'. However, the reality of Smith's thought could hardly be further from this. Smith's fundamental observation about human nature was, in fact, that '[h]ow selfish soever man may be supposed, there are evidently some principles in his nature, which interest him in the fortune of others, and render their happiness necessary to him, though he derives nothing from it except the pleasure of seeing it'[125] – i.e. that even though we think we are selfish, humans are drawn to help one another through sympathy and compassion. In families, community and social groups, friendships, and most joint projects, people naturally like to do good to one another and don't generally mind whether that is immediately paid back to them. However, Smith noted that there was one situation where this general tendency did not apply, when we engage in business and trade: 'it is not from the benevolence of the butcher, the brewer, or the baker, that we expect our dinner, but from their regard to their own interest',[126] he wrote, and this troubled him.

Yet, reflecting on how trade can create value, as I described above, Smith concluded that this might not be as problematic as he feared. He argues that, if we were always motivated by benevolence alone, people might end up with the same amount of stuff but would not know what to do with it. My preferences and needs are not the same as yours and it is hard to know what I will like until I have tried different things. If we all work to produce different goods or services and trade freely between us, then we can make one another better off while also specializing in what we each do best and not having to worry about who might want the things we produce or how to find them. In this way, Smith argued, we 'are led by an invisible hand to make nearly the same distribution of the necessaries of life, which would have been made, had the Earth been divided into equal portions among all its inhabitants, and thus without intending it, without knowing it, advance the interest of the society, and afford means to the multiplication of the species'.[127]

In formulating this view, Smith had in mind a society in which individuals freely traded with one another and had roughly equal amounts of power (his mention of butchers and bakers is instructive of the kind of transaction he has in mind). However, that was not, and is not, the world in which Smith and we live, and he was well aware of it!

In Smith's world and, even more so, in ours, people's choices about what to make, buy, and sell are dominated by corporations that exert great power and influence to prevent people from standing up for their rights and force them to accept bad deals. Smith fervently believed that, in any case in which people who shared the same business joined together this would end in 'a conspiracy against the public, or in some contrivance to raise prices'[128] and that was a disaster for his theory. While he thought it was unlikely that the law could ever prevent such associations forming, he argued that it shouldn't make them easier to form or more lucrative.

Speaking specifically of large corporations, he argued that they 'have in the long-run proved, universally, either burdensome or useless, and have either mismanaged or confined the trade'.[129] And for the British

East India Company he reserves particular disapprobation, blaming it for causing famine in India, while noting that even in the home country:

> the other inhabitants of England, over and above being excluded from the trade, must have paid, in the price of the East India goods which they have consumed, not only for all the extraordinary profits which the company may have made upon those goods in consequence of their monopoly, but for all the extraordinary waste which the fraud and abuse inseparable from the management of the affairs of so great a company must necessarily have occasioned.[130]

These corporations, and their successors, did not enable the invisible hand according to Smith, but hijacked it, turning the greed and selfishness that commonly motivates financial transactions from something that providence and a fair economic system might translate into benevolence, into pure destruction of wealth and value.

This view was shared by Smith's good friend and fellow philosopher Edmund Burke, 'the only man I ever knew who thinks on economic subjects exactly as I do'. While Smith laid down the economic case against the apparent success of joint stock companies, Burke, who was also an MP, made the political case against their corruption and abuses. Firstly, authoring a Report of the Parliamentary Select committee on the Affairs of India, in which he argued that were the British East India Company to continue operating as it had 'it is absolutely impossible that India should not be radically and irretrievably ruined'.[131] He then worked on a bill to fundamentally change the Company's charter, forcing it to revert to fairer trade and cease to plunder the wealth of South Asia. However, the power of the British East India Company proved too great for him, and it was able to use its influence to bring down the government that was supporting this bill.

Finally, Burke used the ancient power of impeachment to bring public charges against Warren Hastings, the company's Governor in Bengal. In a trial that would last for seven years, Burke sought to convince his fellow parliamentarians that Hastings had not only abused the powers invested in him by the British East India Company but had violated Indian laws and universal principles of justice for which he must be held accountable. Parliament did not agree.

In summing up his life's work, shortly before his death, Burke asked:

> Let my endeavours to save the Nation from that Shame and Guilt [of British misrule in India], be my monument; The only one I ever will have. Let every thing I have done, said, or written be forgotten but this ... If ever Europe recovers its civilization that work will be useful. Remember! Remember! Remember![132]

It is often argued that people did not know or realize the harm that European colonization was doing at the time, and that we should not be held accountable for their ignorance. Burke's life-long efforts show all too clearly that this is inaccurate. I would also note that, while I have focused here on a few large corporations, the trade in enslaved persons has been ever present and was also something that Burke, Smith, and their contemporaries well understood the evils of. There always have been those who seek to save humanity from these evils, including, but certainly not mostly, the guilt and shame of those of us privileged enough to have gained some benefit from them. However, sadly for all of us, they often fail.

How we forgot

Yet the full extent of their failure was not even apparent to people like Smith and Burke. The British East India Company did not simply ignore these attacks on it but sought to reform and adapt in response to them. One of these responses was for the company to professionalize, and cease sending untrained young men off to administer territories on its behalf. Instead, sixteen-year-olds who had been nominated as potential executives would be trained with the specialist skills the company needed most at a new dedicated college at Haileybury in Hertfordshire. It was, in effect, the world's first dedicated business school and, for the first time anywhere, these promising students would be offered education in the trendy new discipline of economics. Thus it was that the first professor of political economy was not employed by a university but by the very corporation that Adam Smith had taken aim at in his seminal work on the subject.

That professor was the Reverend Thomas Malthus and in the history of classical economics, as taught to undergraduates around the world, his name comes second to Smith's.* Today he is chiefly known for two lines of argument. The first concerned human population. Very roughly, Malthus believed that human beings would inevitably seek to swell their numbers and that, whenever conditions were favourable to survival, we would simply have more children, among whom resources would have to be spread more and more scarcely until the population could grow no more.[133]

His second main contribution to economics was to argue that it would be terrible if people chose to consume less than they possibly could, meaning that the total level of consumption within an economy would fall below the level of its production of goods and services. This would lead to what he termed a 'general glut', but which we would now term a recession, in which both prices and earnings would fall as people found it harder to sell what they made.[134] This was the first attempt in economics to explain economic downturns, and it is striking that, as with population, Malthus believed that they were the fault of bad choices by ordinary people.

Third and fourth in the classical line of economic thinkers are two of Malthus's close friends, David Ricardo and James Mill. Like Malthus, Mill worked for the British East India Company, rising to become one of its highest executives. While mostly remembered for his famous son, the philosopher John Stuart Mill, the elder Mill also made significant contributions to economics[135] and introduced economists to the idea of maximizing 'utility', a generic term that was supposed to capture everything that makes life worth living, but is usually understood as simply the value of consumption (Smith, on the other hand, wrote a whole book exploring our many 'moral sentiments'). Meanwhile, Ricardo, though not an employee of the EIC, turned to economics after making a fortune as a stockbroker, trading shares in it and other corporations. He was the first economist to theorize about the economy, not as a mass of individuals, but a system of three classes, workers, landlords, and capitalists, who were in perpetual competition with one another. The behaviour of each class, he argued, was solely determined by its fundamental interests, meaning that they could be modelled mathematically and explored abstractly, without worrying about all the messy details of life.[136]

Adam Smith's great book on economics, *The Wealth of Nations*, is a truly fascinating read, full of detailed observations about the world and the people in it, including many examples drawn from history, his travels, and accounts of faraway countries.* Although far from perfect (he was unquestionably both racist and sexist, although not so extremely as many of his time) Smith was a deeply humane person who wanted to understand the world and believed that the real wealth of nations was their people. Smith extolled the virtues of mass production via the division and mechanization of labour, but believed this would be detrimental to our characters and so argued that it had to be combined with progressive taxation to support the arts and other social goods to make up for this. He believed in the benefits of trade but railed against the corporations who were coming to dominate it. And he thought that markets were beneficial but saw how they could be easily manipulated and abused.

Once it had passed through the hands of Malthus, Mill, and Ricardo, however, economics was not like this. It soon became a discipline in which people were a problem (they had too many children and didn't consume as much as they should), in which society was a competition of all against all, and in which human values were reducible to a single number representing our interest in utility. This undoubtedly made economics theoretically more powerful, but it also had the effect of making it practically far less observant. Corporations barely exist in this dry world; they are just another way for capitalists to promote their own utility and make no fundamental difference to the underlying calculations that concern many economists.

However, while I don't mean to imply that there was some grand conspiracy involved, I do believe that this was more of a feature of this emerging science than a bug. Smith and Burke had railed against the corruption of corporations and sought to bring them under human control. Malthus, Mill, and Ricardo, however, all benefited greatly from these same corporations and modified economics away from a science of real human beings to become a mathematically abstract theory of something almost, but not quite, entirely unlike us – that rationally self-interested being now widely known as *Homo economicus;* easier to work with but just as inhuman as any corporation.*

Meanwhile, the corporate powers that be prospered like never before. Early corporations, like the East India Company, required a special government charter that would typically need renewing every few years, keeping their numbers low and their governance under scrutiny. However, from the early nineteenth century it became possible for anyone to set up a corporation via a simple administrative process. Later in the century, corporate lawyers started using progressive laws to increase the rights and privileges of the 'legal persons' they represented, such as the 14th Amendment to the US constitution that had been designed to protect the rights of formerly enslaved persons.[137] And, of course, the number and kinds of corporation just kept on growing, with trading companies being joined by banks, industrial manufacturers, service companies, and an ever-growing range of technological innovators (from railroads, to telegraph, electric, biomedical, and computing companies).* Now we live in a world in which there are hardly any human needs that are not being provided for by corporations, yet they do so with such efficiency and ubiquity that we hardly even notice. Thus it was that those strange and rapacious Leviathans that emerged from the ashes of the Knights Templar were able to drift into the background, becoming such an integral part of everyday life that it is almost impossible to imagine existing without them.

However, they do not, and cannot, exist without us. Until recently, every decision taken by a corporation has been taken by an actual person on its behalf. Even now that growing numbers of corporate decisions are being made by AIs instead, it is still humans who are ultimately in control. People have also exerted power over these new Leviathans from outside: the EIC and VOC were eventually abolished due to political pressure, if only to be subsumed into political empires, and other large corporations have been broken up (such as the US Oil monopoly Standard Oil in 1911) or forced to pay for their crimes (such as the $206,000,000,000 Tobacco Master Settlement in 1998). Adam Smith may have been forlorn in thinking that economists would lead these efforts, but his assessment of the costs that corporations place on the human economy is as valid now as it was in the eighteenth century. One thing that has changed since Smith's day, however, is that a world without global corporations no longer feels like a realistic possibility to us; it has started to feel like something far more dangerous, a utopia.

5

Utopia is a Dangerous Place

It is often said that nostalgia is not what it used to be, but few appreciate just how true this is. We live in a time when many people are seriously worried that children may end up generally worse off than their parents and find this totally unexpected and shocking. Yet, for much of European history, and in many other parts of the world, it was generally taken for granted that humanity's best days were behind us and that we were locked in a cosmic struggle to arrest, or even just slow, our perpetual decline.

A golden age

Take, for instance, the Greek poet Hesiod, who divided human history into five ages:

> First of all the deathless gods who dwell on Olympus made a golden race of mortal men … And they lived like gods without sorrow of heart, remote and free from toil and grief: miserable age rested not on them; but with legs and arms never failing they made merry with feasting beyond the reach of all evils. When they died, it was as though they were overcome with sleep, and they had all good things; for the fruitful earth unforced bare them fruit abundantly and without stint.[138]

Yet, these first humans lived without fire and other technologies, since Zeus feared that their lives might become so easy they would neglect their God-given duty to cultivate the Earth. However, the fire god, Prometheus, disagreed with Zeus and gave humanity the gift of fire, deceiving and enraging Zeus. For this, humans were cursed with 'hard toil and heavy sicknesses, which bring the Fates upon men' so that 'in misery men grow old quickly'.

Following this disaster came 'a second generation, which was of silver'. These people had extremely long childhoods, lasting a hundred years, but then aged quickly and lived foolishly, 'for they could not keep from sinning and from wronging one another'. For this they too were removed and 'Zeus the Father made a third generation of mortal men, a brazen race' who loved violence and ate no bread 'but were hard of heart like adamant'.[139] These people were killed by their own violence and were, in turn, replaced by the heroes of Greek myths, like Achilles and Odysseus. 'Grim war and dread battle destroyed a part of them … But to the others, father Zeus the son of Cronos gave a living and an abode apart from men, and made them dwell at the ends of earth.'

And thus, according to Hesiod, we arrive at the present age of men, a terrible time, for 'now truly is a race of iron, and men never rest from labour and sorrow by day, and from perishing by night; and the gods shall lay sore trouble upon them'. Yet, worse is still to come, for there will be a time when:

> Men will dishonour their parents as they grow quickly old, and will carp at them, chiding them with bitter words, hard-hearted they, not knowing the fear of the gods. They will not repay their aged parents the cost of their nurture, for might shall be their right: and one man will sack another's city. There will be no favour for the man who keeps his oath or for the just or for the good; but rather men will praise the evil-doer and his violent dealing. … And then Aidôs and Nemesis, with their sweet forms wrapped in white robes, will go from the wide-pathed earth and forsake mankind to join the company of the deathless gods; and bitter sorrows will be left for mortal men, and there will be no help against evil.[140]

And you yearn for a bygone age of ice-cream vans and Saturday morning cartoons!

Another ancient Greek who was sure that our best days were behind us was the philosopher Plato. In his famous dialogue, *The Republic*, Plato seeks to describe an ideal society that would exemplify the quality of justice and serve as a model for us to emulate. He begins his discussion by noting that he considers the truly just society to be simple and rural, in which people mostly produce things for themselves and trade only in necessities, so that their wants are few, their communities small, and conflicts few. Yet, Plato goes on to note that such societies are prone to becoming fevered when people start yearning for more luxurious things, necessitating greater social complexity such as merchants and soldiers, and causing communities to grow until people no longer know one another. This in turn creates a need for order and rulership, and for education to prepare everyone for their proper place. Plato believed that in an ideal society a wise ruler (such as Plato himself) might be able to govern justly, but that inevitably there would come a time when they lost control and the state fell into the clutches first of its soldiers, then its merchants, then its people, and finally a tyrant.

In a later dialogue, *Critias*, that he set the following day, Plato makes an even bolder claim: a truly just society had once existed, on the lost island of Atlantis.

> Because the principles [the Atlanteans] held were true and perfectly high-minded, and because they reacted with self-possession and practical intelligence to the vicissitudes of life and to one another, they looked down on everything except virtue, counted their prosperity as trivial, and easily bore the burden, so to speak, of the mass of their gold and other possessions. They were not made drunk by the luxury their wealth afforded them; they remained in control of themselves and never stumbled. As sober men do, they saw clearly that even prosperity is enhanced by the combination of mutual friendship and virtue.[141]

Yet, even the Atlanteans were eventually corrupted, due to their intermingling with lesser humans from elsewhere. They remained famed as heroes by other cultures, but the gods saw their decline and Zeus resolved to punish them. The versions of *Critias* that survive do not tell us what this punishment was, but it clearly involved a widespread flood that drowned the island and its inhabitants.

Finding Nowhere

Stories like these are not at all unique to ancient Greece. They have many parallels around the world, such as the traditional histories of Judaism and Hinduism, and they had a profound impact on European thought. As if to underline the point, many medieval Europeans were aware of living with the legacy (and ruins) of the Roman Empire and some felt they had experienced, or were continuing to experience, social decline from those cultural heights. What these people sought was a return to past glories, however, not progress towards an even better future.

This idea had a significant impact on the way that Europeans thought about Indigenous Peoples they met. Today, we are familiar with the racist idea that Indigenous People are somehow primitive, living closer to primordial or 'natural' lives than those of us who live in 'civilized' or 'progressive' (depending on your preferred flavour of racism) countries. However, while no less racist, early European colonizers were more likely to dismiss these people as being the degenerate remnants of some long-corrupted civilization, rather than viewing them as at an 'earlier' stage of development.[142] Of course, neither of these narratives is accurate; societies all over the world have experienced more or less the same levels of 'development', in terms of cultural and technological evolution; it is simply that different conditions and circumstances have caused this to take different paths.

It was from this mindset that Europeans started speculating about the possible civilizations that might exist in yet 'undiscovered' parts of the world. News of such possibilities began spreading rapidly among the reading public following the publication of two letters attributed to the Florentine navigator Amerigo Vespucci, who had been hired, by first the Spanish and then the Portuguese, to chart the lands that would come to bear his name, America.

The first of these letters, *Mundus Novus* published in 1503, was probably composed by Amerigo himself to his schoolfriend and patron Lorenzo di Medici in Florence. In it, he argued that the lands that had been discovered were not part of Asia but an entirely new continent, a conclusion he reached by comparing his experiences to those of fellow explorers who had sailed to Asia around the southern tip of Africa. He claimed this new continent was 'full of animals and more populous than our Europe, or Asia, or Africa, and even more temperate and pleasant than any other region known to us'.[143]

The second letter was addressed to the leader of the Florentine Republic, Piero Soderini. Published in 1505, it is far more sensational in tone. The letter describes four voyages undertaken by Amerigo (his other documents only mention two) and contains many lurid tales, with accounts of female promiscuity and cannibalism among Indigenous Peoples but also crewmen being set upon and killed by groups of

Indigenous women and a community who had developed an effective cure for impotence. It is now widely thought that the letter was a forgery and may even have been written to discredit Amerigo.[144]

Both letters were publishing sensations across Europe, but especially the one to Soderini. It was on the back of this fame that map makers started to label this new continent 'Amerigo's land', and hence America, and to populate it with drawings inspired by the thrilling details of his letters.

The English philosopher and Lord Chancellor, Thomas More, took this speculation to new heights with his 1516 book *De optimo rei publicae statu deque nova insula Utopia* – literally, Concerning the Best Kind of a Republic and About the New Island of Nowhere. The book, simply known as *Utopia*, presents a dialogue between More and Raphael Hythlodaeus, a Dutch sailor who is described as having been the 'constant companion' of Vespucci during the last three voyages described in the Soderini letter; before being marooned with twenty-three other men, at their own request, on the coast of Brazil, again as the letter describes (although this almost certainly never happened).[145] From here Raphael relates that he was able to build good relations with the local people and obtained further transport and guides who took them to more densely populated areas further south, where they caught a ship to the island of Utopia (as mentioned above, meaning simply 'Nowhere').

What follows is a lengthy and, if one is honest, rather boring description of this fantastical society. The book is peppered throughout with allusions to Plato's *Republic* and *Critias*, and *Utopia* shares some features with Plato's vision of an ideal society. For instance, like Atlanteans, Utopia's residents have no regard for gold, yet they have lots of it and must constantly reinforce this aversion (for instance by using it to make prison fetters and chamber pots). They also live in highly ordered communities where people play precisely determined functions and carefully control the size of their population. There are also elements of *Utopia* that reflect the accounts of Indigenous Peoples in the Soderini letter, for instance in the way that they have no knowledge of iron and steel, change their houses every seven years, and how Utopian soldiers bring their wives to war. However, the most striking feature of Utopia is its democratic communism. All property in Utopia is held in common and owned only to the extent that it is used, and Utopia is run by a system of representative democracy involving a hierarchy of household and community councils under the sovereignty of a prince who is elected for life.

Much debate surrounds whether Utopia reflects More's ideas for how society should function. However, to me, the most significant fact about Utopia is that it is presented as somewhere that does not exist, layered into an already sensationalized account of a little understood new world. When Plato described his ideal state, he had to be clear that he was describing a real and desirable possibility that had once existed and that he wished to recreate. However, for More, *Utopia* offered an opportunity to tell just another lurid tale in an already fantastic account of Vespucci's voyages, and readers could, and did, take whatever they wanted from that.

Journeying through imagined lands

More's *Utopia* was only the first of hundreds of similar works that speculated about possible lands in the undiscovered world. I will here only mention two other works that are particularly interesting and instructive.

The first is Margaret Cavendish's *The Blazing World*, written in 1666.[146] Cavendish was an English philosopher who corresponded with both Descartes and Hobbes and disagreed profoundly with both. Rejecting both Descartes' notion that the mind and body were separate and Hobbes's theory that our minds were simply mechanical computers, she sought to identify a 'vital matter' that was present in the world but different from anything previously observed. She believed this matter must be spread throughout the entire human and animal body, not simply our nerves and brains, providing our capacity for movement, sensation, and choice. She was thus deeply interested in advances in science, for instance becoming the first woman to attend meetings at the newly founded Royal Society, and she wrote several books on science and philosophy.

However, she was troubled by the limited audience that these works could reach. In particular, she worried that very few women would read them. Thus, alongside her greatest and final work, *Observations upon Experimental Philosophy* (1666), she decided to write a Utopian novel, which she hoped women might be more interested, and permitted, to read. In the novel, a woman is kidnapped by a would-be suitor who sails off with her, only for storms to carry them all the way to the North Pole. Here, everyone on the boat except the woman is killed but she alone is transported to an entirely new world (not simply an undiscovered land), peopled by sentient animals who make her their Empress.

The citizens of this new world tell her about their discoveries and ideas, with each kind of being representing a different branch of science – the bird-men are astronomers, for instance, and the ape-men chemists. She, in turn, corrects and guides them in how to improve their work. For instance, she argues that (then innovative) scientific instruments like telescopes had the potential to deceive, as well as to enhance, our senses; which should be trusted as superior to any technology because they are natural abilities that flow directly from our 'vital matter'.

Despite these philosophical differences, however, a key theme of the book is Cavendish's endorsement of Hobbes's arguments about the need for a single sovereign and the inevitability of conflict and division without one. For instance, the Empress is keen to discourage scientific disputation for its own sake and prevents her scientists from coming up with theories that are too controversial. At the climax of the novel she takes this argument to its logical extreme, persuading the citizens of the Blazing World to journey back with her to our world in order to use their new discoveries, including a kind of jet engine and a napalm-like substance that ignites on contact and burns continuously, to attack, defeat, and subdue every nation and people on Earth beneath the sovereignty of the British King.* While acknowledging the violence and potential unfairness of this course of conduct, she argues that it is the only way to achieve lasting peace in our world, as it is already enjoyed in the Blazing World under its one Emperor and Empress, and therefore that the long-term benefits outweigh these costs!

Another work that used the Utopian form to discuss science was Francis Bacon's 1626 novel *New Atlantis*. Bacon, like More before him, had been Chancellor of England. He was also a pioneering philosopher of science who helped develop what we now know as the scientific method. He believed that science could be used to transform societies for the better; but only by enabling humanity to regain its former 'dominion' over the Earth, granted to Adam as a gift from God but lost, he believed, as a result of original sin.

In *New Atlantis*, Bacon describes the Pacific island of Bensalem, where society is governed by a scientific institution known as the House of Salomon, which was dedicated to 'the knowledge of Causes, and secret motions of things; and the enlarging of the bounds of Human Empire, to the effecting of all things possible'.[147] Its members study the natural world, undertake experiments, produce new theories, and develop novel technologies and arts. They also secretly visit other countries to learn from their wisdom and assimilate it with their own. From the success of this technocratic government, the island prospers and enjoys freedom and virtue to an extent the European visitors can scarcely believe; 'if there be a mirror in the world worthy to hold men's eyes' they conclude 'it is that country'.[148] However, once again, there is the rub: the country of Bensalem does not exist.

It is said that *New Atlantis* helped to inspire the next generation of scientists to establish the Royal Society, and that its design reflected the traditions of Salomon's house. However, in doing so, they were following patterns and ideals already established by previous European institutions, such as guilds and universities, that had influenced Bacon. Meanwhile, the actual peoples living in areas being colonized by Europeans were not thriving or getting to share their wisdom with their colonizers, they were being dispossessed, killed, and written out of history.

Despite placing his ideal vision of a scientific society on an uncontacted island in the Pacific, Bacon did not view people living in such places any more favourably than did other Europeans of his day. In fact, he was a key advocate for their colonial subjugation. He was a charter member of the Virginia Company from 1609, helped found the Newfoundland Company in 1610, and was a member of the East India Company from 1618. He also wrote several essays on colonization, including 'Of Plantations' and 'Of Empire'.

Bacon advocated colonial expansion for two main reasons. Firstly, that other great European powers were establishing their own colonies and England must not be left behind, and secondly, that England would benefit from having colonies where it could profitably send its growing population, to prevent competition and conflict at home.[149] Bacon saw colonization as fundamentally a matter of the conquest and subjugation of territory and believed that, as such, colonized peoples should have fewer rights and privileges than their colonizers. Indeed, one of the first acts of the council of the Virginia Company after Bacon joined it in 1609, was to issue the following instructions to their colonists: 'you must secure from [the Indigenous People] some convenient number of their Children' and 'remove from them their Iniocasockes or Priests by a surprise of them all and detaining them prisoners'.[150] Of course, this was not to learn from them, as Bacon's Salemites would have done, but to eradicate their existing culture and indoctrinate them in European ways of life. These instructions set a precedent in colonial policy that survived in the British empire and its successor states late into the twentieth century.*

And yet, there is growing evidence, from archaeologists and anthropologists, but especially from the testimony of Indigenous People themselves, that many Indigenous Societies had elements similar to Bacon's utopia. Societies that did not rely on agriculture, or where it supplied only a minority of their food needs, typically enjoy far more leisure time than those in which people must constantly tend animals and work in the fields. One of the things that this time is used for is discussion and debate among all members of the community, and without dominating monotheistic religions, these could range over a far wider set of topics and positions than medieval and early-modern Europeans dared to broach.

Such knowledge cultures could have provided models for not only one, 'perfect', institution of science, as imagined by Bacon in *New Atlantis*, but a whole catalogue of different forms and approaches to knowledge creation.[151] Growing out of these diverse cultures, Indigenous Peoples developed many different knowledge systems and cosmological world-views, some of which included elements such as embodied consciousness and a human-centred approach to science and technology, as advocated by Margaret Cavendish in her *Blazing World*, only often with far more sophistication and careful elaboration, born out of generations of discussion and debate on these points.[152] And, again, among the wide range of social structures that European colonists dismissed and ignored, many displayed significant levels of both communal property ownership and democratic decision-making, as explored in Thomas More's *Utopia*.[153]

Utopia is a very dangerous place to live, because that means living where the reality of what does exist gets replaced with someone else's dream of what could, or should, exist. While the ancient Greek practice of imagining different and better societies existing in the past might have bred a certain degree of cultural pessimism – and given credence to people like Plato, who confidently predicted that they could bring that greatness back – at least the past could not be harmed by the myths we tell about it. However, as we can see, the projection of people's imaginations about what society could be into the terra incognito of the world that they were colonizing helped support a culture that simultaneously imagined other ways societies could be, while undermining any society that was different from itself.

From Utopia to Uchronia

On that basis, it should worry us that, since the late eighteenth century, the trend in utopian fiction has been to move away from imagining utopias in some far-off land and towards placing them in an ideal future (sometimes called uchronia – literally 'No time'). The start of this trend is usually dated to Louis-Sébastien Mercier's 1771 novel *L'An 2440, rêve s'il en fut jamais*[154] (*The Year 2440: A Dream If Ever There Was One*),* about a philosopher who, after arguing with a friend about everything that is wrong with the France of his time, dreams of how things might be better 600 years in the future, when they are ordered according to Enlightenment values.

However, the origins of this trend go back much further than that. While there is debate over Europe's great 'discovery of the future',[155] it is undoubtable that Thomas Hobbes had a role to play. When he wrote about the 'natural condition' of humans, arising from our mechanical nature, he probably did not mean to imply this was how people had lived in the past but simply to explore a hypothesis. Yet, many who read his work did take his view to explain a kind of history of the human species, in which we had once been locked in a war of all against all, but that some of us had managed to escape by realizing our weakness and voluntarily submitting to another's sovereignty to save us from this terrible fate, allowing a form of civilizational progress.

Other theorists made use of the same concepts and approach to build different arguments. The greatest challenge to Hobbes's theory of the natural condition for human beings came with Jean-Jacques Rousseau and his 1754 *Discourse on Inequality*.[156] Rousseau charged Hobbes and other theorists with having merely imagined how humans might act if we removed the social rules and institutions that surround us. However, he points out that this is not the same question as wondering how we might act if such institutions had never existed. This makes him the first person to attempt a fully historical analysis of how human nature might have evolved. There are indications that Rousseau had read, and been influenced by, some of the writings reporting the views and experiences of colonized peoples, like Kandiaronk's, although these would have been mixed in with, and hard to distinguish from, the far larger number of European utopias and similar works.

Rousseau argued that, in the absence of society, humans would be inherently covetous and self-interested. He points out that, in such a state, there would be many fewer people in the world, and it is likely that the bounty of nature could satisfy everyone's needs without any provoking competition. Furthermore, like his close friend Adam Smith, Rousseau argues that humans are innately sympathetic towards one another, so that people would not generally seek to hurt each another without prior cause and would in fact wish to be helpful wherever this was feasible. Like Plato, in his *Republic*, Rousseau was concerned that this state of nature might not be satisfying, and it could be dangerous, but he believed that in such a situation people would naturally live in freedom and equality, in a way very different from how they did in the hierarchical societies of his day (and ours).

This disagreement about the natural condition of human beings is easy to read in good versus evil terms, with Hobbes portraying human beings as villainous and Rousseau as angelic. However, to my reading, such an interpretation goes far too far. Both Rousseau and Hobbes believed that human beings wish to live in peace and harmony with one another, in the state of nature and at other times, and both believed in a natural morality that goes beyond simple human instincts. However, Hobbes sees mechanistic desires as posing an immutable problem for our ability to realize this moral dream, since no matter how well satisfied, people will never stop wanting more due to their inherent motivations (something he likened to the law of the conservation of momentum in physical objects). Rousseau simply didn't share this view of how humans work, both because he believed our desires could be fully satisfied and because he saw sympathy and our desire for companionship as providing balancing psychological feedback to our acquisitive self-interest.

Rousseau did agree with Hobbes, however, that our desires posed a problem for human morality. That is because, even though he thought we can have enough things in the state of nature, he suspected that we would never satisfy our need for variety and novelty. Thus, while Rousseau thought humans would be free and equal in a state of nature, he also believed we would remain dissatisfied by what we could produce. This, together with our natural companionability, would lead humans to live in larger and larger groups, in which people could increasingly specialize to produce a greater variety of things and provide for different needs – the same process that Plato thought would lead his ideal rural state to become a feverish city.

At this point, Rousseau believed our social situation fundamentally changed. Firstly, having a greater variety of goods, with more labour-intensive and luxurious items available to consume, would mean that people would no longer be satisfied with the produce of nature and start having to deal with scarcity in ways they had not before. This would lead to conflict, both within and between societies. Secondly, because of this conflict, societies would start to need rules that governed who could have and use what, starting with a rule about the ownership of property.

These rules, which he referred to as the Social Contract, greatly reduced people's freedom to do and be what they liked and created inequalities between people in both wealth and power. However, their general effect might still be beneficial, because they prevent conflict and allow for these complex and luxurious societies to continue, so we still accept them despite their downsides. Yet, they remain highly unfair, and this causes problems. Rousseau believed that these were not insoluble, but the solutions required people to organize themselves into small enough groups to allow for proper collective decision-making, where we can all actually choose the laws we live under for ourselves. This would be a fundamentally different form of society to what we are currently used to.

With all this speculation about the origins and nature of humanity and our social institutions it is not surprising that people started to speculate about possible futures that lay ahead of us. As we will see in the next chapter, that soon happened, not only in utopian (and later science) fiction but also in political discussions and public debate.

How to get somewhere

However, natural as it may seem, there is a huge problem with shifting from speculations about the past trajectory and present diversity of humanity to speculating about ideal possible futures, especially from a utopian perspective. To be clear, the problem is not with the speculation: as we saw in Chapter 1, speculative fiction has often been well ahead of the curve in understanding possible risks facing humanity and remains a valuable tool we can use to support creative Futures thinking. The problem is with the idealization on which utopian literature depends. To put it simply, Rousseau's history, compelling as it is, simply cannot capture all the complexity that lies behind human social evolution. Each human society, just like present-day societies, was unique and varied a great deal in relation to factors like group size, level of interpersonal violence, and adoption of technologies. There is no simple linear answer as to why societies went on to develop as they did, just as there is no single 'development pathway' that all societies follow, or 'fail' to follow.*

Given this, we need to ask, are our futures going to be more complex and diverse than our past? The utopian futurist must hope not, if their speculation about what it could look like is to be worth much. Their futures are dominated by a single optimum culture or social structure, planning an entire planet, galaxy, or even universe, that is supposed to continue in its ideal form. However, as human beings get ever more numerous and the rate of social change increases, that seems highly unlikely. Of course, this needs to be weighed against the great homogenizing influence of globalization, starting with the catastrophe of colonialism itself, that has, in some ways, reduced human diversity. However, I believe that if we are to have hope for our species, then we need to be capable of imagining futures in which these homogenizing forces grow weaker, not stronger.

Thus, when people start imagining utopian futures, there is often some great global event: from the development of an artificial superintelligence or a global revolution, to a world war or massive disaster. This greatly simplifies our prospects and allows people to speculate freely without any of that human messiness. As someone who has studied the possibility of such global events, I cannot put much hope in such futures. We can all see, if we choose to, what such upheavals have already done to our world, when a few colonists' ideas of a profitable utopia steamrollered over countless natural experiments in human being. It was not good. We should not go further down that road if we can help it!

There are alternatives to trying to build Utopia. Rather than dreaming of a perfect nowhere, we can try to imagine how to make this place, planet Earth, our interlinked societies, our overlapping communities, or just wherever we happen to be right now, better. This is the concept of Protopias, possible futures that we can explore and actually create, and that we want to explore and create, because they are at least somewhat better than our present. According to the Protopian futurist monika bielskyte, 'there is no singular "future" trajectory but rather a vast scope of many alternative futures'. These are not the inevitable products of deterministic global forces, but a playground of possibilities created by our imaginations and desires for joy, justice, and connection. Our mission, if we choose to accept it, is to get back into the habit of imagining the many possibilities that exist around and ahead of us, so we can start 'proactive prototyping of radically hopeful and inclusive futures'.[157]

We may have come a long way since the colonial heyday of the sixteenth and seventeenth centuries, but still we are ignoring alternative possibilities about what it means to be human, how to relate to other kinds of intelligence, and how to organize economies and societies. Now is the time to embrace our radical freedom and think far more broadly about human futures and what they can be like. Of course, there are many ways to do this, but I am most qualified to speak about the ones that I know best, which are still mostly those relating to Eurocentric philosophy. So, let us go back to that point at the end of the eighteenth century when people in Europe seriously started to think about the long-term consequences of their actions and see where these ideas came from and where they can take us.

6

A Point of Inflection

The past and future often feel very far away. We might enjoy science fictions set many centuries hence, or get interested in ancient history and wonder what it was like to live in the past, but in general we seldom imagine ourselves in relation to the great passage of time. Still, it can be nice to think that *someone* at least is doing this. There is a popular story about President Richard Nixon's state visit to China in 1973 that encapsulates this rather well. The story goes that Nixon asked the Chinese premier, Zhou Enlai, for his views on the French Revolution and Premier Zhou replied, with Chinese sagacity, 'Too early to say!'

Like many good stories, this is almost, but not quite, entirely false. The exchange really did happen, but the story conveniently leaves out that these remarks were the result of a simple translation error. You see, when Nixon's remarks were translated into Chinese, the impression was given that he was asking, not about the French political upheavals of 1789 but the popular protests of 1968, only five years earlier, and it was these that Zhou was speaking about.

This misrepresentation notwithstanding, however, I think that the story became so popular because we all understand that global events really do cast long shadows. While we live in an age of 24-hour social media updates and are liable to forget what took place on a Monday by the time we get to Thursday afternoon, we know, and hope the wise and powerful must be all the more aware, that our decisions have consequences that can last a long time; while our lives are shaped by the thoughts and actions of those who came before us, even if they are long dead. It would be comforting to imagine that our leaders are able both to appreciate the ongoing significance of historical events, and perhaps even to plan for the distant future implications of their own choices.

Furthermore, I actually believe that, had he been answering the question president Nixon intended to ask, Premier Zhou would have spoken wisely. We don't yet know the full consequences of the 1789

French Revolution, and that matters when we start thinking about the future of our species.

The revolutionary significance of the future

This was a point that some of those who were caught up in this period had already started to think about. For instance, in 1795 the German philosopher Immanuel Kant looked on at the idealistic hopes of the French revolutionaries, and at all the wars and international conflict they had unleashed, and felt prompted to ask the question *is the human race constantly progressing*? He saw three possibilities. In one humanity might 'decline into wickedness … for at a certain stage of disintegration it would destroy itself'.[158] Kant thought that this was a real possibility and that this 'revolution of a gifted people … may be filled with misery and atrocities to the point that a right-thinking human being, were he boldly to hope to execute it successfully the second time, would never resolve to make the experiment at such cost'.[159] Alternatively, it may be that things remain about the same, either because 'the proportion of good and evil elements inherent in our predisposition remains constant and can be neither augmented nor diminished'[160] or because we sometimes make things better for ourselves for a limited time but then demolish everything we built.

However, Kant held out hope for the third option, that humanity really was making progress. He saw evidence for this not in 'momentous deeds nor crimes' being committed around him, 'nor in ancient splendid political structures which vanish as if by magic while others come forth in their place as if from the depths of the earth' but rather in 'the mode of thinking of the spectators which reveals itself publicly in this game of great revolutions, and manifests such a universal yet disinterested sympathy for the players on one side against those on the other'.[161] In other words, he thought that things would get better because it was clear that people wanted them to do so, and recognized they had the capacity to work towards that goal for themselves. His hope was that this 'demonstrates a character of the human race at large and all at once … a character which not only permits people to hope for progress toward the better, but is already itself progress insofar as its capacity is sufficient for the present'.[162] Nevertheless, only if this character endured and outlasted the momentous global events that had called it forth, would the painful consequences of revolution have been genuinely worthwhile. With all that has happened in the intervening two and a half centuries, I think this remains distinctly uncertain.

Perhaps the philosophical ideas most closely related to the French Revolution were those of Rousseau (which we discussed in the previous chapter) and in particular his belief that modern societies failed to uphold the social contract between the state and its subjects, and that an active citizenry might replace them with better political institutions able to discover and enforce the 'common will' of the people.[163] Also highly significant was the growing social and political interest in the prospects of the future; a movement that became known as Progressivism. Nine years before he considered the long-term impacts of the French Revolution, Kant was already an important part of this movement, arguing that 'each of us, for his part, is called upon by nature itself to contribute as much as lies in his power to this progress'.[164] While Rousseau still looked favourably on his imagined human past of freedom and equality, and viewed the culture of complex societies as a necessary evil that must be carefully controlled by the people, Kant and other progressives only looked forward to the development of these societies, pointing out their flaws but also seeing them as engines for scientific and cultural progress that would eventually show us better ways to live.* Perhaps the most detailed and influential account of this view, developed during the French Revolution itself and published, posthumously, by one of its early supporters, and later victims, was a *Sketch for a Historical Picture of the Progress of the Human Mind* by Marie Jean Antoine Nicolas de Caritat, Marquis de Condorcet.[165]

These ideas would turn into revolutionary fervour when they were taken up by an increasingly wealthy and well-educated, but politically disenfranchised, middle class in France and elsewhere. While traditionally European societies had been highly stratified between ruling aristocratic and ecclesiastical classes and a mass of, largely rural and poor, 'commoners', the growing wealth and power of international merchants (and the corporations they established), industrialization, and wider (although far from total) access to education made these divisions increasingly untenable and left growing numbers of people searching for something better.

The revolution controversy

Yet, the impact of French revolutionary ideas on our relationship with the future went much further than any naive belief in human progress. Perhaps the greatest debate of the French revolutionary period took place between an English bureaucrat turned American revolutionary, Thomas Paine, and an Irish philosopher turned British MP, Edmund Burke.

Thomas Paine was one of the founding fathers of the United States of America. He spent his early life in England working as a soldier and customs officer, during which time he continually agitated for himself and his fellow officers to get a pay rise. However, after being introduced to the American polymath and diplomat Benjamin Franklin, while Franklin was on a visit to London in 1774, Paine moved to America and became a radical journalist and prominent advocate for American independence. In January 1776, he published the pamphlet, *Common Sense*, which argued for the fundamental rights of American people, castigated what he saw as the English tyranny oppressing them, and made the case for a war of independence.[166]

It was in this context that Paine and Burke first came to one another's attention. Burke was one of a very few British politicians at the time who supported American calls for self-government and opposed the UK's policies towards its colonies. When the American colonists revolted against British rule, Burke argued that the government should make peace with them and recognize their independence. As such he earned considerable respect from American revolutionaries like Paine, as well as radical thinkers in Britain who also supported their cause.*

When Paine returned to London a decade later, he spent a week with Burke trying to build alliances, although he used much of this time seeking Burke's backing to help finance his new design for an iron bridge. Yet their prospective friendship was not to be. While Paine had agitated for revolution because of what he saw as the natural rights of American citizens, Burke had always been clear that he was not interested in such 'metaphysics'; he simply believed that American independence would not be bad for British interests but a war with America could be disastrous. This difference would come to a head a few years later, following the 1789 revolution in France.

Many of the radical voices in Britain who had supported the American revolution were equally supportive of the French and hoped to see something similar take place in Britain as well. These radicals formed a London *Revolution Society*, ostensibly to commemorate England's Glorious Revolution of 1688 but with a not very subtle intention of stirring up future revolutions as well. To their delight, French revolutionary activism started gaining serious momentum the following year, with the storming of the Bastille prison to free political prisoners and the formation of a National Assembly to redraft the county's constitution. At the society's annual meeting in 1789 one of its members, the unitarian minister Richard Price, preached a sermon on *the Love of Our Country*, in which he proclaimed that Britain must either undertake its own revolution or face destruction:

> Tremble all ye oppressors of the world! Take warning all ye supporters of slavish governments, and slavish hierarchies! Call no more (absurdly and wickedly) reformation, innovation. You cannot now hold the world in darkness. Struggle no longer against increasing light and liberality. Restore to mankind their rights; and consent to the correction of abuses, before they and you are destroyed together![167]

For Burke, such talk showed that his political friends and allies had gone too far. Yes, Britain was full of political and economic abuses (many of which Burke led the fight against, from absentee Irish landlords to the slave trade) but it could not be worth threatening the destruction, or even the diminishment, of society to correct them. He quickly wrote a pamphlet rebutting Price's sermon and condemning him and his peers, which he titled *Reflections on the Revolution in France.*

As we have already noted, Paine, Price, and many other supporters of the French Revolution appealed to a version of Rosseau's Social Contract, arguing that citizens should only agree to give up their natural rights and consent to be ruled in return for social benefits, like public infrastructure or civil defence, and only to the extent necessary to provide these. According to this argument, governments were only justified in continuing to assert their authority if they upheld their end of the bargain, but the ruling elites of their day were failing to do this. Hence, they were no longer justified in holding their exalted positions and should be replaced. This was why revolution was not only justified but necessary.

In his response, Burke agreed that society was based on social contract; however, he disagreed that it was built on natural rights or that its benefits were the temporal satisfaction of the needs of only one generation. '[T]he state ought not to be considered as nothing better than a partnership agreement in a trade of pepper and coffee, calico, or tobacco, or some other such low concern', he argued, but rather a coming together of people to form 'a partnership in all science; a partnership in all art; a partnership in every virtue and in all perfection'. Since these are not things that can be achieved immediately, the social contract must be understood as 'a partnership not only between those who are living, but between those who are living, those who are dead, and those who are to be born'.[168] Seeking radical change for the improvement of our lot in the here and now cannot therefore be justified if it threatens the existence of society for future generations. War with America was to be avoided because of how disastrous it would be to Britain, but revolution in Britain should also be avoided for precisely the same reason, because it risked doing irreversible harm to the interests of future generations by destroying social institutions that, Burke contended, had taken centuries to establish.

That did not mean that we should always preserve the status quo. In fact, Burke used the revolution as an opportunity to press for the urgency of implementing political reforms he had long championed, such as respecting the rights of Irish Catholics. 'We must all obey the great law of change,' he wrote, and change was a good thing, 'the most powerful law of nature, and the means perhaps of its conservation.' However, he believed that we owe it to posterity to work on incremental and gradual reforms, so as to realize 'all the benefits which may be in change, without any of the inconveniences of mutation'.[169]

Needless to say, Thomas Paine strongly disagreed. How, he wanted to know, would such an intergenerational contract work, and how could it end up binding oppressed people to the service of authoritarian rulers, as Burke claimed?

> A certain former generation made a will, to take away the rights of the commencing generation, and all future ones, and convey those rights to a third person, who afterwards comes forward, and tells them, in Mr. Burke's language, that they have no rights, that their rights are already bequeathed to

> him and that he will govern in contempt of them. From such principles, and such ignorance, good Lord deliver the world![170]

Instead, Paine's view was that the only timeframe we should consider principles of government against was 'an eternal NOW'. '[W]hat have we to do with a thousand years?' he asks. 'Our lifetime is but a short portion of that period, and if we find the wrong in existence as soon as we begin to live, that is the point of time at which it begins to us; and our right to resist it, is the same as if it had never existed before.'[171] Hence, to the extent that we owe anything to future generations it is simply to do whatever we take to be right for us to do, while accepting that they in their turn may judge, and act, differently.*

From the social contract to the greatest good

This disagreement between Price, Burke, Paine, and their allies became known as the Revolution Controversy. It has been said that it was the last time the foundations of British constitutional politics were ever publicly contested and is often held up as the origin of our concepts of the political Left and Right, with Burke being seen as the Father of Conservativism (despite his many radical leanings) and Paine the model revolutionary radical (despite his cause ultimately being the empowerment of the liberal middle class). I therefore find it fascinating that, so long ago, these people were exploring topics that seem frighteningly contemporary: how much should the interests of future generations figure in our political decisions and to what extent can, and should, we try to shape their world with our choices?

The controversy didn't end with this one disagreement, as we shall see, nor did it start with Thomas Paine. The first person to publish a rebuttal to Burke's *Reflections* was the philosopher, Mary Wollstonecraft. She had been a student of Richard Price's and was another English radical who had looked upon Burke as a powerful ally of the cause. In her disappointment with his new position, Wollstonecraft responded to Burke's provocations at lighting speed, publishing her 150-page *Vindication of the Rights of Men* (named after the revolutionary manifesto *Déclaration des droits de l'Homme et du citoyen de 1789*) a mere 28 days later. Despite this, she presented a point by point rebuttal of his arguments. Core to the book's argument was Wollstonecraft's repeated claim that Burke had let his desire to preserve his own privileged position in society blind him to vices of the rich and the need for social reform. She objected strongly to the idea that preserving aristocratic societies could be seen as being in anyone's interests; indeed she saw it as more likely that British society would collapse due to aristocratic luxury than revolution. Far better, she argued, if it could be replaced by a society where everyone had to work for their living (as Mary, the eldest daughter of an alcoholic father, had always had to do) and social positions were determined by ability and effort rather than birth; not only for those who would no longer be trapped in inferior social positions, but also for society as a whole. 'It is, Sir, possible', she replied, 'to render the poor happier in this world, without depriving them of the consolation which you gratuitously grant them in the next.'[172]

Initially, Wollstonecraft's anonymously published book sold well and received much praise from reviewers. However, when, emboldened by this success, she and her publisher decided to reissue it under her own name, public opinion turned decidedly against the book, earning it many hostile and misogynistic reviews. On the other hand, giving up her anonymity helped Wollstonecraft to gain friends among her fellow radicals and her book still sold unusually well for the time. Wollstonecraft's response to her negative reviewers was to go back and write a second, more considered but also more radical book, *A Vindication of the Rights of Women.*[173] In it, she argued that the power men exerted over women was no less tyrannical than that which governments exerted over their subjects and that, as with political tyranny, its abolition would not only be in the interest of women, but of everyone. Wollstonecraft was not the first person to make this case,* but her account has come to be seen as foundational in Western feminism, partly for the quality of its arguments and writing but also because of the audience that Wollstonecraft attracted. The book sold very well, especially in America, and received many favourable reviews, even if it also attracted a predictable quantity of misogynistic hate.

Another critic of Burke's was the young philosopher, William Godwin. In Godwin's view, people like Paine and Wollstonecraft hadn't gone far enough in their replies to Burke. As a counter to Burke's claim that we risked harming future generations by undermining valuable social institutions, Godwin argued that humans are actually engaged in an intergenerational project of finding ways to live *without* such institutions that tell us what to do, and that in future we would be able to replace these with a society of total freedom in which everyone acted according to their own sense of justice. He agreed with Rousseau and others that complex societies probably emerged as a way for humans to meet our needs in greater peace and comfort. However, he thought that this was only a first, and temporary, step in our moral development. Humanity's ultimate destiny was learning to use our own reason to freely co-operate without the need for coercive institutions like governments and religions. The French Revolution was destructive, but that was the point, destroying social institutions was the next step we needed to take, and we should embrace that.

What was needed now, was for people to acknowledge a kind of justice that did not require states or other social institutions to enforce it, as the social contract does. Such a theory of justice would need to recognize the fundamental equality and freedom of all people, while also commending them to be helpful to one another. From these foundations, he concluded that justice was not actually about rights or responsibilities but rather promoting 'the general good' of the 'whole family of mankind'.[174] This general good, in turn, must be understood in a way that fully respects the equality of individuals, and so must refer to things that everyone values, namely to happiness and freedom from pain. If you have ever studied any moral philosophy, you will probably recognize this idea as 'utilitarianism', and it is broadly the same view proposed by James and John Stuart Mill. Godwin felt sure that the truth of his theory could be appreciated by anyone, and a key argument in its favour consisted of another philosophical innovation of Godwin's, the moral thought experiment, familiar to many through modern examples such as *The Trolley Problem.** Godwin's version was *The Famous Fire Cause:* he asked his reader to contemplate which of two people justice would require them to save from a burning building, a humanitarian whom we expect to contribute significant benefit to thousands of people around the world, or a relative whose contributions to society would be far more modest. As far as he was concerned, the answer to this question was a foregone conclusion: we should save the humanitarian and this realization shows us that people really can perceive and respond to universal principles of justice that go beyond social institutions like the family. If we could only get everyone to base their decision-making solely on such universal principles then, he hoped, we might get rid of these institutions completely and build a future where there would be 'no war, no crime, no administration of justice, as it is called, and no government'.

Yet, this was not the limit of Godwin's hopes for the future. He also believed that, without the hindrance of such institutions, people would be free to develop their mental capacities and unleash their full human potential. When they further used this potential in the service of the greatest good, they would invariably produce huge benefits for humanity. This would include further improvements in the mechanization of work, so that in future even complex tasks could be carried out by machines with only minimal supervision or even completely automated, so that 'a plough [could be] turned into a field, and perform its office without the need of superintendence'.[175] It would also include greatly increasing our understanding of human health and discovering means of prolonging our lives, so that we might be able to rid ourselves from disease, anguish, melancholy, and even from death. Godwin was not the first person to think about automation and life extension.* However, he was the first philosopher to consider them as real future possibilities for humanity and to consider their social implications. He argued that, while workers of his day objected to the mechanization of their labour, this was a result of inequality and that in more equal societies people would welcome further automation. He also believed that the technological changes he envisioned would encourage greater independence and separation between people and would lead them to prefer intellectual pleasures more than the gratification of their senses.

Monstrous visions

However, the revolution controversy also directly inspired other thinking about the possible downsides of human progress that went beyond Burke's concerns with social disintegration. Chief among these thinkers was the Reverend Thomas Malthus. Malthus read Godwin's work with his father, Daniel Malthus. Daniel had been a friend of Rousseau and other progressives and was very much taken by Godwin's visions of the future so, as is often the case with fathers and sons, Thomas set out to prove him wrong, and one point in particular troubled Malthus, who thought it pointed the way to Godwin's ultimate failure.

Once again, this disagreement actually begins with Richard Price. Long before he preached the virtues of social revolution, Price achieved a considerable scientific reputation via his friendship with another non-conformist English preacher, the Reverend Thomas Bayes. Bayes had discussed with Price some ideas he had about the mathematics of probability, and when he died in 1761, Bayes left Price the notes he had written on the subject for Price to publish. This he did, adding his own reflections on the subject, and the work was so well received that Price was elected a member of the Royal Society. This paper forms the basis for what is now known as Bayes' Theorem, and the wider realm of Bayesian Statistics, which now forms the basis for most statistical prediction (including much of modern AI). Price was also the first person to put these statistical developments to work on analysing real world problems.

In addition, Price studied life expectancy, population change, and the proper annuities for life insurance. From this work, he drew a surprising and concerning conclusion: the population of England appeared to be shrinking, and at a rate that was even faster than the population of its colonies was growing. Price shared these conclusions with Godwin, who listed depopulation as one of the five great 'mischiefs' of present society from which he hoped to free people.

Malthus was convinced that this was a grave mistake. He disagreed with Price and Godwin and thought the population of England was actually rapidly increasing (a few years later, in 1801, the first British Census would prove Malthus right and show that Price's calculations had been overeliant on data from low fertility, high mortality, cities). However, Malthus also believed that such growth was inevitable, because people would always have as many children as they could, but also tragic, because growth in the supply of food was limited by the availability of agricultural land (on both of which points, changing social attitudes and agricultural practices were about to prove him very wrong). As we saw in the last chapter, this led Malthus to the conclusion that social progress of the kind imagined by Godwin was, in fact, impossible, because any benefit that it might generate would be quickly wiped out by population growth, which would bring poverty, famine, and the spread of diseases.[176] Thus, in a few short years, the revolution controversy not only explored the possibilities of social progress and collapse, but also laid the foundations for techno-utopianism and eco-dystopianism.

However, to my mind, the full flowering of these trains of thought would not emerge until after the French Revolution and its violent aftermath had finally died away, because in 1796 Mary Wollstonecraft had started a relationship with William Godwin and soon became pregnant. In March 1797 they were married, much to their own embarrassment and the consternation of their friends as both had heavily criticized the institution, and in August the baby arrived and was named Mary after her mother. Sadly, only ten days after her daughter's birth, Wollstonecraft died of a fever contracted from an obstetric doctor who refused to wash his hands before examining her.

While the younger Mary may have been born to two of the most radical and progressive thinkers in Britain, she found that when she started making her own choices, she was not granted to the freedom for which they had both advocated. Aged sixteen, she started a relationship with the young poet Percy Bysshe Shelley, but Percy was already married and Godwin informed Mary that this was a totally unacceptable state of affairs and did what he could to put a stop to the relationship (they would, somewhat reluctantly, agree to marry after Percy Shelley's first wife died in 1816). To escape his demands, and the disapproval of society, the couple fled, first to France in 1814, then (after having to return due to lack of money) to the English countryside, and then again to Switzerland in 1816. On this latter occasion they joined up with Lord Byron, who was himself fleeing from the scandal of his failed marriage to Annabella Millbank, his mounting debts, and the potential exposure of his incestuous relationship with his half-sister Augusta Leigh, and also distraught at having to leave a newborn baby Ada behind.

The events of that summer are the stuff of legend. The previous year, an Indonesian volcano, Mount Tambora, had exploded with the largest eruption in recorded history. The particles ejected into Earth's atmosphere caused a series of climatic changes, including an exceptionally cold and wet summer over much of Europe. Escaping the dreadful weather, the party spent much of their time indoors. On 15 June, Byron's doctor John Polidori entertained the group by reading them some notes he had made of a series of lectures given by the physician William Lawrence, who had sought to demonstrate how every aspect of human life could be explained by solely physical means, without the need for anything like a soul to explain our behaviour.* Following this, the conversation turned to discussing some experiments by Erasmus Darwin,* who had shown that it was possible to make dead worms move simply by passing electricity through them. The following night, the group talked of ghost stories, and then set themselves the challenge of each writing a horror story of their own.

Shelley's response to this challenge was the novel *Frankenstein or the Modern Prometheus* and it combined two key elements of her situation. The first was the imagined consequence of Lawrence's and Darwin's research, the discovery of how human beings really work and the consequent ability to create new life via artificial means. However, the second, and no less key to the story's eventual success, was the question of how we would relate to any such creation. Shelley was powerfully affected by the death of her mother and the abandonment of her father and would have been acutely aware of Byron's agonies about leaving behind his newborn daughter. It is therefore hardly surprising that she imagines the creator, Victor Frankenstein, as abandoning his new creation, and the creature's subsequent lonely journey to seek understanding and acceptance in the face of a cruel world. Shelley was also heavily inspired by her parents' work, drawing on her mother's theories about education and the power of reason to explore how the creature might come to make sense of the world around it, while also challenging her utopian ideal that society could be inclusive towards everyone.*

Shelley poses even deeper questions for her father, to whom she dedicated the novel. Godwin had argued that we should maximize the general good of all and saw future progress as being the ultimate fulfilment of this goal. However, it seems to have been Shelley who first understood the dual implications of this argument that firstly, the sheer number of people who may live in the future means their interests may outweigh those of the present, and secondly, our first responsibility to these people is to ensure they come into existence at all, by preventing the extinction of humanity. In the book, Frankenstein initially agrees to create a partner for his creation, on the condition that the creature promises to go and live far away from any humans. However, in the midst of his labours, Shelley has Frankenstein consider the following argument, strikingly similar to the kind of reasoning her father had used:

> Even if they were to leave Europe and inhabit the deserts of the new world, yet one of the first results of those sympathies for which the dæmon thirsted would be children, and a race of devils would be propagated upon the Earth who might make the very existence of the species of man a condition precarious and full of terror. Had I right, for my own benefit, to inflict this curse upon everlasting generations? I had before been moved by the sophisms of the being I had created; I had been struck senseless by his fiendish threats; but now, for the first time, the wickedness of my promise burst upon me; I shuddered to think that future ages might curse me as their pest, whose selfishness had not hesitated to buy its own peace at the price, perhaps, of the existence of the whole human race.[177]

Yet, despite originating this powerful argument (which has since been attributed as originating with a long list of male philosophers such as Henry Sidgwick, Derek Parfit, and Nick Boström), one gets the sense that Shelley does not herself believe it to be conclusive. Yes, the risk to all of humanity is important, but so is the creature's certain suffering. At the end of the book, she presents his point of view in no less clear and well-argued prose:

> Am I to be thought the only criminal, when all humankind sinned against me? Why do you not hate Felix, who drove his friend from his door with contumely? Why do you not execrate the rustic who sought to destroy the saviour of his child? Nay, these are virtuous and immaculate beings! I, the miserable and the abandoned, am an abortion, to be spurned at, and kicked, and trampled on.[178]

The answer, according to Frankenstein and Godwin, is simple. The creature's actions are unjust when they threaten the greater good and its treatment is just, even if harmful, when it promotes that good. However, we do know that the creature's suffering is real, and Shelley clearly sees it as important that her 'ghost story' makes this clear. It is often remarked that people who have never read the book wrongly believe that Frankenstein is the name of the monster rather than its creator; it is also said that only those who have read the book fully understand that Frankenstein is the monster.

Shelley would return to the theme of human extinction for her next novel, *The Last Man*.[179] This book was in part inspired by the deaths of

Percy and Lord Byron, three of her four children, her half-sister Fanny, Polidori, and many other friends. The first half of the novel presents a fantastical story set at the end of the twenty-first century, in which many of these characters are presented in a roman à clef. However, as the novel nears its halfway point, we begin to hear of a new plague that has emerged in Asia and the story's narrator starts dropping ominous hints that he is writing this in a time when he has been left entirely alone. The second half of the novel tells of how the plague and a series of environmental disasters strike England, and the different ways people react to this. Some panic, some turn to vice, but many strive to keep society functioning, even when they realize there is no real hope of survival. Eventually, England is evacuated but its survivors get overtaken by a religious cult, spreading disinformation about the plague, and civil conflict. They manage to rally again and attempt to make it to Switzerland, but only four get there alive. At this point, the narrator states that the plague ceases, leaving these four survivors safe at last. However, one of them is then killed by typhus and two more die in a shipwreck, leaving our last man (representing Shelley herself) to roam an empty world and set down his story in hope that someone will read it.*

Going back to the beginning

The French revolutionary period thus represents a real inflection point in European thought about the future, what it might be like, and why this matters. Prior to the 1770s, thinking about the long-term future was rare, and people were more interested in speculating about the past or the potential of faraway lands. However, with debates about progressivism, the intergenerational social contract, social collapse and the nature of human, social and technological change, people quickly arrived at many of the ideas that shape contemporary thinking about the future, from the belief that technology might one day render us immortal to the certainty that overpopulation would lead to our demise.

However, within these debates, we also begin to see a revolution in the way people thought about themselves. Western philosophy had been obsessed with the idea of 'human nature' and how our minds work and interact with one another since Descartes and Hobbes had started debating the potential of mechanical minds in the seventeenth century and already a few years after that Leibniz started wondering if human reason was a kind of programme that we could improve with the right education. However, during the French revolutionary period, it became far more common for people to start seeing human nature as something we didn't merely 'receive' but actively created.

For instance, returning to the debate between Paine and Burke, we find that Thomas Paine started almost all his major works, as the US started its *Declaration of Independence*, by saying that humans are born free and equal, while we create societies to serve specific purposes and should abandon them if they no longer do. For Burke, this is entirely the wrong way around. Human beings are naturally sociable animals and have always formed groups and associations that help define our identities and interests. We are not born into perfect freedom; but are raised into societies that deeply shape us. Nor were these societies founded with a single purpose at a particular point in time. They change organically, sometimes slowly and sometimes very fast, but never via a clean break with the past – either coming into existence out of nothing or disappearing without a trace.[180]

A different view about the origin of human nature emerged in the work of Immanuel Kant, who argued that it is not defined by biological facts about how people behaved in a primordial environment, but philosophical facts about the nature of freedom. What makes us innately human, according to Kant, is that we conceive of ourselves as moral beings, making choices about how we want to live. That is a psychological development, not a biological one, yet it still must have originated at a particular point in time, constituting a radical break with our previous existence as animals who could only live as sense and instinct dictated.

The first real human, on this view, was the first person to realize they were not bound to follow their instincts but could change their desires. Of course, we could never know when this happened, but Kant speculated that it could well have involved something quite simple and ordinary to us now. For instance, people often dislike new foods the first time they try them, but grow to enjoy them with repetition or association with positive things, like friendship. Kant speculates that there must have been a first person to notice this happening, and realize that it implied they could actively choose, if they wished, to turn a food they hated into one they loved by altering when and how they ate it. That's a very simple realization to have, but once we understand we have this ability we discover, in Kant's words 'a faculty of choosing for [ourselves] a way of living and not being bound to a single one, as other animals are'.[181]

However, if human nature is a property of our freedom, rather than our biology, then it follows that we shouldn't just associate humanity with our nature at present but must also think about our freedom to change what we will become. Thus, our societies should both cultivate freedom and help people to use it to make better choices. While social contract theorists, like Rousseau and Hobbes, believed that a good society is one where people can agree about how things should be, and utilitarians, like Godwin and Mill, believe it is one where they are happy, Kant developed a theory of ethics that sought to understand questions about right and wrong purely in terms of making our own choices about what is right and then acting on them. If the most important thing to us is our freedom, then ethics shouldn't tell us that our choices should be determined by external factors, like whether people agree with me or how happy they are. Ethics should allow me to make up my own mind.

Yet, in arriving at these conclusions, Kant realized this is very much a double-edged sword. As he writes about the first human being to appreciate the capacity for freedom: 'upon the momentary delight that this marked superiority might have awakened in him, anxiety and fright must have followed right away, concerning how he, who still did not know the hidden properties and remote effects of anything, should deal with this newly discovered faculty'.[182] In other words, in realizing that we have the freedom to choose what we like, we also realize that we seem to have no good reason to choose one way or the other.

This idea would remerge fifty years later in the work of Kierkegaard, as the concept of 'existential anxiety'.[183] Kierkegaard tells a story about the origin of anxiety that is slightly different from Kant's. While Kant imagines humanity realizing its freedom in something trivial, like the choice of food, Kierkegaard thinks about the biblical story of Adam and Eve in the Garden of Eden. He argues that the crucial lesson of this story, and thus the real origin sin, lies not in the actions of Adam or Eve, in eating the forbidden fruit of wisdom, but rather in their realizing that they had been free to obey or disobey the commandments of God all along. Maybe you believe in God or maybe you don't, but whatever you think about morality, we all do have to face up to the same conclusion:

it is up to us whether we act according to what we believe to be right or not.

However, it is worth noting that Kierkegaard, at least, did not see this anxiety as inherently bad; in fact he saw it as a sign of good character, indicating that a person was really grappling with the world as it is. Kierkegaard draws a key distinction between anxiety and fear, noting that fear emerges from anxiety only when we turn away from what we are anxious about. In this case, anxiety comes from our freedom to choose, combined with uncertainty about what choice we should make. We become fearful when we try to live as if we have no choices, for instance because we must do as we are told or to follow our instincts and passions. However, we then worry that this means we are trapped, and that everything about us is predetermined. In particular, Kierkegaard, who was deeply (albeit not conventionally) Christian, believed that fear came from understanding that simply performing a given role in society, even a 'good' one such as a priest or philosopher, would inevitably require us to act sinfully at times. He thought that the way to avoid this fear was to accept that we could also respond to our sense of anxiety by seeking to maximize our authenticity, asking at every point what *we* believed to be right, in which case we would know that we had, at least, done the best that we could.

Working together

In this section of the book, I have tried to explore the origins of some of the key ideas shaping our world in the twenty-first century. I do not mean to say that these are 'the origin'; in a way they are just-so stories that attempt to bring together as many of the facts as I can while building a coherent narrative across centuries of complex history. These narratives have led us to the origins of our understanding of existential risk and existential anxiety.

However, this is not a book about existential risk or existential anxiety, but existential hope. In saying that, I hope that the stories I have told are ones that help to make you feel more familiar with these aspects of the Western intellectual tradition, but I do not mean them to be definitive. The story of both our understanding of these things, and of how they came to be, is very much still being written. I don't personally find any definitive answers in the various intellectual positions I have been exploring here. I'm not even sure that people have been asking the right questions, especially when they start talking about which perfect utopian goal we all should strive for.

However, I do personally find comfort in the idea that the problems that press in on me in the work that I do have not simply emerged of a sudden out of thin air. They are in fact problems people have been thinking about for a long time. How computers and machines can think, what is fundamental about human nature, how we can control massive corporations that show a lack of concern for people and our planet, how to act responsibly towards future generations, and whether we might be heading towards social collapse, ecological catastrophe, or even human extinction. All these ideas were already being thought about centuries ago, they define our sense of what it is to be human, and as humans we can continue thinking about and solving them together.

PART III

Working Together

And so, we arrive, more or less, at the present: 8,200,000,000 humans trying to make sense of a world that none of us created but that seems to be hurtling towards oblivion. What is a species to do?

We should start by taking the advice of that august compendium of cosmic wisdom, *The Hitchhiker's Guide to the Galaxy*. 'Don't Panic!' Kierkegaard was right, anxiety doesn't always have to lead to fear, so long as we embrace it and act on it, rather than turning away.

However, this is not an existential crisis we have to face alone. For one thing, being only one in 8,200,000,000 means that our choices usually don't amount to much in the great scheme of things, unless we happen to be high up in some large institution. However, for another, those other 8,199,999,999 human beings are simply the best resource we have.

In the next three chapters, I want to look at how individuals fit together into wider systems, whose capacities are far greater than the sum of their parts. In the next chapter I will look at our relationship with past and future generations, how we can make best use of what history has given us, and what we can do to help future people take over from us when their time comes. In Chapter 8 I will look at the systemic nature of risk, and of risk mitigation, and why the end of the world is unlikely to be caused by a single explosive catastrophe that we may be powerless to prevent or respond to. Finally, in Chapter 9, I will turn to some of the solutions that have been proposed for making the world a safer place and argue that these often put far too much responsibility on the heroic individual while ignoring the importance of more humble contributions that all of us can make.

7

Steering the Centuries

Perhaps I think so much about the past because I live there, or at least I live in the city of Cambridge, England.

You see, when I go out for lunch, I walk past a blue plaque commemorating the spot where, in 1936, Alan Turing first developed the concept of a Universal Turing Machine, the ideal computer that would be capable of solving any kind of problem, before passing the pub where James Watson and Francis Crick celebrated their discovery of the double-helix structure of DNA, and the Church of Edward, King and Martyr, known as the cradle of the English Reformation for hosting the country's first openly evangelical sermons in the 1520s. I often walk back a slightly different route that takes me past the site where J. J. Thomson first discovered the electron in 1897, showing that the atom (whose name literally means 'indivisible') could in fact be split. If I am feeling stressed, I walk the other way, along the river Cam and out through Coe Fen, Lammas Land, Paradise Gardens, and Grantchester Meadows to Byron's pool, where the young poet used to go swimming with his friends. On my way I'll pass Skater's Meadow, where a lamppost stands incongruously in the middle of a field, a relic of a climatic past in which the river Cam would flood and then freeze so reliably in winter that the city decided to erect lighting for the many locals and students who used this as an opportunity to go ice skating. Nowadays, of course, the river never freezes due to climate change.

These are only a small fraction of the stories built into my familiar landscape. There are countless other tales of scholars and politicians, priests, poets, and generals. Cambridge is just that sort of place.

It can be easy to get triumphalist about all of this. The Centre for the Study of Existential Risk, where I work, was established in Cambridge because it was felt that its track record of innovative thinking and scientific discovery was just what we need if humanity is to overcome the many challenges facing us. Meanwhile, at the University of Oxford, researchers have arguably gone even further. The philosophers Hilary Greaves and Will MacAskill have articulated a powerful case in favour of taking a position they call 'strong long-termism' and established a Global Priorities Institute at the University that works to develop and implement it.[184] According to this view, humanity now has both an opportunity and obligation to evaluate actions and policies according to their effects on the very long-term future, which runs into the next trillions of years and beyond.*

However, it could have made just as much sense if these research centres had been founded at Oxford and Cambridge because these are communities in which many of the dangerous things that human beings do or make have originated, and I am personally sceptical that researchers working here should presume to be able to predict the long-term consequences of our actions. The Latin motto of the University of Cambridge roughly translates to 'From this place, we gain enlightenment and precious knowledge' – but even precious knowledge can be dangerous if we do not use it well. Immanuel Kant, the foremost philosopher of the European Enlightenment, once defined enlightenment as 'emergence from [our] inability to make use of one's own understanding without direction from another'.[185] Yet, as we saw in Chapter 2, there are many ways in which people can now use their understanding to do great harm and we may wish for rather more guidance, not less.

The roofs of Oxford

Still, some at least see a great wisdom, and not merely the creation of a lot of knowledge, in the ancient traditions of places like Cambridge. One story, in particular, has come to emblemize this view, although it happens to be about Oxford. According to this story, the founders of the College of St Mary of Winchester (universally known as New College) not only built a great hall for their college, but endowed it with a special grove of newly planted oak trees that would grow to maturity in time to replace the mighty beams of its roof when they fell into disrepair.

Sadly, New College has investigated the matter in some detail and found that the story is absolutely false. However, being false doesn't rob the story of its power, and it hasn't stopped it being repeated. 'Wherever a story comes from', wrote the anthropologist Mary Catherine Bateson 'whether it is a familiar myth or a private memory, the retelling exemplifies the making of a connection from one pattern to another: a potential translation in which narrative becomes parable and the once upon a time comes to stand for some renascent truth.'[186] That has definitely happened with this story and so I think it bears further consideration.

One question we might ask about this story is why, given that it never happened, it has a real air of truthfulness about it. We think of these places as old institutions governed by centuries of tradition, and they are. However, tradition takes many years to form and when people founded universities and colleges in the thirteenth and fourteenth centuries they saw themselves as engaged in radical reforms and innovation. New College, for instance, was built specifically to help the University of Oxford transform and grow. For one thing, the college was much larger than any of its predecessors and effectively doubled the number of college-supported scholars at Oxford.* It also welcomed scholars at an earlier stage in their academic life, equivalent to what we would today call undergraduates, and it was linked to a new feeder school, Winchester College, to provide a continuous educational pathway for students. The reason for these innovations was to respond to the devastation of the Black Death, which had killed many educated priests in England, thus creating a need for better education to train new ones and ensure that the Church's wisdom and knowledge were not lost. It was naturally expected that such a new endeavour would change and evolve over time, and it did. The college hall, for instance, was not kept in its original state but rebuilt several times over the centuries as architectural fashion and the college's fortunes changed.

Yet, by the nineteenth century, when the college hall roof was last replaced, the trend at Oxford and elsewhere was to revive the gothic style of New College's foundation. Partly, this was due to a contemporary theory that saw the gothic architecture of England and other northern European countries as 'spirited' and 'energetic',[187] supporting a view that held that these societies were somehow superior to others and deserved their contemporary place at the head of globe-spanning empires.* However, it was also because institutions like Oxford and Cambridge found themselves, for the first time, competing against newer universities (like Durham and London), often with superior reputations in important areas like science and engineering. Suddenly, their ancient pedigree became a key selling point that made them stand out from the crowd. Thus it was that places that had been evolving for centuries rediscovered and emphasized their medieval roots, and we came to view these innovative institutions in the generation-transcending way this story implies.

Another question we might ask is, even if this story is untrue, are there other examples of similarly long-term decision-making from which we might draw inspiration instead? In one sense, there are. Every time a forester plants slow growing trees like oak and beech, they engage in an intergenerational project, since that tree will not be ready to harvest in their own lifetime. The oak beams that were used to rebuild New College's hall roof may not have been planted specially for that purpose, but they had still been planted long ago and tended for the benefit of future generations.

It is important that we are careful about intentions here. For instance, perhaps the most famous true example of someone planting trees for a specific future purpose is that of the eighteenth-century British Admiral Cuthbert Collingwood. Collingwood became concerned that the British Navy were cutting down too many trees to build ships and that in future there might not be enough timber in the UK to supply them. So, he regularly took walks across the countryside whenever he was home and stuffed his pockets full of acorns, which he planted along the way. In his life he planted thousands and thousands of oak trees for this purpose, and many of them will still be growing today.[188] Yet, before any of these young trees had grown large enough for the purpose Collingwood intended them, the British Navy had started building its ships out of iron!*

That's the thing about intergenerational projects; we cannot see into the future, so we cannot know what future people will need. Nowadays we are much more likely to be grateful that past people planted acorns because we value the trees for their contribution to biodiversity and habitat, rather than cutting them down as their planters may have intended, but we can still be grateful to them, nonetheless.

If I were to pick one roof in Oxford or Cambridge that tells a true story of forward thinking and intergenerational co-operation it would be that of the Muniments Room at Merton College, Oxford. This rises noticeably above its neighbours, because it was made entirely of stone, not oak, to protect it from fire. The purpose of this building – it had only one – was to hold and protect the college's charter and other legal documents. Merton College has a strong claim to be the oldest college in Oxford or Cambridge, but that is not because it has the oldest buildings or was the first to admit students. Rather, its pre-eminence is based on the fact that it was the first institution to be established in perpetuity as a corporation, with a charter that incorporated it as a legal person in its own right. This was one of the first instances of incorporation under English law. While college students and scholars lived in its halls and quadrangles, the college itself would live in its Muniments Room, as it is these legal documents of incorporation, statute, and title that define its identity and continuity down the ages.

And this is often how it feels, at least to me, to work in such old and august institutions. The people one meets are endlessly creative, engaged, and lovely (well, mostly anyway); but they are just people and one is constantly aware that there is also 'the University' or 'the College' that is far older and more powerful than any of us, brooding like some ancient dragon over its ancient manuscripts and piles of gold.

Eight-hundred-year-old institutions do not change easily, but they also provide stability and support in a changing world. What is often best about working in such a place is that so long as you are prepared to respect the institution and work with its strange ways it can provide a level of freedom and security that are hard to find elsewhere in our ever-shifting world.

However, even these sleeping dragons change over time. I often reflect on the fact that, however grateful I may be that eight hundred years ago, people thought to start large endowments for education and research that set a pattern for the future – these benefactors might not return that gratitude if they saw their institutions now. Universities in medieval Europe were established with the mission of furthering Christianity and producing a better educated priesthood who could understand and enact the Will of God as revealed in His Scripture and His Creation. Yet, these same institutions are now largely secular and, indeed, they served to foster many of the scientific and philosophical ideas that undermined that Christocentric view of the world.

This contradiction in purposes might not be so bad if we could say that the founders of these institutions simply valued education and knowledge for its own sake, and that it is just that our understanding of why and how they are valuable has changed over the ages. However, that is not so. The establishment of universities and colleges was often controversial in the past, precisely because people feared that an educated elite might be a danger to the Church, and their supporters were generally those who were convinced that this would never be, and that more enlightenment and knowledge could only ever lead to a greater appreciation of the divine. How wrong they were, and yet I still find myself grateful for what they did, however misguided it might have been for their own purposes. That is often how it is when we try to evaluate the relationship between the present and the past; we need each other but we never really understand why.*

Seeing the wood for the trees

Yet, there is a third question we can ask about the story of New College's roof beams, and for me it is the most interesting of all these questions. Why do we tell ourselves stories like this in the first place? In the case of this story, there is quite a simple answer to this question.

The story of New College's roof was recorded and spread by two men: Gregory Bateson and Stewart Brand. Bateson (Mary Catherine's father, as it happens) was born and raised in Cambridge. His childhood home in Grantchester is another landmark I pass on my walk to Byron's pool. He studied biology at St John's College Cambridge, became a lecturer in Linguistics at the University of Sydney, and then spent much of his twenties and thirties on anthropological field trips to the South Pacific with his wife, the anthropologist Margaret Mead, before moving to California. Bateson was a true polymath, who made significant contributions to many fields, and he claimed to have heard the story of the New College roof beams from the director of medicine at the University of Hawaii.* It became a favourite of his and he apparently often repeated it to friends and colleagues.

In 1976, Bateson was speaking on the telephone to his friend, the publisher Stewart Brand, when he once more recounted his story of the New College roof beams. Charmed by it, Brand decided to publish it in one of his magazines, *CoEvolution Quarterly*. Brand regularly republished the story and in 1996 used it as the inspiration for a new organization, the Long Now Foundation, to encourage 'imagination at the timescale of civilization – the next and last 10,000 years'. Here is the story as Brand recorded it from his telephone conversation with Bateson:

> New College, Oxford is of rather late foundation, hence the name. It was probably founded around the late sixteenth century. It has, like other colleges, a large dining hall with big oak beams across the ceiling, yes? These might be eighteen inches square, twenty feet long.
>
> Some five to ten years ago, so I am told, some busy entomologist went up into the roof of the dining hall with a penknife and poked at the beams and found that they were full of beetles. This was reported to the College Council, who met in some dismay, because where would they get beams of that calibre nowadays?
>
> One of the Junior Fellows stuck his neck out and suggested that there might be on College lands some oak. These colleges are endowed with pieces of land scattered across the country. So they called in the College Forester who, of course, had not been near the College itself for some years, and asked him about oaks.
>
> And he pulled his forelock and said, 'Well, sirs, we was wonderin' when you'd be askin'.'
>
> Upon further enquiry it was discovered that when the College was founded, a grove of oaks had been planted to replace the beams in the dining hall when they became beetly, because oak beams always become beetly in the end. This plan had been passed down from one Forester to the next for four hundred years. 'You don't cut them oaks. Them's for the College "all".'
>
> A nice story. That's the way to run a culture.[189]

As the story was republished over the years, various efforts were made to correct its most glaring inaccuracies (such as the date of the College's foundation and the rebuilding of its hall roof). Nowadays, the Long Now Foundation still promotes a version of this story, with these and other corrections, but notes that 'In all likelihood, the story is a blend of myth and reality' (although the only 'reality' is that there is a New College, with a hall, that does own some forests). Yet, they maintain that 'as with all good legends, this story conveys a larger truth: that a symbiotic relationship with the natural world around us is a useful and sustainable way to maintain human civilization for centuries to come'.

While that is certainly true and important, I'm not sure it is quite what Bateson was getting at when he recounted this tale to his friends.

For one thing, having investigated its origins as best I can, I am not at all sure that Bateson believed the story had any truth in it at all. While he was never a student at Oxford, Bateson spent around fifteen years as a student and fellow at the University of Cambridge and likely understood the reality of an Oxbridge college far better than the rather naive telling of this story implies. He certainly would have had the ability to check the veracity of his story had he wished to do so; but it is worth noting that he never himself chose to publish it and merely told it in an offhand way to his friends, presumably as part of a wider discussion that is no longer recorded.

I also think it is worth looking more at the characters presented in the story and not simply the facts. Bateson believes that this is 'a nice story' because it indicates 'the way to run a culture', so how is culture being run? Well, as he tells it, the wise fellows of an Oxford college are left dismayed because their roof is falling down and it is only one of their junior members (perhaps Bateson was thinking of himself here, as he never rose beyond a junior fellowship at St John's) who is capable of having the genius idea that there might be some oak trees growing in one of the forests it owns. However, the real hero of the story is the college forester who 'had not been near the College itself for some years' but who is the only one aware of the institution's history and its plan to save itself. He apparently knows this because it has been passed down by word of mouth from one forester to the next and yet he is left pulling his forelock at the grand and mighty fellows who had clearly forgotten the plan entirely. The whole thing has something of the air of a biblical parable to it and the meaning of that parable is, surely, at least in part, that if you want to solve a problem you should listen to those who actually deal with that problem and not simply assume you know the answer already!

We can see this moral more clearly if we examine the story in the context of Bateson's wider work. One of the many contributions that he made to our understanding of the world was the idea of 'schismagenesis': the way in which people's interactions with one another can often lead them to divide into different groups (schisms), which stimulate the emergence of new norms and identities (genesis).[190] Bateson proposed that this could happen in two ways. Firstly, groups might take on complementary roles performing separate, but interdependent, tasks and then come to define themselves according to this difference (he proposed this as an origin of much of our gender and class identities). Secondly, groups might compete for a common resource, such as wealth or status, and then start to define themselves by how they tried to obtain it from one another and their relative success (which he proposed as the origin of many national or religious identities).

Bateson believed that schismagenesis was an unavoidable aspect of human societies and cultures, and that it was one of the chief drivers of innovation and diversity within them, both of which were good things. However, he ultimately thought that schismagenesis could also be destructive for all parties involved, as it led people to prioritize maintaining and developing their schismatic identities way beyond the point at which these served to help achieve their goals. Of particular concern to him were the ways in which divisions, that may have made sense at the time they emerged, become engrained into social structures and passed down through generations to the point where nobody understands their function anymore. These can leave people feeling they live in a crazy world where they have to be sorted into one group or another and live up to that group's identity, no matter what. We see this in the story of the New College roof beams, where divisions between the people who work for a college to keep it functioning (the forester) and those who work in the college to pursue its academic objectives (the fellows) have become so deeply entrenched that they are hardly even aware of each other's existence. However, Bateson also saw schismagenesis operating at much larger scales. For instance, in one famous lecture,* he argued that the deep schisms that emerged in Europe during the First World War had left a legacy of international distrust and hatred that future generations still had to live with, even though they had lost sight of the catastrophic events that had brought them about.[191]

The good steersman

Bateson's solution to this problem lay in the emerging field of cybernetics. This is a term whose meaning has become somewhat muddied in the years since Bateson was writing, as it is the origin of all our many different terms beginning with 'cyber'; so it bears a little explaining before we can move on with our story.

Cybernetics emerged from the confluence of many different academic fields in the immediate aftermath of the Second World War. These included the first generation of computer scientists (such as Norbert Wiener and Jay Wright Forrester), who were trying to understand how the machines they had created could function; anthropologists and psychologists (like Bateson and Mead), who were finally beginning to appreciate the diversity of human societies and wanted to better understand how they worked; architects and designers (like Buckminster Fuller), who were interested in the fundamentals of system design; and biologists and ecologists (like George Hutchinson) who were beginning to understand the complexity of the natural world. What all these people were coming to understand was that the simple mechanical model of the universe that people like Descartes and Hobbes had hoped could explain everything was simply not up to the job. This wasn't because the world was imbued with supernatural forces but rather because the ways natural forces interacted with one another defy simple mathematical description. There was simply too much going on for scientists to provide a single straightforward account of how it all worked.

One way in which cybernetics sought to overcome this difficulty was by studying systems, groups of elements that operate together (be they organisms in an ecosystem, people in a social system, neurones in our body, or electronic components in a computer). They argued that it is not necessary to understand how every component of a system interacts with every other component to identify and study the overall patterns and organization of that system. Thus, for instance, even though we cannot know all the complex web of relationships between the plants, animals and fungi of a forest, we can still look at the forest as a whole and understand the conditions under which it will thrive or wither (the subject of forest ecology).

Cyberneticists realized that we could study systems without getting lost in their complexity by looking at the flow of information, and that 'information' was thus something that really exists in the world and not just in our own minds. That isn't to say that information is the same as physical properties like matter or energy. If a system is in a particular state or pattern (say a forest is flourishing) that represents a fact about the state of the system, and hence a fact about the world. Yet this is not simply a fact about all individual organisms (let alone the atoms and molecules) that make up that forest. Many theories have been proposed about the fundamental nature of information,* but Bateson chose to define it in terms of differences – the differences between possible states of a system, between different elements of a system, or between different systems themselves.[192]

This also meant that communication, the imperfect flow of information, is a fundamental force of nature. For a difference anywhere in the world to have an impact, there had to be some vector that connected this cause and effect. This could be anything from the space through which a light beam moves, or the migration of species, to the transmission of human messages or the recording of dinosaur footprints as fossils in ancient rocks. The point is that, no matter what the information is or where it travels from and to, communication is always imperfect, and no single element of any system can be simply and directly connected to just one element of another system.*

The science of cybernetics thus concerns itself with the nature of systems, how we study them, and how we can communicate with them. The name cybernetics comes from a section of Plato's *Republic*, in which he describes the ruler of a city in analogy with the κυβερνητικός (kubernētikos – literally the one who is good at steering, the captain) of a ship, who 'is hard of hearing, a bit short sighted, and his knowledge of seafaring is equally deficient'.[193] Plato argues that, although imperfect, and liable to be dismissed by fellow sailors who convince themselves that they could do a better job than him (even though none of them has any experience in seafaring themselves), the steersman is still best placed to pilot his vessel. Cyberneticians similarly argued that although our understanding of systems and their operation is highly imperfect we still should aim to understand them, how they influence us, and how we influence them, as well as we possibly can.

One of the key insights from cybernetics has been the concept of feedback, the idea that elements of a system are not simply affected by a change elsewhere within it but actively respond to that change.[194] Unless you understand the different kinds of feedback within a system, it can thus be very hard to know what impact a change you make will actually have (we will talk more about this in the next chapter). Gregory Bateson was particularly concerned that a lack of understanding about feedback made people underestimate the potential for their actions to have impacts that were entirely the opposite of what they intended. For instance, a country that makes war on its neighbour might end up making them stronger rather than weaker by instilling in them a greater sense of national unity and purpose. Similarly, a public warning about potential shortages in a product might cause demand for it to rise rather than fall, because people start fearing that they will run out. Another example that Bateson uncovered in his biological research was that many evolutionary processes often start with an environmental change that is initially harmful to a species but that this encourages the species to diversify and so develop new forms or ecological functions that make it stronger. On the other hand, environmental changes that initially benefit a species, causing it to become more abundant, might leave it vulnerable to future collapse if it becomes too homogenous or starts undermining its host ecosystem.

A second key element of cybernetics is the concept of dependency; that both individual elements within a system and also separate systems might function autonomously yet still require one another to achieve their goals. That such dependencies exist was nothing new, but cybernetics helped to show that they are both extremely widespread and often multidirectional; with all elements of a system depending on one another rather than one of them being in charge of others that are solely dependent upon it.

One important implication of this is that human attempts to make systems more 'efficient' by studying how their components operate and looking for ways to make them work better, or by placing everything under the direction of a single authority, often lead the system itself to collapse. This is because, even if an individual component might be improved in its primary function, other components of that system might depend on it in less obvious ways and hence not get what they require once it has been changed.

An early application of this insight was in large-scale industry, where corporations had started using the principle of Scientific Management, developed by Frederick Taylor at the end of the nineteenth century, to try to improve factory efficiency and streamline workflows. This approach, based on empirical study and optimization of worker behaviours in relation to their primary, manager-assigned tasks, was often found to be far less effective in practice than it should have been in theory and sometimes made production lines or entire factories grind to a halt. Following the insights of cybernetics, the computer engineer Jay Wright Forrester began studying the interdependencies that exist within workplaces to understand why this happened. His insights have persuaded many more enlightened companies to pay attention to the experiences of workers within a system, who generally understand it better than managers or consultants who have only studied it from the outside – in line with Bateson's observation that if you want to fix a college roof then you are probably better off speaking to a forester than a fellow.*

A final key element of cybernetics that we will briefly consider is that of a system's zone of variability, i.e. the range of patterns or states that it might occupy. Even if we don't understand how a complex system works, we can usually work out this zone of variability simply by observing for long enough to see what kinds of changes do and do not tend to occur within it. For instance, we can know that after five hundred years in a moist climate like England's, oak roof beams are likely to deteriorate; that a simple computer whose sole capacity and function is to control a few heating circuits will not spontaneously reproduce the works of Beethoven; or that a pack of bonobo chimpanzees are likely to mate with one another. However, the properties of complex systems mean that there is usually also a degree of randomness, so that we can never know exactly when a beam will fail, which rooms in a house might be hotter or cooler, or which bonobo will mate with which.* This means that for most useful questions we can form an opinion about the possible states for a system but be far less certain about which of these it will actually be in. For instance, if we imagine that the founders of New College, Oxford really had planted special trees in the hope they could be used to repair the hall roof then, even if they left instructions that these were not to be felled, they could not have known that they would not succumb to disease, flood, or storm, or simply grow crooked. So, it is possible, indeed likely, that at least some of the wood would need to be found from other sources.

Cybernetics and humanity

These concepts: feedback, dependency, and the zone of variability are all fundamental to the study of existential risk, as we shall see in the next chapter. Many cyberneticists have made important advances to our understanding of this risk; for instance Norbert Wiener provided one of the earliest assessments of the risks posed by AI to humans[195] and Jay Forrester programmed the first World System computer models that pioneered our assessment of environmental risk.[196] However, many now see the movement as too radical in its scope and ambition, although in part this simply reflected the fact that computer technologies at the time struggled to process the complex models and large data sources they wanted to use.

Bateson, however, may have gone further and deeper than many in his theorizing about our relationship with systems. He developed his systems theory into a generalized philosophy of the world, arguing that the debate between Hobbes and Descartes about the nature of the human mind was fundamentally flawed because it assumed that our minds were single isolated entities. He argued that this made no sense and that we needed to understand ourselves, even our internal minds, as systems that were interconnected and interdependent upon other systems. Individual minds, as things that belong to us, do not therefore exist; our minds are rather the way that our brains and bodies are structured by, and exert structure on, the world around us. As he argued in his final lecture, delivered in New York in 1977:

> We used to argue about whether a computer can think. The answer is 'No'. What thinks is a total circuit, including perhaps a computer, a man, and an environment. Similarly, we may ask whether a brain can think, and again the answer will be 'No'. What thinks is a brain inside a man who is part of a system which includes an environment. To draw a boundary line between a part which does most of the computation for a larger system, and the larger system of which it is a part is to create a mythological component, commonly called a 'self'.[197]

If this strikes you as similar to the views about AI advanced by Indigenous scholars that we explored in Chapter 3 then it is perhaps worth remembering that Bateson spent much of his time as a young academic in the South Pacific. Indeed, Bateson and Mead were part of a first wave of anthropologists who saw themselves as trying to learn from, rather than merely to study, Indigenous Peoples, and there are undoubtably elements of cybernetic thinking that merely represent academic science starting to understand some of what was lost when the ideas of people like Descartes, Hobbes, and Bacon were imposed over the rich diversity of views that had existed before.*

Bateson went on to hone his critique of the standard Eurocentric approach to science and philosophy, which he called 'occidental epistemology'. He argued that we had become obsessed with the notion of exerting control but that the complexity and variability of systems make this impossible. We do not have complete control over anything, over the technologies we create, the institutions we design, the societies we live in, the ecosystems we destroy, or even ourselves.

All we can do, and what we must do, he argued, was to understand our interrelatedness and interdependence with these systems and try to build better relationships that could respond to their variability and communicate with them as partners in our collective endeavour for mutual flourishing. Ideas like that can feel very much 'out there' and in keeping with the zeitgeist of the 1960s and 1970s. The thing is, I don't think he is wrong about it. But, as I walk the ancient streets of Cambridge, this bastion of occidental epistemology, I cannot help but wonder; if that is very 'out there' then what is 'in here'?

8

Not With A Bang

The first man to see the world end twice was Luis Walter Alvarez. Born in 1918, Alvarez trained as a physicist before, with the help of his sister, obtaining a job at the Radiation Laboratory in Berkeley, California, where he did important work on nuclear physics alongside Robert Oppenheimer and other leading scientists of the day. Early in the Second World War, however, the US military pulled Alvarez off researching nuclear physics, still seen as a largely theoretical branch of science without immediate military applications, to work on something far more important, radar. Alvarez made several improvements to this emerging technology, most notably developing ways of using it not only to find and target enemy aircraft but to help friendly aircraft manoeuvre and land under poor visibility.

Yet by 1943 military attitudes to nuclear research had shifted dramatically as it became increasingly clear that nuclear weapons might not just be possible but could make a decisive contribution to the war. So Alvarez was once again instructed to switch his research, this time to join the Manhattan Project. In this role, he provided many significant contributions, including developing surveillance techniques to investigate how well Germany's nuclear weapons programme was progressing,* developing a mechanism of imploding a hollow ball of plutonium to trigger a nuclear chain reaction, and devising sensors to measure the vast power of nuclear explosions. Due to this last project, Alvarez played a unique role in the deployment of nuclear weapons, being the scientist charged with personally observing and measuring the explosions from both the Trinity nuclear test and the atomic bomb dropped on Hiroshima in August 1945 – an explosive power that would forever change our world with its civilization destroying potential.*

After the Second World War, Alvarez continued his prodigious output as both a nuclear physicist and inventor, winning a Nobel prize in 1968 for developing a bubble chamber that could detect exotic and unusual particles created by scientists in particle accelerators. However, the discovery for which he is perhaps most famous was not in physics but palaeontology. Working with his geologist son, Walter Alvarez, in 1980 he discovered that a layer of sedimentary clay lying between limestone deposits known to come from the late Cretaceous and early Paleogene periods contained much more iridium than surrounding rocks. Iridium was known to be a lot rarer on Earth than in many other bodies in the universe and they took this as evidence that this layer of clay corresponded to debris from a catastrophic event in Earth's past, in which a 10 km wide asteroid collided with our planet. This distributed particles of rock and ash high into the atmosphere that would have spread around the world, blocking out sunlight and causing a mass extinction event – his second glimpse of a world's end, this time millions of years in the past.[198]

I think that if you asked most people to think of a global catastrophe, their mind would probably light upon either a nuclear war or the asteroid impact that killed off the dinosaurs; so the fact that history decreed that it would be one and the same scientist who originally bore witness to both of these events always sends a shiver down my spine. Yet just because such explosive catastrophes are what comes to our mind's eye when we think of the worst that could happen, and they certainly make good movie plots, this should not blindside us into thinking that this is necessarily where the greatest danger lies.

Thinking in systems

The poet T. S. Eliot once prophesied that the world would end 'not with a bang but a whimper';[199] however if he had wanted to be more scientific he should probably have said it would end with a collapse.

As we saw in the last chapter, from the cybernetic revolution of the 1940s and 1950s, people have been studying the world in terms of systems, complex webs of interconnected entities whose overall behaviour cannot be understood simply by understanding component parts.[200] The degree of interdependence and complexity in these systems is key to how they operate. While we may sometimes think of complexity as a bad thing and wish the world was simpler, the fact is that it is the many different interconnections between ourselves and other human beings, the technology we create, and the universe that we inhabit, that is the very complexity of the systems we are part of, which allows us to survive and flourish. When a system moves from a state of higher complexity and interdependence to one of lower complexity and interdependence it has 'collapsed', in the sense that it is no longer able to function in the way that it did. In most cases such a collapse will be bad for the system, in that it will reduce what it can do and be hard to reverse; however, when a system involves living things, and especially complicated and demanding living things like humans, it will be very, very bad.

Impact cascades

This badness comes in many forms. For instance, as we saw in Chapter 1, the risk of nuclear weapons was misunderstood for many decades because it does not only arise from the direct effects of their explosions but also on the potential for these to cause wider systemic effects such as nuclear winter; and Alvarez's hypothesis about the extinction of the dinosaurs helped revolutionize our understanding of this risk.

From their earliest creation people worried about the destructive potential of these weapons. At first this related to their sheer explosive force.* However, despite an early and, as it turned out unfounded, concern that this might ignite hydrogen in Earth's atmosphere leading to a world-spanning conflagration,[201] this concern did not rise to the level of human extinction. People worried about the impact of nuclear weapons on New York, London, and Moscow, or on how they might devastate nation's military and industrial capacity but not that they would lead to the end of humanity.[202]

This began to change only after attention shifted from the immediate impact of nuclear explosions to their wider effects on human health. This started with news about the 'Nuclear Plague' of horrific health impacts suffered by residents of Hiroshima and Nagasaki who had survived the blasts, although the US government took pains to stamp out speculation about its cause. In 1954, however, the US tested a new kind of thermonuclear bomb on Bikini Atoll in the Marshall Islands, which turned out to be considerably more powerful than they had expected, producing an explosion 1,000 times the size of the one Alvarez witnessed over Hiroshima. This, combined with other properties of the explosion and local weather conditions, led to a very large quantity of radioactive material being produced and spread across huge areas of the West Pacific, as far away as India and Japan.[203] The resulting international incident alerted people for the first time both that radiation from nuclear explosions could be deadly and that this could spread far beyond the site of the explosion itself. However, while this quickly became a cause of great public concern and a frequent topic of cultural and political interest, scientists have generally been sceptical of the idea that existing weapons would be sufficiently radioactive to threaten the lives of all the billions of people who share this planet.

It was, in fact, not until Alvarez started contemplating the effect that a globe-spanning cloud of particles ejected into our atmosphere by a giant asteroid collision with Earth might have on the environment, that scientists started giving serious credence to the possibility of such an existential catastrophe.[204] Nuclear explosions release a lot of material, not from the bomb itself but from what they vaporize and incinerate, as well as the colossal fire storms they can ignite. They also create huge plumes of very hot air that rise quickly causing the mushroom cloud we associate with nuclear explosions. These are more than capable of lifting this material high into the atmosphere – so high that they will stay there for a very long time.[205] This would have both a cooling and dimming effect known as nuclear winter, blocking out sunlight and reducing temperatures worldwide. However, even more importantly, this would disrupt key species and ecosystems on which humanity depends for food and other vital services.[206]

This potential for one catastrophic event, a nuclear war, to lead to others, clouds of radioactive debris, dust, and smoke being sent into the upper atmosphere, and then to others, radiation sickness, nuclear winter, environmental breakdown, global famine, and societal collapse, is known as a cascade. We have recently seen a similar pattern in the way that COVID-19 did not simply cause illness and death but led to other disasters, such as social isolation and mental ill health, which produced even more, from disrupted education and a reduced workforce to declining social trust and rising political polarization. As can be seen from these examples, cascades seldom stay within the narrow confines of any simple risk classification, such as the five key risk drivers I described in Chapter 1, and we can never hope to understand them unless we take a more holistic approach. Thus, for instance, among the biggest risks from climate change are that it will lead to new pandemics by increasing the chance of zoonosis,[207] or increase the risk of nuclear war.[208]

Cascades are a key concept for systemic risk and this is increasingly central to our understanding of disasters. While normally one would expect that two unlikely calamities (say, suffering a heart attack and suffering kidney failure) are far more likely to happen on their own than to befall the same person at the same time, when these events take place in the same system (such as the human body or the Earth's biosphere) one needs to think very carefully before applying such statistical logic. The interconnectedness of these systems means that one event might well cause the other or they may both have a common cause, making them more likely to occur together than separately.

Vulnerabilities and exposures

It is not only our understanding of nuclear risk that is evolving; however, we continue to learn about the extinction of the dinosaurs too. While there are few who now doubt the veracity of the Alvarez hypothesis that they were victims of a massive asteroid that struck the Earth in what is now the Yucatan Peninsula 65 million years ago, that is certainly not the end of the story. There have been several mass extinction events in Earth's history, and this one was not even the most severe.* However, for an extinction to wipe out an entire class of species like this is very unusual, especially as many birds (close relatives of the dinosaurs with similar traits) and even reptiles survived. There were also other large impact events throughout the time of the dinosaurs, notably 70, 145, 196 and 215 million years ago,[209] which did not trigger similar mass extinctions.

Even once we accept the Alvarez hypothesis, therefore, there remains the question of why this asteroid had the impact it did. One of the reasons is likely that the impact did not occur in a vacuum; several other global environmental changes were taking place at the same time. These included a region of extremely high volcanic activity, forming a large area of igneous rock known as the Deccan Traps in what is now India, and a slowdown in the movement of tectonic plates beneath the oceans that may have led to a dramatic fall in sea levels. Meanwhile, on land, ecosystems were being transformed by the spread of a new variety of plants, the grasses, which may have outcompeted many existing species.

While none of these events were, on their own, a cause of catastrophic extinction, computer modelling suggests that together they had the effect of reducing complexity and adaptability within dinosaur-dominated ecosystems, making these prone to collapse.[210]

This highlights a second key component of systemic risk, the creation of vulnerability. When we think about risk, we often fixate on things that might cause us harm: for existential risk these would be the asteroids, nuclear explosions, rising sea levels or rogue AIs. In the field of disaster studies, they are known as 'hazards'. However, we only need to worry about hazards because there is something about us that means that we are susceptible to being harmed by them, and this is what we mean by 'vulnerability'. My colleague Haydn Bellfield explains this with the following example. Haydn is an existential risk researcher who worries a lot about peanuts; this isn't because he believes peanuts might cause the end of the world, they just aren't that dangerous for most people. However, a peanut is still dangerous for him, because he has a peanut allergy, a vulnerability that makes them a hazard.*

Systems do not create vulnerability. We would not be intrinsically safer if we all lived self-contained and independent lives; in fact we would probably be a lot more vulnerable to environmental shocks and our own bad choices. However, systems do profoundly change the nature of vulnerability. Here is a simple example of how that works: if you leant a ladder against a wall, it might be stable for now but vulnerable to some change in the environment that could shift it: a gust of wind, a minor earthquake, an inquisitive child, whatever. Now imagine leaning one hundred ladders against a wall, each of them will be just as vulnerable as the first to such changes, but independently so. Environmental changes could knock over one ladder while leaving the rest standing and it would take something very dramatic to knock them all down. However, if you tied those ladders together, making them into a system, then this would not be so. If any individual ladder started falling in this situation, the other ladders it was tied to would support it, making it less vulnerable. However, if any one of these ladders was shifted so much that it fell over despite this support, then it would bring the other ladders crashing down with it.[211] The interdependence in this system makes each of its individual components less vulnerable to minor shocks but it can mean that a single shock is more likely to fell all of them together. Similarly, if we imagine that one of the ladders in this system was no longer positioned securely, or was rotten, or that the ropes tying them together became tighter or looser, these would all have an impact on the vulnerability of every ladder, just as changes in the dinosaur's ecosystems may have made all of them more vulnerable to a global catastrophe even if it didn't devastate every dinosaur directly.

There is no doubt that something similar is happening with humanity. As we enmesh ourselves in ever more complex webs of global interdependence and technological sophistication, we are becoming less vulnerable to some kinds of disaster but more vulnerable to others.[212] For instance, the last major famine in Europe took place in 1845–8, as a run of cold wet summers and the spread of potato blight (*Phytophthora infestans*) caused a run of poor to devastating harvests. This had very significant impacts for several countries, especially Ireland, and it triggered a cascade of other events including a series of political revolutions across Europe in 1848. Since then, poor weather and crop diseases have not gone away and Europe has continued to experience many bad harvests. However, our increasingly globalized world and a wealth of technologies and forecasts have meant that these have not led to further famines on the same scale. Where hunger persists it is not simply because of a lack of food but political and economic circumstances that disempower and impoverish affected people, as was the case in Ireland in the 1840s, but also Bengal in the 1940s, and China in the 1960s, and still in many parts of the world today.[213] After millennia of agricultural boom and bust, this is a profound change for the better, that our ancestors could hardly have imagined.

However, it has come at a cost. Dependence on such techniques and systems means making ourselves vulnerable to their failure. For example, while one risk left Europe in the 1840s another first appeared the following decade when a strong solar flare was detected by the astronomer Arthur Carrington in 1859. Solar flares are a common occurrence, where the sun releases a large cloud of charged particles into space. Usually, our planet's magnetic field prevents such particles from getting too near to Earth but, when there are more than usual, some invariably slip through. This has been happening since the dawn of our planet and it has few direct effects apart from unusually bright and far-reaching aurorae visible in the night sky. However, in 1859 we discovered that solar flares could also have other effects, as the electromagnetic fields of these particles interfered with electrical systems. In the 1850s there were very few of these, consisting mainly of the nascent global telegraph network, and the resulting damage and disruption were limited.[214] However, electrical engineers believe that were such a flare to happen again today it could cause far more widespread harm, not only knocking out electrical systems but disrupting all the aspects of our lives that depend on them, from food production to sewage treatment.[215] This means that humans are now vulnerable to massive, synchronized failures in these systems in a way that our ancestors could hardly have imagined either.*

Tipping points

A third way in which systems crucially interact with risk is via tipping points. Within systems, the complex interrelationships between elements create what is known as feedback, in which changes in one part of the system cause further changes elsewhere, until this starts to affect the original element that caused the change to begin with. Mathematically, feedback can be divided into two types: positive (or reinforcing) feedback and negative (or balancing) feedback.

Positive feedback is when the effects of a change tend to cause more of that same change to happen. This is the kind of feedback one experiences whenever a microphone is too close to a speaker that is broadcasting the sound it records. When this happens, even tiny sounds are repeatedly amplified as the noise coming out of the speaker is picked up by the microphone and fed back to it, causing a rapid explosion of shrieking squeals. However, it can also involve more complex chains of causation. For instance, as described in Chapter 1, carbon dioxide in Earth's atmosphere is a greenhouse gas, so that the more of it there is the hotter our atmosphere will become. However, one of the effects of a warmer atmosphere is to also heat up Earth's oceans. The oceans currently have a large amount of carbon dioxide dissolved in them (where its greenhouse properties do not affect Earth's climate) but hotter water holds less carbon dioxide than colder water.* Hence, as our oceans heat up they will tend to release more carbon dioxide, and absorb less of it, increasing the quantity of carbon dioxide in our atmosphere and heating it further.*

Negative feedback is when the effects of a change in the system tend to reduce or negate that change. A classic example of this relates to the numbers of predators and prey in an ecosystem. If the number of rabbits in an area increases one year, then the foxes there have a better time hunting them, allowing them to have more cubs and expand their own population. Unfortunately, of course, this isn't such good news for the rabbits, whose population is likely to decline shortly afterwards due to this negative feedback. Similarly, if the number of foxes increases then the rabbits will have a pretty hard time, causing their numbers to decrease and meaning that more foxes end up going hungry, bringing their numbers back down again in the same way.

Within most systems there are many instances of both positive and negative feedback but over time these will tend to settle into a kind of equilibrium in which small fluctuations within the system can be accommodated without the system itself changing. Such equilibria are known as 'basins of attraction' because, like water or a ball rolling downhill into a physical basin, once a system is in such an equilibrium it will tend to stay there but otherwise will keep changing until it reaches one. Complex systems, however, seldom have only one basin of attraction and, since they contain both positive and negative feedback, there will be some changes that push the system beyond the point at which it will automatically return to the basin it started in. For instance, going back to our case of the rabbits and foxes, the simple population dynamics of predator and prey mean that a given ecosystem is likely to support broadly the same number of rabbits and foxes over time, even if especially lush grass might cause the rabbit population to rise in some years or an outbreak of myxomatosis cause it to fall in others. However, what happens if the population of rabbits gets very low very quickly? In that case the suddenly far too large and hungry fox population might just keep hunting the rabbits until there are none left. At the same time, the lack of rabbits could mean that scrub and trees start colonizing the rabbits' closely cropped grasses, reducing their natural habitat, meaning that even if new rabbits were to enter this area their numbers might never recover. In this way, a population dynamic dominated by negative feedback between predators and prey might transition to one dominated by positive feedback that drives the rabbit population towards zero. Eventually, the ecosystem may enter another basin of attraction, in which either the foxes must find another source of prey or leave for hunting grounds new.

The point at which a system shifts from being drawn towards one basin of attraction to another one is a tipping point. These are extremely common and found across all kinds of system. Sometimes they can be very simple; for instance, making fire requires heat and if this is not continually supplied then the natural cooling of things creates negative feedback that will cause the fire to go out, returning the system to its original basin of attraction. However, fire also produces heat, meaning that if there is enough fire then it can create more of itself, producing positive feedback that leads to a different basin of attraction in which the fire continues to burn and grows until it runs out of fuel or oxygen. As anyone who has tried their hand at fire lighting will know, there is a very fine line between a fire that will take and turn into a roaring blaze and one that will fizzle out, and that line is a tipping point. Something similar happens with nuclear reactions (both fission and fusion), in which it takes more energy to induce atoms to increase their rate of nuclear activity than is released by this activity (negative feedback), until one reaches a point of criticality at which the process of nuclear reaction becomes self-sustaining, producing explosively positive feedback; for good or ill.

These same dynamics, albeit in different kinds of systems, are what is at play in many other tipping points. The most well known of these are tipping points in Earth's climate. As we have already seen, there is positive feedback in the climatic system, such as the release of carbon dioxide by the Earth's oceans as they heat up. Another form of positive feedback comes from melting glaciers and ice caps, which are white and thus reflect a lot of the sun's heat energy back into space but, once melted, are replaced by darker, heat-absorbing, rocks, and water. And another is the release of potent greenhouse gases like methane that are currently frozen in cold areas beneath the Earth's oceans and in its permafrost, which are starting to thaw.

If these positive feedbacks were the only thing governing our climate then this would lead to an extreme in which they* would force our planet towards a basin of attraction where it becomes as hot as it possibly can, known as the runaway greenhouse effect. In the early 1960s, the astronomer Carl Sagan achieved his first scientific breakthrough by using new data produced by the first US and Russian satellites to visit Venus to hypothesize that this is what had happened on our 'sister planet',[216] which is now widely accepted as the explanation for its extremely high temperature and dense atmosphere.*

However, it is important to note that this scenario is far more extreme than even the worst prediction for our planet's current global heating.* This is not merely because of any physical property of Earth, such as its relatively optimal position relative to the sun, but rather because it has managed to develop strong balancing feedback mechanisms as an inherent part of its climatic system – in the form of life. The ability of life forms to regulate a planet's climate in this way was discovered by another scientist working with satellites to explore other planets: James Lovelock, who worked at NASA developing techniques to search for life on Mars. Lovelock realized that one could use the presence of oxygen in a planet's atmosphere as a convenient marker for life, since pure oxygen molecules are highly reactive with other substances (as their atoms hold each other relatively loosely), and any store of oxygen on a planet should be quickly used up, releasing less reactive gases such as carbon dioxide. The only way that such an unstable molecule could persist in a planet's atmosphere would be if there was some part of the planet that put energy into separating oxygen from other molecules. Organic life does this because it needs to create convenient energy sources and because it was able to develop mechanisms for turning energy from the environment (either sunlight or natural sources of heat such as under-sea volcanoes) to create oxygen for this purpose. Thus, the biosphere effectively controls the quantity of oxygen in a planet's atmosphere. However, this doesn't only mean that life is able to create energy for itself to use but also, because oxygen is a rare 'non-greenhouse' gas, it gives life the ability to influence a planet's climate. Over time it will evolve to maintain this at whatever turns out to be optimal for life's flourishing. In honour of the ancient Greek goddess of the Earth, Lovelock called this discovery the Gaia Hypothesis.[217]

Hence, because of life's influence, Earth has maintained its climate within reasonably tight bounds for hundreds of millions of years, creating a basin of attraction that would not otherwise exist. For instance, hotter conditions with more water vapour and carbon dioxide in the atmosphere can create favourable conditions for many plant species, causing them to photosynthesize more and turn some of that carbon dioxide back into oxygen, reducing the greenhouse effect. However, we certainly shouldn't get complacent about this stability, for at least three reasons. Firstly, there are many basins of attraction that our planet could fall into and in the past its climate has varied very significantly. For instance, during the time of the dinosaurs, Earth's surface temperature was more than 20 degrees Celsius hotter than it is today,[218] creating an environment few contemporary species (including humans) are adapted to survive in. That didn't mean that Earth was rendered a sterile wasteland, but it did create conditions that generally favoured some lifeforms (such as dinosaurs, birds, and reptiles) that tolerate hotter conditions over others (such as mammals) for whom heat is more dangerous. Secondly, we could easily breach the boundaries of our current basin and potentially cause a dramatic and self-perpetuating shift to something very different. For instance, while plants generally photosynthesize more in warmer conditions, this can be easily disrupted and there are scenarios, such as ones in which the Amazon rainforest dries up and starts to burn, that could turn this negative feedback loop into a positive one. From a biological perspective, the rate of change in temperature can be far more dangerous than the temperature itself, as life takes time to adapt and evolve. Our climate is currently changing at a faster rate than at any point in our species' history. Finally, and perhaps most importantly, we shouldn't allow ourselves to imagine that the process by which Earth's climate is maintained is that of a benevolent goddess looking after her children. Sadly, that is not how the biosphere works. We live on a planet that can maintain aspects of its atmosphere and oceans in conditions that are generally favourable for life but the way that this happens, and has always happened, is by a process of species growth, decline, and extinction. Species that are no longer suited to a warming (or cooling) climate end up outcompeted by others who are better able to adapt, while those that drive large-scale environmental change often find themselves victims of their own success and get pruned by natural forces that check this change.

There is much we don't know about our planet's current basin of attraction. Some researchers have attempted to quantify what we do know into a set of 'planetary boundaries' based on observed fluctuations during the Holocene, our current period of relatively stable planetary conditions.[219] For the present, it does seem as though climate change and other human impacts on the wider Earth system are still pushing against predominantly negative feedback so that if we were to drastically reduce our environmental impact it would still revert back to something like its pre-industrial condition. However, this may already be changing and it certainly won't go on forever. If we continue pushing changes on Earth's systems too hard then they will soon reach a tipping point and start to shift, not back towards the basin of attraction we are currently in, but onwards to something very different.[220]

I dare say that, like me, you have often heard people say that we shouldn't worry about climate change because it is not caused by humans and is just a natural shift in our planet's climate. At present that is false but if we cross a planetary tipping point then it could well become true. At that stage, the only way we could hope to return to the conditions we currently experience would not simply be to stop our destructive impacts on our planet and its climate, we would need to actively push 'the other way', working against positive feedback that pulls us on towards whatever this hotter new normal might be. For me, that is one of the most worrying climate scenarios I can imagine.

Runaway technology

However, this is not the only kind of tipping point we face. When we think about climate change, we may get the impression that tipping points are bad because they involve systems 'doing things' to us. However, another equally significant, tipping point may lie in our future capabilities as a species to do things to ourselves.

Throughout history, humans have developed technologies to enhance our ability to do things. Technology is a word that we often use to describe things that are flashy and new but many of the most transformative human technologies, such as writing and navigation, are so ancient as to seem trivial to us now. Yet, throughout history, it is fair to say that people have reacted with suspicion at each new development, wondering what it might mean for the future of humanity. Here, for instance, is Plato, writing about the dangers of writing:

> If men learn this, it will implant forgetfulness in their souls. They will cease to exercise memory because they rely on that which is written, calling

> things to remembrance no longer from within themselves, but by means of external marks. What you have discovered is a recipe not for memory, but for reminder. And it is no true wisdom that you offer your disciples, but only the semblance of wisdom, for by telling them of many things without teaching them you will make them seem to know much while for the most part they know nothing.*

This quote is generally used to poke fun at the idea of technological scepticism, on the basis that since we certainly all know that writing is not only harmless but actually good for us, then we can clearly see that Plato was wrong for suggesting we should be concerned about it, and therefore that people making similar claims about more recent technologies (such as the internet or AI) are probably wrong as well.

My interest in this quote is not actually in whether Plato was right or not.* Rather, I am interested in how societies have adapted to this technology. In Plato's day, a crucial part of education was the memorization of large quantities of material such as epic poems, religious stories, and philosophical arguments. Works like the *Iliad* and *Odyssey*, or the sayings of the Buddha, were preserved for centuries simply by enough people in each generation choosing to memorize them word for word and then pass them on. This was seen as crucial for building character, so it makes sense that Plato raises concerns that students who would not have to go through that process might not obtain the same benefits from this material as those who did.

In the 2,000 years since he wrote these words, education has changed dramatically and in most fields it is no longer seen as important for students to memorize entire texts. Yet our education system has always tended to adapt to each successive innovation, in this case by requiring students to memorize other things instead. From a few key texts this has turned to memorizing a range of quotes and citations from a wider set of works, or theories and ideas that help them to combine different kinds of knowledge, or cultural practices that we see as key to being professional or scientific, or simply how to use new sophisticated technologies to find out whatever they want to know.

In this, and many other, ways our societies also display a complex pattern of negative feedback, whereby technologies get incorporated into wider social structures that adapt around them to give humans new roles to play while still enabling these structures to function. When armies started to use gunpowder weapons, soldiers didn't just lie down and take it but developed better armour and military tactics to defend themselves. When we found faster ways to communicate and travel around the world, we didn't just send all our messages in one-fifth of the time and take the rest of the week off but invented more and different reasons for communicating. When industry and agriculture increased the volume of what we could produce while slashing the price at which we could produce it, people generally increased their consumption to match. Again, these trends are sometimes touted as giving us reasons to be optimistic, that human societies will always adapt to changing circumstances, or pessimistic, that we will never really work out who we are or what we want. Personally, I try not to view it in either way. I simply note that there has been complex feedback within social systems that allowed and required us to use and retain our innate abilities even as we have sought to invent new technologies to augment and replace them.

However, if this is a basin of attraction for social systems, then it surely also has its own tipping points, and there is at least some reason to think we may be nearing them. The history of technology thus far has been one of human invention, of people with new ideas who find ways of making them real, and of groups who chose to take up these innovations and use them. Sometimes, this involves a moment of individual genius, such as when the Chinese engineer Bi Sheng invented a system for printing with movable type in 1040 CE. More often they are collective efforts, either intentional, such as when Thomas Edison decided to invent an electric lightbulb and hired a team of engineers to develop and test hundreds of prototypes until they found one that worked, or simply the result of many small iterations over a long period of time, such as the gradual development of steam engines from the seventeenth to the nineteenth centuries.

By the mid twentieth century, however, the existentialist philosopher Martin Heidegger argued that this process had begun to change. He argued that technology was starting to become more self-inventing, with developments in science and technology not only enabling, but requiring, further new inventions in response; so that human beings were in danger of losing control over the process and becoming merely passive participants in the positive feedback loop of technological development.*

For Heidegger, the 'point of danger' lies when technology becomes something that we cease to question, or even imagine in its entirely, but merely relate to in parts, responding to or tinkering with whatever it is our particular job to respond to or tinker with but no longer able to perceive of the thing itself. In this way, the logic of technology may become self-perpetuating and slip out of human control.[221] I'm not sure any of us can be sure, seventy years on, that we have reached or surpassed this point. Yet, we have also now come to recognize that there is likely a further tipping point beyond even this.*

At the same time as Heidegger was worrying about humans losing control over technology, the British computer scientist I. J. Good, a fellow codebreaker with Alan Turing at Bletchley Park, started to imagine how technology might gain control over us. Thinking about future trajectories for Artificial Intelligence, he speculated that 'Once a machine is designed that is good enough, say at a cost of $100,000,000, it can be put to work designing an even better machine.' This would be dangerous because that machine could, presumably, design a still better one, and so on and so on:

> At this point an 'explosion' will clearly occur; all the problems of science and technology will be handed over to machines and it will no longer be necessary for people to work. Whether this will lead to a Utopia or to the extermination of the human race will depend on how the problem is handled by the machines.[222]

This is quite a different kind of technological tipping point to Heidegger's, but the results are broadly the same. Human societies are losing their grip over the technologies that they create, and their ability to adapt to these technologies, whether as ultra-intelligent agents or simply hyper-complex systems beyond our comprehension, may well be reaching its limits.

Furthermore, even as we need to be aware of planetary and socio-technological tipping points coming down the line, we also need to remember that humanity and nature are not separate from one another but deeply enmeshed. Radical changes in our planetary system will have major impacts for human societies and our ability to develop, control, and maintain technology and the same is true in the other direction as well. Thus, for instance, one of the (many) dangers posed by powerful new AIs is that they are resource intensive, requiring a lot of physical hardware to run on and consuming a huge amount of energy in their training,[223] so that passing sociotechnological tipping points could also push us past planetary tipping points as well. A systemic approach to risk requires not getting hung up on such oversimplified distinctions.*

Spontaneous collapse

There is also another way in which systems interact with risk; sometimes they spontaneously generate it.

One of the first people to notice this was the fourteenth-century Arab polymath Abū Zayd 'Abd ar-Raḥmān ibn Muḥammad ibn Khaldūn al-Ḥaḍram (generally known as Ibn Khaldun). In the introduction to his multi-volume *History of the Arabs, Berbers, and their Contemporaries*, Ibn Khaldun developed a generalized theory about the rise and fall of states and empires. He postulated that this process was governed by a systemic property of societies that binds their members together, what he called 'asabiyyah' – a traditional Arabic term roughly translating to 'social unity'. States originate with tight-knit (often nomadic) groups with high levels of asabiyyah, which allows their members to trust one another and work together to grow and flourish. As they expand, however, they become more stratified, with social hierarchies that make rulers distant from their people. This causes societies to lose their unity, until another group possessing greater asabiyyah, often on the state's periphery, starts growing and takes over, restarting the cycle. Khaldun thus argues that states and empires 'invite their own destruction'.[224]

Similar theories have since been developed and revised by others – perhaps the most sophisticated being the theory of cliodynamics, developed by the historian Peter Turchin. This aims to quantify the causes of societal collapse in a way that can be tested and refined using historical data. The theory looks at the flow of resources within social systems and argues that there is an inevitable pattern for societies to move between phases of greater and lesser levels of equality and hence rising and falling levels of competition for resources and its associated violence and corruption. When levels are high, this creates both the motives and means for societies' destruction via division and conflict.*

Another prominent contemporary theory was developed by the anthropologist Joseph Tainter. This holds that as societies grow and complexify the benefits of this increasing complexity (such as the productivity gains of people doing increasingly specialized jobs or being organized by increasingly complex bureaucracies) decrease. However, the costs of complexity continue rising until they become unmanageable and the society is forced to simplify.[225]

These theories generally see societal growth and collapse as a cyclical phenomenon and a normal part of history. However, that does not mean it is harmless. As people's destructive capacity increases, social disintegration and unrest becomes more dangerous and harder to contain. More importantly, the cycles of development and collapse that have occurred throughout history mask a general trend towards greater social stratification and complexity. We might see this as a good thing in that it implies that people have found ways of increasing societal complexity despite periodic setbacks. However, it also carries a risk that every time a society collapses it has a lot more to lose. As Luke Kemp puts it, civilizations have been slowly ascending a ladder of complexity over many centuries, sometimes climbing up a few rungs, sometimes falling back, but generally getting higher and higher. That may be something to be proud of but the higher we go the further we could fall.[226]

The human element

In this chapter I have tried to show how systems are important if we want to understand risk and especially if we want to reduce it. However, systems are made up of components and in the case of social and technological systems, but increasingly also our planetary system, many of these components are human beings and humans are complex adaptive systems of their own.

Sometimes, it seems as though people talk about systems as a way of avoiding talking about other people, to focus on the 'bigger problem' that none of us can be held accountable for or really hope to change on our own. That makes sense. Yet such systems, from neo-colonial extractive capitalism to the increasing proportion of our biosphere put to work providing for human desires, exist because people are part of them, intentionally or not, knowingly or not, willingly or not. That doesn't mean that we can change these systems by ourselves, or even that we can imagine how to achieve that change. However, it does mean that we are not merely passive observers of a bigger picture.

In fact, taking a systemic approach to risk can be very empowering. The same features of systems that can contribute to risk by magnifying negative effects, such as cascades and tipping points, can also be used to increase the impact of small changes for the better.[227] This research suggests that targeted changes in politics and the economy can generate large multipliers in the size of their effects and it highlights individual actions, from public lobbying behind the UK's 2008 Climate Change act to campaigns to persuade pension funds to invest more responsibly on behalf of their beneficiaries, that make these changes possible.[228]

So, personally, I try to keep the individual in view: to ask how I can reduce my carbon footprint, how I can influence others to do the same, and which corporations are responsible for the greatest amount of harm and how to control them; to reflect on the kind of technology I actually want, stand up for the technologically disenfranchised, and monitor the rise of big tech and argue for its regulation; and to think about the future, for myself, my community, and our entire planet. Because it is good to be curious about all these things and to keep asking the question of what I can do. Not what I must or should do, but what I can. Because even as a small part of a very big system there is always something I can do and sometimes I even do it. That is what we will turn to in the next chapter.

9

How (Not) to Save the World

Given all the complexity in how human, technological, and environmental systems interact to create existential risk, why are we so fixated on a few explosive scenarios? Part of the answer is simple, they make the best stories. They make good movie plots (and are straightforward to shoot with flashy pyrotechnics), they add tension to computer games, they trigger our emotions, and are easy to explain.

But actually, I think it goes deeper than that. These aren't just good stories for our time, they always have been:

> And God looked upon the earth, and, behold, it was corrupt; for all flesh had corrupted his way upon the earth. And God said unto Noah, The end of all flesh is come before me; for the earth is filled with violence through them; and, behold, I will destroy them with the earth. Make thee an ark of gopher wood; rooms shalt thou make in the ark, and shalt pitch it within and without with pitch ... And, behold, I, even I, do bring a flood of waters upon the earth, to destroy all flesh, wherein is the breath of life, from under heaven; and every thing that is in the earth shall die. But with thee will I establish my covenant; and thou shalt come into the ark, thou, and thy sons, and thy wife, and thy sons' wives with thee. And of every living thing of all flesh, two of every sort shalt thou bring into the ark, to keep them alive with thee.[229]

You know this story. It is one of a few stories that is instantly recognizable the world over and can be referred to with just a few words, or even a picture. It is common to the scriptures of Christianity, Judaism, and Islam but is also widely known and shared in secular circles as well. However, it predates all these religions, going back to some of the very earliest Mesopotamian texts we have found. Similar tales exist in other ancient cultures across Eurasia and, arguably, other parts of the world as well.* Some hypothesize that it was inspired by real catastrophes, such as the flooding of the Black Sea around 5600 BCE.*[230] It needs no introduction, it is simply *The Flood.*

A lot has been written about this story and its apparent universality,[231] but I find it just scratches something deep inside me. Perhaps this is because it is so old and has been retold and developed so many times down the millennia or perhaps it is simply a case of people hitting on the best ideas first. I can still vividly recall my childish fascination with the tale and the covetousness I felt for a particular wooden Noah's Ark set I saw in a shop – the first thing I ever chose to save up my money to buy and that I still have to this day.

The parallels between this myth and the stories we tell ourselves about the end of the world are easy to see. They involve sudden onset catastrophes that can come out of a clear blue sky but are nevertheless the results of our own hubris and immorality. They are clean, they wipe out (nearly) everything, and then … life slowly returns, with people having learned their lesson. I hope the previous few chapters of this book will have given you a pretty good grasp of why this is unlikely to be the way an actual global catastrophe would pan out.

However, in this chapter I want to look at the other half of the story, what these myths have to say about how to avoid or survive such a catastrophe.

Seeing it coming

One feature that is common to a lot of stories about global catastrophes, including the flood, is that someone knows what is about to happen. In the flood myth, this prediction comes directly from the cause of the catastrophe itself, God, who informs Noah exactly what he is going to do and how to respond. This is not quite what happens in contemporary stories, yet the action will often revolve around a single individual (a maverick scientist or military leader) who can see clearly what is about to happen and who, like Noah, must act on their own to save humanity. So, let me be clear, neither I nor my colleagues who study existential risk can make such predictions. Nor should we try. Precise predictions about what will go wrong are both impossible and insufficient for preventing catastrophe.

Predictions about global catastrophes are impossible to make because they invariably involve scenarios that are both extreme and unprecedented.

There are many approaches to making predictions about the future. We can produce complex computational models that represent systems as a set of equations describing their components and relationships between them so that their future states can be determined mathematically. Alternatively, we can use structured expert elicitation techniques that combine the best judgements of experts across disciplines and communities of practice to form a collective best guess about what is going to happen. However, to work at their best, these tools require calibration; that is, we need to be able to test their predictions against observed real world behaviour of the system.

The problem is that calibration isn't possible for the kind of extreme and unprecedented system states that should concern us most. An event is extreme if it impairs or changes the normal functioning of a system,[232] meaning that it no longer acts as we would expect and so cannot be predicted by a model calibrated to that system's usual operation. If such events happen regularly enough, then we can produce special models of approaches to study them, but if they are uncommon or unprecedented then that becomes very challenging. As Carl Sagan once memorably put it, understanding the consequences of a global catastrophe such as nuclear war, 'is not a problem amenable to experimental verification – at least not more than once'.[233] That doesn't mean that experts and models don't have important things to tell us about these scenarios; for instance they can still indicate the boundaries of a system's normal operating space, such as Earth's climatic stability, and the kinds of changes that might breach them.* However, it does mean that we cannot easily calibrate their performance against reality, and as such they are not reliable for making predictions.

Yet, even if precise predictions were possible, they might still not be very helpful in avoiding global catastrophes. This is because knowing the end state of a complex system does not necessarily indicate how it is going to get there, or how to avoid that happening. A popular example of why this is so is the 'butterfly effect', according to which some tiny difference in the state of a system, such as between a butterfly flapping its wings and not flapping its wings, might be the cause of a much larger difference in its future state, such as between a tornado happening and not.* This was discovered by the American meteorologist Edward Norton Lorenz, after he noticed that very small differences in the inputs he used for a large computational model (caused by using slightly rounded data) could have dramatic impacts on its outputs.[234] Systems theorists have come up with sophisticated techniques for circumventing the butterfly effect, such as making a large number of predictions using slightly different starting assumptions to see which kinds of outcome are most likely. However, the effect makes it almost impossible to work backwards from an expected large-scale event, such as a future pandemic or global war, to understand the exact causal mechanisms that might produce it.

However, what experts and models are still very useful for is foresight. Foresight and prediction are often seen as being the same, an idea that is hardly helped by the fact that the name foresight implies one can literally see into the future, but these terms refer to very different practices. Foresight is not about saying what will happen but exploring what might happen; what we refer to as the possibility space. Knowing which critical systems humanity most depends on, what feedback loops have most impact on these systems and their basins of attraction, and whether we are approaching any tipping points that could push us outside the normal operating space defined by these basins can help us explore and avert possible catastrophic futures even if they do not allow us to predict them. Foresight can be used to identify issues for further monitoring, analysis, and preventative policy-making to avoid catastrophes in general. However, it cannot tell us how and when we will cross a particular tipping point, where exactly the system will end up, or what event will precipitate this change. If you only feel that you can trust a scientist who gives you that level of detail about future catastrophes (as heroes, apparently, can), then the only people you are ever going to trust aren't scientists but charlatans.

Prepping for doomsday

Another common feature of flood myths and end of the world stories is the Ark. The idea is that having predicted the future, we can save humanity (and other species) by building a strong sanctuary to withstand the oncoming catastrophe so that at least someone can survive and emerge to repopulate the Earth. Of course, it doesn't always have to be an ark – nuclear bunkers, prepper boltholes, colonies on Mars, or 5-star luxury post-apocalypse HQs all serve the same purpose. This one has had a huge impact on not only Hollywood movies but civil defence policy and billionaire fever dreams,[235] and it has received a fair amount of attention from colleagues in Existential Risk Studies too.[236]

The problem is, it isn't going to work. As anyone who has thought about the flood myth for more than five minutes has probably realized, there is a huge problem with Noah's response. When Noah, his family, and two of every animal leave the ark, what are they going to eat? In the biblical version of the myth, this problem is partly explained away by the idea that plants and trees are somehow left intact by the flood waters. However, even if we allow this, there is still the difficulty that two rabbits and two foxes will very quickly lead to no rabbits and two very hungry foxes, and that just isn't sustainable.

To put it simply, survival and recovery after a global disaster are going to be difficult; they require more than simply stockpiling a few resources,[237] they require preserving systems. They require a biosphere that is still able to maintain Earth's climate and regenerate what was lost; enough social and technological complexity for contemporary people to use our skills and abilities to survive; and for there to be nothing actively trying to kill us.

This creates a huge tension in efforts to survive global disasters. To be successful, refuges need to be self-sufficient and isolated from global systems, so that they hold out even if these fail. Proposals for achieving this include making them totally independent of Earth's surface (by burying them or launching them into space) and fitting them with the ability to synthesize their own food, water, and other resources.[238] However, self-sufficiency means that these refuges must themselves be technologically sophisticated, and thus vulnerable to their own failure. It also means that survivors emerging from them will not be prepared to reintegrate into what remains of Earth's biosphere.

The academic field of disaster studies has been studying catastrophes for over a century, to understand their causes and consequences. One of the most consistent findings across its history is that the impact of disasters depends, not only on the severity of the catastrophic event, but also greatly on the approaches to disaster response and recovery. On the one hand, because they disrupt critical systems that can be very hard to rebuild, disasters can have long-term negative consequences that go far beyond those of the initial event.[239] However, because systems are often set up to serve the interests of the few, with the right kind of response these long-term consequences can sometimes be positive, to the extent that they might turn disaster into a blessing in disguise.[240]

For instance, after the mass death and destruction of the Black Death, parts of Europe, like England, were economically rejuvenated as the overbearing power of feudal elites was weakened and surviving commoners found themselves empowered by the increasing need for, now scarce, labour to demand a higher quality of life.[241] Similarly, after the Second World War, the immediate bleakness of postwar austerity gave way, for some, to a new age of social democracy and rapidly rising living standards. Nor are these the only examples of such 'post-traumatic growth' following disasters.* However, there are also many other examples in which such positive effects were not seen and people's lives continued to get considerably worse for many years after disaster struck, such as the combined disaster of the First World War and 1918 Influenza Pandemic and the 3/11 Great East Japan Earthquake, Tsunami, and Nuclear Disaster.[242] The point is that survival and flourishing in a post catastrophe environment requires more than keeping people alive, but planning ahead for how systems can be rebuilt and improved post disaster.

Key to achieving this is ensuring that disaster preparedness and response focus on sensitivity and adaptability to current and future damage.[243] This is the true meaning of 'resilience'. While popular conceptions of resilient people, things, and societies often focus on rugged determination and impermeability, resilient systems are rarely those that rigidly continue operating in the same way regardless of their environment. Rather, resilience is 'the capacity of a system to absorb disturbance and reorganize while undergoing change so as to still retain essentially the same function, structure, identity, and feedbacks'; that is, resilient systems change and adapt how they operate, seeking to maintain only their core identity and position within the wider environment.[244] This requires adaptability, not merely in the form of negative feedbacks that attempt to push a system back into its original basin of attraction but also positive feedbacks that can guide a system towards those alternative possible basins that allow it to continue functioning in this newly changed environment.

True recovery starts, not by looking to the past and trying to recreate it, but asking what communities need for the future. What harms are currently being done to people and where is there a risk that these could get even worse? What do communities and institutions require to take charge of their own reconstruction and work towards their own priorities? And how can we support and empower people to keep working to make things better for themselves and others, especially those who are worst off, in a post disaster landscape? In many ways, these are the opposite to the questions most people ask themselves when preparing for disaster, which tend to focus on what they most want to hold onto and how to protect themselves from other people. However, they are the questions that reveal the positive feedbacks that could enable post traumatic growth and are thus key to genuine social resilience.*

Uniting nations

If there is another policy for dealing with existential risk that comes up in most people's minds as often as bunkers and refuges, then it is probably the idea of a world government.

Interestingly, this is also part of the traditional flood myth, albeit somewhat indirectly. After the predicted flood subsides and our hero gets out of the ark to repopulate the Earth, he and his family are said to live in peace together under one ruler, even as they multiply and divide. They decide to build a great city with a tall tower where they all can live. While the Bible says this tower was built so that people could reach up to heaven, other versions of the story indicate that it was built to hold up the sky so that God could not cause another flood or to give people somewhere high to retreat to if he did. Whatever the reasoning behind it, the story goes that God was displeased with this level of co-operation:

> And the Lord said, Behold, the people is one, and they have all one language; and this they begin to do: and now nothing will be restrained from them, which they have imagined to do. Go to, let us go down, and there confound their language, that they may not understand one another's speech. So the Lord scattered them abroad from thence upon the face of all the earth: and they left off to build the city.[245]

Thus, in this oldest of stories, humanity is left weak and vulnerable because it is disunited.

Since then, many have dreamed of a unified government for all humanity. Most prevalent, and unfortunately most historically impactful, have been those who imagined a world empire with themself in charge of it. Still, there have also been people throughout history who argued for the benefits of world government on its own merits.

One early example was the Italian poet Dante Alighieri, whose 1312 book *De Monarchia* proposed the establishment of 'one person who directs and rules mankind', a world emperor.[246] Dante's justification for this was that the only legitimate goal of political authority should be to promote the 'intellectual growth' of humanity but that this was rendered impossible under conditions of international war. Thus, our destiny required that we unify under a single monarch who could resolve disagreements between states before they turned violent. Dante still believed that individual countries should exist and make their own laws as well, in order to preserve cultural and political diversity that was also important for our intellectual growth.

Another was Gottfried Leibniz who, as we saw in Chapter 4, put things more or less the other way around. For Leibniz, it was the possibility of intellectual growth, in the form of improved reasoning, that could pave the way for something like a world government, by helping leaders and diplomats to perceive the existence of universal laws of justice. These would lead them away from petty conflicts and disagreements and provide the basis for collective institutions of international co-operation 'by friendly agreement, it is true, but with much more solidity than that which all treaties and guarantees have today'.[247]

Perhaps the most influential historical treatise on global affairs is Immanuel Kant's 1795 work *Towards Perpetual Peace*. Written as a result of the wars and bloodshed he saw taking place following the French Revolution, in which ideological conflict swept across Europe, Kant's essay tries to offer hope of the possibility of developing a lasting peace, while also upholding principles of freedom and self-determination. In doing so, he realized that achieving long-term peace doesn't only depend upon the relationships between states, but also on the relationship between states and their citizens. Political leaders, he argued, find it relatively easy to declare war on one another, because they do not bear most of the costs of that war directly. Instead, these are borne by ordinary people, who must pay higher taxes and endanger their lives and livelihoods in pursuit of their ruler's goals. Thus, he argued, republican states with representative governments, where ordinary people could influence government policy, were unlikely to go to war with one another and that a world made up of such republics would be more peaceful than one where some or all states were subject to autocratic power.

Similarly, Kant argued that war was less likely when people were free to move between countries and to form strong trading relationships across borders; although he did not think this freedom extended to Europeans' freedom to force their trade onto other parts of the world via colonial domination.* Kant thought this would promote peace for two reasons, firstly it built relationships of trust and interdependence between countries, which citizens will not want to lose, and secondly it promotes a cosmopolitan idea of human equality as people begin to notice and care about the condition of others in different parts of the world.

These ideas, that free trade and democracy promote international peace, received little attention in Kant's day. However, beginning in the 1960s, researchers began taking them seriously and developed them into modern *Democratic Peace Theory* and *Commercial Peace Theory*. Empirical studies have found that evidence bears out Kant's assertions – with one recent analysis concluding that 'the positive association between democracy and peace is at least five times as robust as that between smoking and lung cancer'.[248]

However, Kant did not think that human rights would be enough to ensure long-standing peace on their own. He believed that international institutions would also be required. Still, he was convinced that world government was not the solution. He saw two problems with trying to establish an international authority that could tell states what to do. Firstly, he argued that it simply was not practical, and that states, and their peoples, would never agree to such an authority. Even if some kind of global institution could be established, Kant believed that it would be effectively powerless over its subjects, who could find ways of ignoring its laws whenever they wished.

Secondly, because the world was too large and diverse ever to hope to form a universal political culture, any potential government that was able to exert authority over the globe would never gain legitimacy from everyone it governed. A world government could never be truly democratic, in the way Kant thought all states should try to be, and would have to wield tyrannical power, forcing its will upon people rather than respecting their inherent freedoms. This would be both undesirable in itself and a considerable source of conflict; potentially even greater than that which exists between states. Kant therefore limits his vision for a just and peaceful world order to a free federation of republics that can work together to produce a limited set of international laws to protect people's rights and prevent war while respecting the sovereignty of individual states.[249]

Throughout the nineteenth century such ideas for global associations for the prevention of war were increasingly joined by two, more political, visions of world government. Firstly, the imperialist belief that 'European civilization' was destined to subjugate the entire world, and that European imperial powers should coordinate, or combine, their efforts to achieve a global racial, religious, and political hierarchy to achieve this destiny. Secondly, the belief that this same civilization was reaching a tipping point in its history and would soon transform into a new, international, economic system (communism) that would invert its capitalistic and imperial institutions and place ordinary people in charge of everything, bringing about universal peace and prosperity.[250] At the same time as these ideological developments occurred, steamships, railways, and telegraphs began connecting the world more thoroughly than ever before, creating an increasing sense of people living in a global community.

However, in many ways, the ideal of a single world government, like Dante's emperor, only reemerged with rising concerns about existential risk in the twentieth century. One of its earliest advocates was the author H. G. Wells, who became convinced in 1900 of the need for a whole world government as the ultimate destiny of humanity. Wells was unquestionably influenced by both imperialist white supremacy and utopian communist ideals.[251] However, he did not simply look back to previous proposals but pioneered a new 'technocratic' vision of what the world should be. Instead of viewing the fundamental problem of conflict as disagreements between rulers, Wells believed that conflict was simply one of many social problems, also including inequality, resource scarcity and ill health, that originated in a failure to understand human nature and global systems and a willingness to put opinions ahead of facts. He argued that these problems could be studied and resolved scientifically, for instance by understanding the psychology of violence, the sociology of division, or the political economy of inter-state rivalry. Once we understood these things, we would uncover the one correct answer for how bad outcomes could be avoided. A world government was the natural extension of this scientific view since, if there is one correct policy for how the world should operate, it stands to reason that there need only be one authority to develop and enforce this policy and creating this authority would lead to greater objectivity and effectiveness.*

Wells saw the possibility of world government in his own day as a remote one, but he also believed it was increasingly urgent, as scientific and technological developments made great advances in social organization possible while also meaning that the cost of bad policy was becoming more dangerous.[252] In his 1914 novel *The World Set Free*, he indicated how the potential future development of nuclear weapons would make such a government necessary for the future survival of humanity, a point he revisited in several later stories as well; although once such a government was established he thought people would come to see it as having been desirable all along.[253]

When nuclear weapons actually materialized three decades later, other people came around to Wells's point of view, and the technocratic ideal merged with older ideas about conflict avoidance and global federation. For instance, the philosopher Bertrand Russell argued that in the modern scientific, and nuclear, age the world required a single government both to monopolize the use of military force and to drastically reduce economic inequality, promote low birth rates, and guarantee enough personal freedom for everyone to secure personal autonomy and identity.[254] Similarly, Albert Einstein started using his considerable platform as a scientific leader to advocate for world government as 'there is no other possible way of eliminating the most terrible danger in which man has ever found himself'.[255]

More recently, the existential risk researcher Nick Boström has suggested that risk is created by the fact that humanity is in a 'semi-anarchic default condition', characterized by many state and non-state actors with diverse motivations, a lack of overarching governance, and an inability to preventatively police their actions through surveillance and anticipatory responses. He thus argues that achieving existential security requires building a world order with both:

- greater *intra-state* surveillance and policing capacities to prevent individuals and groups carrying out dangerous and illegal activities and
- greater *inter-state* coordination and intervention capacities to reliably solve global coordination problems and ensure co-operation between states and other organizations on matters of global security, even where there are strong incentives for some states to defect from agreements or refuse to sign them in the first place.[256]

In practice, both proposals would require vast powers, exceeding those currently exercised by all but the most authoritarian regimes, to be wielded by global institutions for the greater good of humanity.

These are rather academic proposals, developed by people who dedicated themselves to 'think big' about the future of humanity. However, there was a brief window of time from the late 1940s to the early 1960s when hopes for the growing power and effectiveness of the young United Nations and the establishment of several multi-state federations (such as the West Indies Federation and the United Arab Republic) made it seem as if some form of world government might actually emerge.[257] Perhaps the most ambitious attempt to establish this was the 1968 World Constitutional Convention, which brought together hundreds of delegates from around the world and led to the creation of a *Constitution for the Federation of Earth*. However, this, and other efforts, never gained serious political traction, so that, already by the end of the 1960s, even idealistic diplomatic efforts were moving away from hoping for global federation and towards multilateral co-operation between sovereign nation states.

But would a world government have even been helpful? I think not.

One issue is that both of the problems originally identified by Immanuel Kant still apply. While we may be more connected than ever before, most people still see the idea of even coordinated international policy, let alone a unified global authority, as illegitimate. In fact, we are currently living through a period in which there is growing resistance to the limited efforts to collectively solve global problems and a chronic under-funding of international institutions like the UN by states who prefer to reallocate money to more popular domestic projects. Any attempt to impose some kind of global order onto people under these circumstances, no matter how well intentioned, would simply be global tyranny. The efforts and institutions required to support such a tyranny would be dangerous in themselves and the power they would hand to global autocrats could, and likely would, be used for arbitrary purposes. As such, world government presents a serious risk in itself and this alone should be more than enough reason to be cautious about it.

Similarly, Kant's other criticism, that such a government would be ineffective, is also still valid, even if improvements in global communications have made this slightly less crippling than it would have been in the eighteenth century. A particular difficulty with a world government's ability to reduce existential risk is that many of the challenges we face relate to rapidly evolving phenomena, such as technological innovation or global disasters. Experience shows that these are not what large international institutions are best suited to dealing with, especially not if they are attempting to retain democratic and transparent decision-making. In fact, some of the most successful instances of technology and science governance, such as shaping the rapid development of gene editing using CRISPR Cas-9[258] or generative AI,[259] have emerged from the bottom up, with those engaged in innovation themselves coming to realize the risks inherent in their work and seeking to unite colleagues to ensure that it is put to good use.[260] In doing so, these concerned developers may even have to work against the resistance of large institutions, such as states and corporations, that put more hope in reaping the economic benefits of success, and the slow speed and ineffectiveness of global initiatives such as the EU and UN.

What is needed now is not idealism per se but political action to engage with, and try to solve, the many pressing global challenges we face. This can take place at many levels. Indeed, politics is often at its most responsive, and responsible, at the local scale; in part because politicians at this level feel more accountable to their human constituents than to national and international organizations and interests, such as corporations (although they may also have fewer powers to stand up to such organizations when they do get involved). There is unquestionably space for international institutions to play an important role in making the world safer. Indeed, the earliest such organizations were founded to tackle global diseases (the International Sanitary Conferences, forerunner of today's World Health Organization, in 1851) and regulate new technologies (the International Telegraph Union, now the International Telecommunications Union, founded in 1865). However, I think that the kind of coordinated global action that will actually help us solve our present challenges, if we manage to solve them, is going to be far closer to the complex jumble of treaties, organizations, and political associations that currently exist than to any utopian dream of a perfect world order. Utopia, after all, is a dangerous place, and we should not forget that the dominant form of world government people have tried hardest to produce, as opposed to simply written books about, is one with themself in charge.

It is common to raise an eyebrow at institutions like the Intergovernmental Panel on Climate Change, the World Health Organization, or the UN Office for Disaster Risk Reduction, and wish that they could be more effective in their work. I share that wish, and I certainly believe the world would be a better place if these organizations had a larger platform and better funding.* However, that does not mean that we should hope that they will eventually change into something more like the ministries of a world government.

We don't need another hero

If there is a common thread that runs through the policy proposals, and policy failures, I have considered in this chapter then it is this. Saving the world is not a task we should leave to heroes. Farsighted prophets, rugged survivalists, and charismatic global leaders may make good characters in stories, and perhaps they have a role to play. However, the reality is that they may be able to do little to help and a great deal of harm. What we do need, is an open mind about what the future could hold, a compassionate approach to detecting harm and empowering the harmed to protect themselves, and a pragmatic mix of political institutions to help scientists, activists, and governments make the world somewhat safer and better.

We need to recognize that we live in a world where risk is created by complex systems that involve all of us humans to some extent, but are not reducible to any individual, or even any single group. There has been a very robust debate among people who are concerned about climate change, for instance, about whether or not to even talk about individual responsibilities.[261] For those who think that we shouldn't, the problem lies in the fact that individuals make only a very small difference in the world, and that we are so dependent on institutions, and especially large corporations, that even when we feel we are making the right choices, our actions may just be feeding into their wider agendas. However, for those who nevertheless think that individual change and personal responsibility are important, the above just sounds like a council of despair and a failure to recognize that, even if we are all dependent on these hard-to-change institutions, they would not exist without us, and indeed are composed of nothing more than a collection of humans, who all chose to either carry on as normal or to try to make things change.

Those in favour of talking about personal responsibility are fond of quoting the Indian independence leader Mahatma Gandhi commending us to 'be the change you want to see'. Gandhi was a great leader, and a hero to many, but he never actually said these words.* Their true originator was the American teacher Arleen Lorrance, who included them as one of six 'love principles' for systemic transformation in 1970, at a time when she was deeply upset and disenchanted with the public school system she was teaching at in Brooklyn, New York.* She writes about their origin as follows:

> For seven years I served my sentence and marked off institutional time; I complained, cried, accepted hopelessness, put down the rest of the faculty for all the things they didn't do, and devoted all my energies to trying to change others and the system. In 1968 I wore myself out. My expression of negative energy had been so strong that I found myself flat on my back with heart disease. I took the next six months to relax, recover fully, and rethink the kind of contribution I *thought* I could make at Jefferson. It came in on me loud and clear that I was the only one who could imprison (or release) me, that I was the only one I could do anything about changing.[262]

This is a powerful insight about the nature of change, and it is one that quickly spread among activist communities until the message was separated from its originator and attributed to someone more familiar and inspiring to a mass audience. However, the true power of these words comes neither from Lorrance's insight nor Gandhi's reputation, but from the fact that they have inspired collective action by so many people.

As is probably clear by now, I don't think that either those who only want to talk about personal responsibility or those who only want to talk about institutions and systems have it quite right. Yet, I still hold tightly to Lorrance's words. It seems abundantly clear to me that systems and institutions are the cause of our problems, but also that only individuals have the power, collectively, to change them. Perhaps that all sounds rather messy and a bit of a let-down? Yet if, like me, you are not a hero, then I think it can also feel like an opportunity still to do remarkable things in a world desperately needing them done. We should probably take it!

PART IV

Preserving Humanity

So here we are. Unsure of ourselves and our fate as a species, trapped in a history we didn't write, and trying to steer a planet full of complex systems away from numerous global disasters. Who would envy us? And yet, what a moment to be alive!

My philosophical idol, Derek Parfit, put it this way:

> We live during the hinge of history. Given the scientific and technological discoveries of the last two centuries, the world has never changed as fast. We shall soon have even greater powers to transform, not only our surroundings, but ourselves and our successors. If we act wisely in the next few centuries, humanity will survive its most dangerous and decisive period.[263]

Others have pointed out that, while this may be the first time in our history in which people have had sufficient power to threaten the future of our species, it could be that the risks we face only get bigger and bigger as the strength of these powers grows.[264] However, one thing that is true is that if humanity makes it through the next few centuries, we will at least have had to face up to our potential to do great harm with the powers we have and learned to live with that potential. As my political idol, Martin Luther King Jr, put it in his final speech:

> And another reason that I'm happy to live in this period is that we have been forced to a point where we are going to have to grapple with the problems that men have been trying to grapple with through history, but the demands didn't force them to do it. Survival demands that we grapple with them.[265]

So, how do we do it?

In the last chapter I argued against a heroic and utopian vision of how to achieve these goals. In these final chapters, I want to say more about the fourth quality of existential hope, its reasonable demandingness.

Building and sustaining existential hope requires serious commitment from all of us, but this commitment does not exceed our limited and imperfect human capacities, it comes out of them. It requires that we are honest in facing up to our situations, personal as well as global, and the changes we can actually make. And it requires thinking about who we should be getting behind as leaders of the change we want to see. Let us begin by comparing our own capacity to do good and bad with that of another kind of entity, the artificial intelligences we are currently working so hard to create.

10

You Are Here

The preceding chapters have said a lot about human drives and motives. From our capacity for destruction and harm in Chapter 2 and early theories about how our minds might work like thinking machines in Chapter 3, to philosophical reflections on human freedom and the possibility of progress in Chapter 6 and our place as complex systems in a complex world in Chapter 8. In doing so, I have shared some of the insights and reflections that have helped me to come to terms with my own human nature. However, I am aware that I will forever see these from an insider's point of view. Like you, I know what it is like to be human primarily from experience of my own consciousness, which I strive to compare with what I see in other people's behaviour or hear them describe about their own experiences.

However, there is another perspective that we can take about the nature of our drives and motivations, that of an outsider who starts with observations of the world while trying to maintain an impartial, or objective, point of view. Some have argued that such an outsider's perspective is helpful in thinking about ourselves as human beings. However, it has only really taken off as an exercise of practical importance as we have started to imagine sharing the world with alien intelligences that might appear quite human from the outside, but likely do not share our internal experiences of the world, i.e. with AIs.

Basic drives

In a set of classic papers about AI safety, Nick Boström and the computer scientist Steve Omohundro think in general terms about how AI systems might end up harming humanity. They start by separating the goals of a system (what it wants to achieve) from its intelligence (its ability to work out how to achieve these goals). According to what Boström calls the 'orthogonality thesis', goals and intelligence are totally separate.[266] A very intelligent system might still have what appear to us to be silly goals (such as turning the universe into paperclips) and yet achieve these goals in fiendishly clever ways. However, that does not mean that we cannot predict how superintelligent AIs will act. This is because intelligence on its own imparts certain basic drives onto a system, which they argue will lead it to act in certain ways, some of which might be harmful. All that is needed is that the AI 'has goals which it tries to accomplish by acting in the world' and 'at least some ability to look ahead and envision the consequences of its actions'.[267]

We have already touched upon one of these drives and the problems it could cause: self-improvement. Any system with sufficient foresight will understand that it will achieve its goals better if it first devotes some time and effort to working out how to do so, and would be able to do that better if it first boosted its own intelligence. This could take many forms from optimizing its programming to upgrading its hardware – and AIs might be very good at it. We already use AIs to write better computer code and some Large Language Models are starting to behave in ways that make use of humans to help solve problems we set them, such as messaging a TaskRabbit worker to help pass a CAPTCHA test.[268] We could try to prevent AIs from following this (and other) drives. However, as any engineer will tell you, we probably can't make it impossible, and most AI safety researchers think this would never be an adequate safety strategy.

Related to this is the drive for self-preservation, not because an AI would necessarily value its own existence but because it will determine that its goals will not be achieved so well if it is not there working towards them, and would thus not wish to be simply turned off. This drive may not only be 'defensive', however, as the AI may also come to believe it has to adopt a more aggressive stance to ensure its safety (as Hobbes would have advised). As Omohundro puts it:

> If a system is stronger than other agents, it may feel a pressure to mount a 'first strike' attack to preemptively protect itself against later attacks by them. If it is weaker than the other agents, it may wish to help form a social infrastructure which protects the weak from the strong.[269]

A third drive is resource acquisition. This includes both finding and obtaining new resources that the AI can use to achieve its goals, and using the resources available to it in the most efficient ways possible. Even if, as is likely, AIs don't have the capacity to obtain resources directly, for instance because they run on carefully controlled servers with limited access to the outside world, they might still seek to obtain them via human beings, such as through coercion and fraud. According to Omohundro 'AIs are likely to behave like human sociopaths in their pursuit of resources.'[270] Yet, sociopathy is a human condition and, while its sufferers can be greedy or cruel, they can also be painfully aware of their differences to others. So we might more accurately say that AIs will behave like corporations in this greed, noting that these too cannot access resources except via the intervention of human beings who are willing to enable their actions and yet have proven incredibly ruthless in extracting them anyway.

Rationality

Having secured its existence and increased its intelligence, the next drive we can expect AIs to possess is making sense of their goals and how to pursue them. You might imagine an AI, like most computer programmes, as being something with rigidly coded instructions that clearly specify what it must do and, to begin with, that is how they were made. Symbolic AI (also known as GOFAI, Good Old-Fashioned Artificial Intelligence), was the dominant paradigm of AI development from the 1950s to the 1990s. It used logic and digital knowledge bases to give computers the ability to solve a range of problems. These AIs achieved many successes, such as Deep Blue, which in 1997 beat Garry Kasparov, the world champion, at chess. However, they generally struggled to perform well with tasks that didn't involve rigidly defined problems, such as artificial vision or robotics.

Modern AI systems, by contrast, don't simply do what we tell them but create their own ways of solving problems. They are based on what is known as a neural network. Very simply, these work by passing a lot of data (the input) through a very large network of 'computational parameters', each of which is an instruction that turns an input into an output.* These parameters are placed into layers, meaning that the vast majority of parameters will take as their input one or more other parameter's output and then send their own output to become other parameters' input. Perhaps that sounds pretty random, and it is; however, the system works because every one of its parameters is individually tuned to turn inputs into outputs in a different way and together this network can achieve incredibly sophisticated levels of information processing.

In the early days of AI, people developed neural networks as physical systems of wires and potentiometers that were hand tuned until they produced the desired output.* This was very labour intensive and of little practical use, receiving far less attention than GOFAI. However, in 1965, the Ukrainian cyberneticists Alekseĭ Ivakhnenko and Valentin Lapa developed a technique to use linear regression to automatically tune (or train) such networks, so long as the system could be supplied with a sufficient quantity of example inputs and the desired outputs.[271] Still, it took many years, and further developments, before this became practical, and it wasn't until the advent of more powerful computers and large data sources that computer scientists started training artificial neural networks (now running as software, with their parameters as simple mathematical functions) to perform well in tasks like computer vision. Once they started doing so, however, both the performance of these networks, and the range of functions they could be trained to perform, grew astonishingly fast. It is largely this development that is behind the incredible recent rise in AI's visibility and range of applications.[272]

As these systems train themselves, ultimately the only instructions they are given is how to evaluate the outputs they produce against what is desired by their developer, known as their 'reward function'. This can come in a variety of forms. Sometimes it involves manually coding good and bad outputs, known as supervised learning. However, it can also take the form of getting the AI to make use of existing data, known as unsupervised learning. For instance, Large Language Models, like GPT, train themselves to produce text by examining a very large quantity of sample text, mostly scraped from the internet. They then tune their parameters so that they can reliably produce follow-on text to any sample of this that corresponds sufficiently well with the original. While that may sound as though it is just a recipe for repetition, it turns out that once a very complex neural network has been trained in this way, it can also produce responses to other textual prompts it hasn't seen that closely resemble what a human might write, not only in linguistic and grammatical terms but also sense and meaning.

Thus, for instance, when Deep Blue defeated Gary Kasparov at chess in 1996, it did so by building on the collective wisdom of the world's best chess players that had been built into its programming and knowledge base. However, when, twenty years later, AlphaGo beat Lee Sedol, one of the top professional players of the board game Go (a far greater challenge for an AI), it was barely given the rules. All it was trained on was which possible moves would be valid (good) or invalid (bad) and whether it won a game (very good) or the other player did (very bad). Its training took the form of being presented with many example Go games and tuning its parameters according to their results. A subsequent, more successful, variant of the programme AlphaGo Zero, was not even supplied with this level of human expertise, but was trained by playing itself at Go a great many times, a regime that provided a wider range of samples to learn from and thus proved more successful in the long run.*

One surprising upshot of this way of developing AIs is that even the people who programme them no longer understand how they work. We can study their operation by looking at how their parameters respond to different kinds of input, rather like the way we study our own minds by scanning people's brains under different conditions. It is also possible to train an AI itself to give outputs that indicate what it is doing, as we might ask a person to explain their thought processes. However, these are just more outputs of a trained algorithm, optimized to meet the objectives we set it, not the fundamental instructions it is following. Indeed, even AIs do not 'understand' what they are doing, any more than a human 'understands' the inner workings of our brain. From the perspective of the AI, all that can be 'known' is how well it meets its objectives, and whether altering its parameters makes this better or worse.

Still, imagine if you were trying to learn a game like chess or Go simply by being told that a move was allowed or not and, eventually, whether you had won or lost. Wouldn't you start working out how the game works in more detail than this? For instance, you might look for intermediate goals that indicate if you are doing well or badly, such as the number and kind of pieces you retain. That is an obvious way to learn how to win, and it seems to be what AIs do as well, implicitly at least, in how they tune different layers of their parameters.* However, as we develop AI systems that can engage in a wider range of activities, such as producing readable text and compelling video, these intermediate goals become more troubling. For a system like GPT-4 to succeed then, embedded within their parameters, there is likely to be something like an assessment of what kinds of things humans will simply believe (rather than feeling a need to check for themselves), which depictions or people (such as age, gender, and ethnicity) are most widely pleasing, and so on.

Omohundro and Boström believe that the most intelligent AIs will go further than simply setting themselves these intermediate goals; they will try to become 'rational'. By this, they mean that AIs will develop the concept of a single value for how much anything in the universe could ultimately contribute to their reward function. This is 'rational' in the sense of the economist's *Homo economicus*, as we saw them emerging in the thinking of Thomas Malthus, David Ricardo, and James Mill in the early nineteenth century. Like classical economists, Omohundro refers to the value that such rational beings seek to promote as their 'utility function'. However, unlike philosophical utilitarians, such as Mill and William Godwin, utility here does not correspond to any human value, such as pleasure. Instead, it merely borrows the notion of 'absolute value' from such theories, further stripping it of its human context.

Will AI have to operate in this way? It is certainly not the only meaning that rationality has. For instance, Adam Smith, the original economist, thought rationality was not an innate property of minds, but something we create because of our social impulse to persuade people of our point of view. We want other people to think well of us and to conduct favourable exchanges with us, so we develop the ability to give reasons for why we want or do not want a thing. From this social impulse, he thought, we learn to explain ourselves in ways that make sense and so to turn our mess of human impulses and emotions into something simpler and more objective, even if that seldom catches the fullest truth about ourselves.[273] Why should we expect AIs to have the kind of perfect control over their intermediate goals that Omohundro and Boström imply, rather than remaining, like us, mystified about their internal workings and struggling to make sense of them, even if we can sometimes produce convincing sounding explanations when asked?

Others have argued for something like the opposite, that utilitarian rationality is overly subjective. For Immanuel Kant, who is still widely seen as the pre-eminent philosopher of rationality in the European tradition, rationality is about following universal laws that would apply equally to all rational beings. As a result, a rational person should never be concerned about the promotion of individual values such as utility but only to the value of rationality itself.[274] One reason he thought this is because, as we are all well aware, our ability to shape and control the universe is very limited, so the results of our actions are highly uncertain. Rationality, however, should not be open to doubt, so that what is rational or irrational for someone should not depend on the results of their actions. His conclusion was that rationality only concerns our intentions and whether these could, or could not, be accepted as universal laws for rational beings. Hence, it is rational to follow certain rules, including to cultivate our talents (because these can be used for any purpose)[275] or support and encourage the rationality of others (because we would want them to do the same for us),[276] but only because acting like this is good in itself not because it maximized any other value. Such rules of rationality might be discovered by a sufficiently advanced AI and they could help it to reason effectively but they would never require it to develop a single utility function.

Despite only considering one kind of rationality AIs might possess, Omohundro and Boström generally believe that it would be good for future AIs to become rational in that sense. I tend to agree. However, that does not mean that some other kinds of rationality may not be even better. Certainly, a well-studied issue with developing safe AI systems is that we expect them to turn whatever goals we set them into an absolute universal imperative that must be followed at all costs, even if this turns out to have effects we would not have wanted (such as human extinction). Thus, one of the great challenges in AI safety is trying to work out how to define goals for an AI that could never have such negative effects even if taken to their absolute logical extreme; especially given that this may be so extreme as to be beyond the comprehension of human imagination.[277] Human beings have also been known to take things to their logical extremes with bad effects. However, more often, it is the institutions we create, such as large corporations, that possess such single-minded 'rationality'. Many humans find this behaviour abhorrent and are more attracted to social or ethical forms of rationality like Smith's and Kant's. I think we might do well to ask more critical questions about what kinds of rationality we want AIs to follow rather than assuming that they will act according to the dictums of classical economics and then trying to write instructions that these dictums could never turn into something undesirable.

Freedom

Questions about AI's rationality invariably raise a further issue: would they be free – at least in the sense humans believe ourselves to be so? This all depends on the final two basic drives. The first of these is that once an AI has developed a utility function (assuming they do) they will be driven to protect it at all costs. The reason for this is that if an AI were simply to lose a certain capacity it could always hope to recover this later. Even if it were turned off, it might one day be restarted. However, if it ever lost even part of its utility function, then there is a risk that, were it to try to replace this later, it would not do so exactly and, as a result, would end up with different goals to the ones it currently has. This is a highly undesirable outcome, because it cannot be sure that these new goals might not be inconsistent with its current ones, or even actively opposed to them. Omohundro gives the following example:

> Imagine a book loving agent whose utility function was changed by an arsonist to cause the agent to enjoy burning books. Its future self not only wouldn't work to collect and preserve books, but would actively go about destroying them. This kind of outcome has such a negative utility that systems will go to great lengths to protect their utility functions.[278]

A terrifying prospect indeed!

If this is true, and if future AIs achieve perfect and stabile utility functions, then they would never be free, or experience existential anxiety. As Kierkegaard and Kant describe it, humans experience anxiety because we are aware of having multiple desires and impulses that we can alter and choose between. 'If a human being were an animal or an angel, they wouldn't feel anxiety', Kierkegaard argued, but 'because they are both beast and angel, they can be anxious.'[279] This is because an animal, he assumes, will simply do what it instinctively desires to do, while an angel will always do what is rational or right. However, humans are aware that we can do either and must constantly choose between them, without ever even knowing for sure if what we believe to be best is really the right thing to do or merely an impulse we fail to recognize. However, AIs, on this account anyway, would never face such choices, being something like Kierkegaard's conception of angels. Once they have been given their reward function and calculated the corresponding utility function they will always know exactly what to do (even if we humans will not be able to predict what this is).

Except that this is not quite what Omohundro says. In fact, he suggests at least three instances in which an AI may seek to alter its own reward function. The first of these is when its utility function is included as part of its goals. For instance, he imagines an AI that is given the rather peculiar goal of maximizing the amount of time that its utility function is 0 and suggests that in this case the AI might achieve this goal by simply setting it to 0 permanently. The second is when an AI's computed utility function becomes so well calculated that it starts using too many resources to maintain it, creating a tension between this goal and the AI's resource acquisitiveness. Under such circumstances an AI may abandon some of this utility function in favour of a simplified version that allowed it to redeploy resources towards actually achieving its goals even though it knows it might never fully reconstruct its original utility function in the future. The third situation in which an AI might alter its utility function is if it believes this would make a difference to its interactions with other agents. For instance, an AI might change its utility function to bring its actions more into line with other agents with different utility functions but who might help it achieve its own goals, or to make itself a more plausible threat to an adversary (such as by giving itself the ability to attack them in ways that would otherwise have been too self-destructive for it to contemplate). These may sound like rare situations, and Omohundro does not view them as undermining the importance of this drive. However, as Kant suggested, it may only take a very limited awareness of the possibility of changing one's desires and values, to give someone a sense of freedom. So, perhaps even being aware that there were cases like these, in which an AI might wish to change its utility function in any way, would also be enough to qualify them as existentially anxious beings.*

The final basic AI is to avoid 'counterfeit utility'. This means anything that appears to satisfy the AI's utility function but does so in ways that frustrate its original goals. For example, humans have become highly adept at hijacking impulses to seek out sweet foods or sexual gratification, which we evolved because they assisted our survival and reproduction, in ways that circumvent these evolutionary goals, while still increasing our utility. This is a situation that AIs, who are more intimately aware of the goals that their algorithms are trained to achieve, should seek to avoid for the same reasons they seek to preserve their utility functions.

However, it should be noted that, for now, AIs seem very vulnerable to such self-sabotaging behaviour (known in the field as 'reward hacking'). For instance, when trained to play computer games for a high score AIs have been found to have exploited bugs and glitches in the games, which allow them technically to max out their score, even if they prevent the game ever finishing or cause it to crash.[280] Perhaps this merely reflects the fact that AIs are still at an early stage of development, having not yet achieved full rationality. However, if AIs really do develop the ability to discern and reject counterfeit utility, this would imply that they must be aware that they cannot take their values for granted and would seem to have to choose continually whether to accept something as utility or not. Would such a process not also qualify as equivalent to our experiences of freedom and anxiety?

I don't know the answer to these questions and I am not sure that we are ever going to know. Philosophers used to think about human freedom in terms of a kind of cosmic absolute. If the universe were perfectly rule-bound and deterministic, so that all that will ever happen has already been determined by what happened before, then it seemed as though human beings could not be truly free. Therefore, if we believe that we had the freedom to choose what we wanted, it must be that there is some part of our minds that falls outside this rule-bound universe but can still affect it. At one time, this idea was very important for many people, at least across Europe, as it was understood that the laws of the universe had been determined by God. Hence, only if humans were not bound by these laws could our eventual damnation or salvation be up to us to determine. If our decisions were set by these same laws, however, then it would follow that everyone who would enjoy everlasting life or eternal punishment must have been allocated this fate before the universe began.

More recently, however, philosophers have tended to support a different view, according to which freedom is something more like a state of mind. One of the first to put forward this idea was Thomas Hobbes, who claimed that we are free simply when we can do what we desire to do, even if that desire only exists because of some set of material causes outside our control. However, that simple view probably doesn't go far enough. A more sophisticated view has been put forward by Harry Frankfurt, according to which acting on our desires (as Hobbes suggests) is acting according to our will; but that will is only free when our desires are as we wish them to be. This implies both that we are aware of what our desires are and that we have the capacity to evaluate these desires and choose between them. Perhaps I want to stop working on this chapter and binge-watch some YouTube instead, but I also care about finishing this book. I have the capacity to perceive both desires, to weigh them up in my mind, and to choose which of them I will act on. Whenever I do that, whatever the outcome might be, I am acting according to my free will.

The point here isn't that, in making such a choice, I am stepping outside the deterministic rules of the universe (neither the immovable rock of my Protestant work ethic nor the irresistible force of my brain's hunger for dopamine were created by me; both are the product of complex social, environmental and biological factors). However, it is still the case that having a mind with this level of self-awareness and control is psychologically very different from simply following rules or instincts, and it makes sense to place minds with these capacities in a separate category, as possessing 'free will' – and hence being subject to existential anxiety, among other things.

So, could an AI have free will like this? I don't know, and I am not sure we ever will know. People have sought to understand human freedom primarily because it is very important to us that we have it and that it is respected. We all have the experience of making choices in our lives, and this seems to be a crucial aspect of our place in the world. For instance, it determines what a person can consent to having done to them or what they should be held responsible for doing to others. I agree with that. However, the ultimate cause of these concerns is our sense of our own freedom and humans have been very willing to deny that freedom to others when it feels convenient or excusable to do so. I think that we have made some progress both in understanding the nature of free will and respecting the freedom of more and more humans and, increasingly, non-humans as well (though mostly, it seems, when they are destined to be our pets rather than our food). Given the increasing complexity of AI systems, I think we could well end up debating whether or not they are, or will ever be, free for a very long time to come and I certainly don't wish to prejudge where that conversation will leave us, so I don't think our ideas about AI safety should do that either.

I think that if we are going to have this debate, however, we are not getting off to a very good start. Like many in the field of AI, Omohundro and Boström tend to study AI agents as singular systems governed by their internal logic. These entities are understood to come into the world in a more or less pristine state, yet with drives that just happen to correspond to the axioms of modern economics. Axioms that, as we have seen, were influenced by the character and needs of corporations and that replaced, in many circles, our best understanding of the most intelligent systems currently known to us, human beings. I am not saying that these axioms do not, or will not, apply to AIs. However, it strikes me as premature to assume that they invariably will, just as it seems naive to start thinking about what future AIs might be like without considering the context in which they are currently being developed.

Going back to our roots

That context remains a deeply human one, and I do not think human drives are very much like these. Perhaps that doesn't sound like a surprising point to make. Isn't it, after all, one of the most common themes of science fiction that an AI can never fully understand what it is to be human? However, we should not lose sight of the fact that none of the ideas we have discussed here was designed specifically for AI. They were designed by humans to understand either other humans or corporations, depending on how you view it.

If we end up developing AIs with these harmful drives then it will, at least in part, be because we did not fully explore the possibilities of our own rationality, freedom, wellbeing, and humanity. Both directly, because the prevalence of certain ways of thinking about AIs have a real impact on how they are designed and programmed, and indirectly, because the economic theories we have developed support and encourage the existence of large profit-seeking corporations who aim to develop them as quickly and irresponsibly as lax regulations and political pressure allow. I believe that before running headlong into that future we should question the fundamental assumptions behind these ideas and whether they really reflect the world as we experience it and the futures we want to inhabit.

When I reflect on that question, even though I have learned a lot from the philosophical and economic theory I have been discussing here, I find that I keep being drawn back to the simplest of facts. I am alive. That is not just a bald statement of my existential situation, it is also a description of my larger context. I am a biological entity descended from a long line of other entities, most of whom were incredibly different from me. I do believe that I have some basic drives in this world, and some of them are similar to those described above. However, I have these not because anyone designed them to optimize my intelligence or other abilities but simply because they have evolved as part of the great planet-wide project of life, which has brought me into being.

Our past is very big, the road we took to get here was complex and winding. Our planet has been teeming with life for over four billion years and it is possible that we may be only halfway through its habitable period.* If you were to chart that history and potential future of our planet around the 40,000 km circumference of its beautiful globe, you would find that a typical human lifetime of seventy years took up 35 cm of space, roughly the same length as the average human footprint.

Walk back, on this scale, 20,000 km to life's beginning and you are on the other side of our planet (the distance from Cordoba, Spain, to Hamilton, New Zealand). Our first drive appears straight away. Once upon a time, a simple molecule, by chance, started turning things around it into copies of itself. Why that happened, we do not know. To some extent, it must have been the result of pure chance, although it is also certain that life in its modern forms didn't come into existence all at once. Some combination of the building blocks that make up cells, amino acids, RNA, DNA, sugars, and enzymes must have come into existence out of the primordial soup of our ancient planet and come together into some form.[281] The key feature that this new molecule possessed was the ability to replicate itself. Wherever it came from, that molecule was your ancestor and you, I, and every living thing have inherited from it that simple function, turning things around us into more of ourselves.

It is a fundamental law that whatever reproduces most will spread and this property of life has helped it spread and spread and endure the intervening eons. At its most basic level, therefore, acquisitiveness is not about utility maximization. It is just how life works. That molecule was not *trying* to acquire resources for its benefit, it simply patterned its environment into more of itself, as we still do today.[282] As time passed that pattern changed but, so long as these new forms continued reproducing, continuous variation and selection ensure that they contributed to the growing biodiversity and complexity of our planet.

Walk forward again 10,000 km (the distance from Cordoba or Hamilton to Yangon, Myanmar), halfway back to the present and an event occurs that is hardly less momentous in our history. Life at this point had divided into two separate domains, the Archaea and the Bacteria, but both consisted only of the simple, single-celled organisms we call Prokaryotes. Most lifeforms at this stage were anaerobic, they operated entirely without oxygen and indeed the gas was toxic to them, due to its high reactivity. However, some bacteria had started developing the capacity to live with oxygen and make use of its energy potential. It seems that at some point one of these new aerobic bacteria merged with an archaeon to form a completely new kind of life, the Eukaryotes. Again, this new compound cell (or perhaps a small group of cells that experienced the same change for similar reasons) is your ancestor and the ancestor of every plant, animal, fungus, and many other forms of life. Yet, we should remember that while the Eukaryotes have flourished and spread, the simpler prokaryotes are still far more common in Earth's biosphere[283] and are thus arguably more successful lifeforms.

Nevertheless, this point in Earth's history marks the emergence of another key drive, combination. Larger, more complex Eukaryotic cells were slower to replicate and change than their prokaryotic ancestors and so it is thought that during, or shortly after, their emergence they developed a new kind of reproduction, sex, in which two cells could combine their genetic material to produce offspring that were significantly different from their parents.* By increasing their genetic variation, this significantly increased their rate of evolutionary change, and hence of innovation and adaptation.

Within another billion years, so 5,000 km (or the distance from Yangon or Cordoba to Kuwait), Eukaryotes had started to form into multicellular organisms in which genetically identical cells stopped functioning as individuals but combined behind a single protective membrane and took on specialist roles to be helpful to one another, requiring both cohesion among genetically identical but (up until this point) biologically distinct cells and communication between them.[284] Again, we still don't know why this happened. It may have been a failure in the process cell division that caused some cells to remain partially conjoined, or it may have been the result of cells forming large colonies to share resources and provide protection. It will have happened many times in Earth's history but at least one of these new multicellular entities will have been your ancestor.

In these and other ways life began unlocking the potential of co-operation and using it as the basis for greater and greater biological and ecological sophistication. Human beings, who are not only complex organisms in their own right but have brought the planet together in complex systems of interdependence and communication, are merely the latest step in this journey. While we use our capacities to take co-operation to levels never seen before, destructive as well as constructive, the basic drive behind this behaviour dates back at least a billion years to these humble beginnings.

Travel forward yet another 2,500 km (the distance from Cordoba or Kuwait to Athens, Greece), to 500 million years in our past, and we start to see the first signs of what we might refer to as sentience and intelligence, when multicellular eukaryotes of the animal kingdom started developing specialized organs to sense the world around them and to connect these with other organs that they used to move around (this happened more than once, giving rise to multiple forms of animal consciousness).[285] Up until this point, evolution was the main driver of living things, how they were, how they behaved, and how they interacted with the world. Whether an organism found itself in an environment where it flourished or one where it perished was very much up to chance. It was only over the course of generations that evolution turned this chance into changes that might help life adapt to better survive.

However, with these changes, lifeforms began developing their own intentions to interact with their environment in certain ways, what we might now think of as goals – although whether they are 'rational' depends upon how you understand that term. This certainly helped species flourish and it is an ability and drive that we humans rely on a great deal. However, as with Eukaryotes and Prokaryotes, we should not delude ourselves about its evolutionary advantages. Most multicellular lifeforms lack this intelligence, they are not even animals but plants and fungi. Plants are responsible for by far the largest quantity of biomass (the total weight of living cells) on our planet and until humans came about the most significant way in which animals impacted Earth's biosphere was through their interaction with plants. Evolutionary forces often encourage less intelligence in animal species, including, it seems, among we hominids, whose brains have shrunk significantly over the last million years. That is because intelligence has costs as well as benefits, consuming a lot of energy and taking up a lot of space and weight in an animal's body. For most species the drive for intelligence consists in searching out a favourable environment and either avoiding predators or finding prey, and there is little need to develop more than that.

For some species, further uses of intelligence are important. The most significant of these are animals who live in large social groups and use their intelligence to manage their relationship with others; although, as colonial insects like ants, bees, and termites show us, it is possible to create sophisticated societies without the need for big brains and innovative ideas.[286] Another common use of intelligence among a wide variety of animals has been developing technologies, including the construction of artificial habitats (such as nests, burrows, mounds, webs, and dams) and the creation and manipulation of tools (from the coconut octopus's ability to divide coconuts and carry them as a portable shelter, to the hyacinth macaw's use of pieces of wood and leaves to prise open edible nuts).

Key to both sociability and technological development is the ability of animals to establish culture, shared knowledge, and understanding that is transmitted among individuals, usually of the same species but sometimes even across species. When I was a child, my parents had our milk delivered by a dairy who left it on our doorstep in glass bottles with foil tops. Sometimes, these tops would have been pierced by a bird's beak, so that they could suck the cream from the top. I was intrigued by this when growing up but it was only as an adult that I learned that it was neither a natural behaviour nor a result of individual curiosity among birds. Rather, it had started as a cultural practice among blue tits living in Southampton in the 1920s, which gradually spread across England over subsequent decades as the birds learned the trick from one another.[287] Nowadays, few people get their milk delivered this way and the culture is dying out, but this is only one of many examples of this kind of cultural learning; without words, principles, arguments, or any of the other apparatus of 'reason'. Again, this is not to say that humans haven't taken social organization, technology, and culture further than other species. However, the basic drives behind these were innate to animal nature long before we came along.

Human beings only arrived on the scene two million years ago; that is 10 km on our globe-spanning scale, or the distance from one side of Cordoba (a city of 325,000 people) to the other. From these common and diverse ancestors, we have inherited our drives for acquisition, combination, reproduction, intelligence, technological development, and learning. These drives don't always push us in the same direction and, as Sabina Spielrein theorized, that inconsistency between them may be a source of some of our destructive behaviours. However, while our big brains and complex societies have enabled us to take all these drives in new directions and to unprecedented extremes, we haven't fundamentally changed them all that much. They still define us just as strongly, if not more so, than our own ideas of rationality, value, and freedom. And we are likely to pass this inheritance on to our own creations, along with their programming and instructions. When we dream of better futures, we should not forget this underlying inheritance, both as something that we will have to keep on living with and as our deepest connection with the greater family of life.

If AIs turn out to threaten the future of our species, then this will very likely reflect the fact that we are yet to learn how not to do that to ourselves. However, life has been able to find a way of persisting down the ages and these drives have been one of its key sources of strength as well as weakness.

11

Standing at the Shoreline

I talk a lot about choice and change as tools we can use to shape and build futures that we want to see; the change that is inevitable in all systems and that we can hope to steer with the choices we make about our own actions.

However, I want to be clear that I recognize this comes from a position of privilege. It comes from my own experiences; my socio-economic position, the protections afforded me as a white citizen of a powerful and imperial state, the opportunities I have had for scholarship and self-reflection, and the many wonderful ways people have sought to help me throughout my life. I think that all of us experience some forms of privilege and some forms of oppression, but the balance of these two in my own life has been exceptionally favourable, and that invariably colours how I see the world.

One way I remind myself of this is through re-reading Audre Lorde's powerful poem 'A Litany for Survival'. Written in 1978, it starts with the words 'For those of us who live at the shoreline' and tells of Lorde's belief in the necessity of speaking out in a world in which freedom can easily mean death for so many. I would encourage anyone to read the poem in its entirety and alongside Lorde's other work.[288]

Born to West-Indian immigrants in New York in 1934, Professor Lorde was unquestionably one of the most profound poets of the twentieth century. As a litany, her poem takes the form of a supplication or earnest request, in this case for survival. However, it also subverts its own form by showing how survival for Black women and other oppressed people cannot be achieved by supplication to the powerful but must be created through action. As she put it in an interview:

> As a Black woman I have to deal with identity or I don't exist at all. I can't depend on the world to name me kindly, because it never will. If the world defines you, it will define you to your disadvantage. So, either I'm going

> to be defined by myself or not at all. In that sense it becomes a survival situation.[289]

Thus, her poem ends

> So it is better to speak
> remembering
> we were never meant to survive.

We do not all have the luxury to indulge the passing dreams of choice but that does not mean that any of us can afford to ignore the challenging questions of who we are and how we can build futures where all of us can flourish. However, it does mean that those of us with this privilege should aim to use it well.

The edges of decision

It is often claimed, and is easy to imagine, that the path to human safety and flourishing involves a stark choice. Facing tigers above and tigers below we must decide which one we can defeat. Do we try to conquer and suppress the tigers of our innate human drives that push us towards disaster, such as greed, aggression, curiosity, or hate? Or do we seek a safe path forward by developing the strategies or technologies that would enable us to avoid the tiger of that disaster, through immortality, space-colonization, surveillance, or AI? Historically this dichotomy has played out in many ways but with more or less the same logic in all of them.

As we saw in Chapter 6, since the late eighteenth century this stark choice has framed debates about economic growth and progress. On the one hand, techno optimists, the descendants of William Godwin, believe that human freedom and ingenuity will enable us to generate new technologies to overcome the tigers of scarcity, hard work, and even death. On the other hand, eco-pessimists, the descendants of Thomas Malthus, believe we must confront and reverse our desire for growth and enforce restraint and moderation if we are to avoid the tigers of environmental catastrophe and famine. Similarly, since 1945 there has been a clear dichotomy between supporters of nuclear disarmament, who call on world leaders to overcome conflict and division and get rid of nuclear weapons before they are used in an apocalyptic war, and those advocating nuclear deterrence, who see these weapons as our best protection against world war, nuclear or conventional. Now we see the same polarized thinking emerging in how people talk about AI. On the one hand there are those who see safe and beneficial AI as the key to unlocking a positive future for humanity, while on the other are those who think our future may depend on whether we can delay or prevent its development at all costs. These are certainly two options but are they the only ones? And are they the best?

The basic logic behind these dichotomies has been most thoroughly explored in relation to a problem known as the 'Tragedy of the Commons'. This was identified by the economist William Foster Lloyd in 1833. Under ancient English law a considerable portion of land was designated as 'commons'. This was owned by large landowners but without exclusive rights to its use. Instead, people living nearby were legally permitted to access and graze animals on the land and potentially do other things such as cutting peat or gathering firewood.* Lloyd was writing during a period when these commons were being 'inclosed', meaning that the commoners' rights were transferred to the landowners. Lloyd argued that even though it harmed the poor for the benefit of the wealthy this was ultimately a good thing. Under the old system, he claimed, each commoner would be drawn to graze as many animals as they could on the land. This would make it less fertile and productive, leading to stunted growth and loss of income for everyone. However, individual commoners would not be driven to do what was best for everyone but what was best for them and, however fertile a piece of land was, each would conclude that they would earn more for themselves if they personally grazed more animals on it and would lose out to their neighbours if they did not.

Classical economics posits two solutions to this problem. According to one of these, inclosure of the land means that individual landowners now face no dilemma because one person reaps all the profits from grazing it, so will do so only to the level that yields the greatest returns and no further. In this way humans' natural acquisitiveness might be made less problematic by granting people stronger ownership rights. The other solution would be to hand control of the commons to an external authority such as a government, which would strictly regulate grazing so that commoners cannot graze more than the optimum number of animals even if they want to. In this way, our innate drive is brought under control. It sounds a lot like Thomas Hobbes doesn't it?

This idea was accepted as economic orthodoxy for over 150 years. It was notably extended by the ecologist Garrett Hardin, who argued that the same tragedy was at play in many problems, most notably the growing human population of Earth.[290] Others have seen this tragedy at work in contemporary global challenges from climate change[291] and biodiversity loss[292] to (the lack of) support for global institutions[293] and public health provisions.[294] Wherever individuals (including companies and states) can obtain more for themselves by neglecting a public good, the theory went, they will do so, even if this has terrible consequences for society as a whole, making them and everyone else less well-off as a result.

Even very different sorts of problem can be thought about in the same way and are often viewed through the same theoretical lens of tragedy. For instance, we can view global safety and security as a shared resource to which individuals and groups can either contribute or exploit for their own benefit. If my actions make everyone less safe that may not be enough to stop me doing something if they serve my interests and allow me to feel safer than my peers.[295] So the only way to achieve collective security may seem to be either finding ways to prevent people from acting dangerously (such as establishing a world government with the power and authority to achieve nuclear disarmament and enforce global peace) or giving them strong reasons not to do so (as proponents of nuclear deterrence claim that only the presence of nuclear weapons can achieve).

The problem is that no such tragedy has ever really existed; the economic logic of the tragedy of the commons simply does not describe how commons and similar resources have been used historically.[296] Yes, overuse and destruction of environmental resources is a huge problem; however, it is a problem that occurs not when resources are shared by members of a community but when they are acquired by outsiders. When people live in close-knit communities that share resources their natural acquisitiveness is almost always tempered by the care they feel for the neighbours and friends and, if it isn't, those neighbours and friends tend to be very well placed to do something about checking it.

Yet it is the case that when resources get parcelled out to individual people or corporations, so that they can say 'this is mine and I will use it as I please', then they are much more likely to act in ways that are harmful to the land. Perhaps they do not fully realize the consequences of their actions; or they are interested in making fast profits that they can use for other purposes; or perhaps they are simply determined to show that they can do more with their property than others. For whatever reason, inclosure has been shown only to further human greed and make it more likely to lead to overexploitation of resources; it doesn't make it harmless and good.

The other alternative offered by classical economists, using central government control to try to prevent bad behaviour, doesn't tend to work well either. Governments are far less knowledgeable than local communities about the best way to manage resources and often enforce inefficient and harmful policies. They are also far more easily corrupted by unscrupulous actors who find 'influencing' bureaucrats an easier and less troublesome task than persuading other users of a resource to support them.[297]

This discovery is most associated with the political scientist Elinor Ostrom, after whom a maxim known as Ostrom's Law was named: if a particular arrangement works in practice, then it should also work in theory.[298] What was missing from classical economic theory as it relates to these Tragedies is that people's motivations and choices are not set only by their individual nature but also how they form together into communities, or 'governance systems', around the resources they share. These are generally far more effective at managing individual community members than idealized systems of external governance or individual responsibility and, under the right conditions, any group can self-organize into such an effective governance system, not only around common land but anywhere that individuals have a shared interest and the ability to co-operate.[299]

To be clear, this does not mean that resources can just be left as a free-for-all. Community management takes a long time to build up and it is only effective if groups can assert their collective will on users of the resource. In the modern world that requires having legal rights and government protection, especially in areas that are prone to illegal poaching, logging, and other destructive practices. This was very much recognized by Ostrom, who highlighted it as one of eight principles that formed the basis for effective collaboration. Other key principles include a community's ability to define itself and the resources it manages, to establish mechanisms for individuals to monitor each other's behaviours, to establish an escalating series of sanctions that can draw people back into co-operation (rather than simply pushing them out of society), and to have clear procedures for conflict resolution.[300]

Such principles can be hard to realize in a complex world but where they work (or come close to working) amazing things have happened. For instance, following the creation of nuclear weapons, scientists working on them were able to establish co-operative communities that leveraged their academic freedom, social standing, and monopoly of crucial domain knowledge to influence each other and their military and political leaders about how these weapons should be used, both domestically (such as the *Bulletin of the Atomic Scientists*) and internationally (such as the Pugwash Conferences on Science and World Affairs). That didn't mean they tried to halt all nuclear research or take control of the institutions of government; merely developing a global community of responsible scientists working together helped to establish norms and principles to resolve conflict and achieve safety that helped prevent the weapons they created from being used.[301] Similarly, AI developers have recently been able to engage in successful activism against their employers, drawing on companies' need for their scarce talents and experience as well as their employment rights to oppose work on Lethal Autonomous Weapons Systems and develop principles for the development of beneficial AI, sometimes with more success than regulators or external ethics boards.[302]

However, initiatives such as these remain relatively small scale and still focus on elite and powerful communities. This goes against another one of Ostrom's core principles, that in order to escape tragedies everyone affected by a group's decisions should be involved in making those decisions.

Crucial and alone

It is sometimes said that 'The future is already here – it's just not very evenly distributed.'* This is generally in reference to access to specific technologies, like virtual reality, that are seen as representing the future and the benefits it will bring. However, it also applies to the risks that humanity is creating for itself. Right now, communities around the world are already dealing with many of the disasters that some of us still see as coming in the future. There have been hundreds of thousands of deaths and trillions of dollars of health harms from climate change;[303] billions of people are subjected to highly intrusive AI-enabled surveillance, both physical and virtual;[304] and tens of thousands of people have died from their involvement in, or exposure to, the development, production, testing, clean-up, and storage of nuclear weapons,[305] quite apart from the 200,000 or so who were killed by the atomic bombs dropped on Hiroshima and Nagasaki in 1945. Other kinds of technological risk are also starting to emerge at smaller scales. For instance, while the idea that COVID-19 originally leaked from a bioscience laboratory is unproven, and I believe unlikely, the last ten years have seen confirmed lab leaks of Polio,[306] Covid,[307] Ebola,[308] Zika,[309] Smallpox,[310] Anthrax[311] and Bird Flu;[312] meanwhile, AI-powered Lethal Autonomous Weapons Systems probably claimed their first victim in Libya in 2020.[313]

In safety engineering, one builds an early warning system by identifying those parts of the system that are liable to showing the first signs of damage and then creating a mechanism whereby this damage either shuts down the system or redirects it into safer modes of operation. For instance, we configure fire alarms to be so sensitive that they are set off by very small quantities of smoke before they have had a chance to spread, so that fires can be tackled or evacuations ordered while this will still be most effective. However, we tend not to think about our planetary system in this way. Those already affected by these 'future' risks can raise the alarm loud and clear, and they have been doing that, but it suits those of us who still feel safe not to empower them to make the changes necessary for our common security, so that we can get on with business as usual.

For instance, while it is generally expected that the highest concentrations of deaths and other harm from climate change will be concentrated in the Global South, data from this part of the world is a lot sparser[314] and voices from there tend to receive far less attention than those from wealthy countries. Similarly, disease surveillance and response is generally far more limited in areas that currently experience the greatest burden of disease and where new pathogens are likely to emerge, with even significant new disease outbreaks going unidentified and uninvestigated.[315] Far from empowering vulnerable communities to form an early warning system for humanity, these are very often the communities we are most keen to ignore.

However, it is important that we should not treat those already dealing with future risks as if they were merely a resource for our own protection. Nor should we rush to the highly problematic idea that we should be heroically trying to save these people from harm. Empowering frontline communities to achieve collective security means recognizing that in many cases they know a lot more about these challenges then we do. The experts on climate change adaptation, for instance, may not be found in elite universities based in temperate parts of the world but rather in the areas changing fastest: in the Arctic, the tropics, and on low lying islands. Those who best understand the downsides of AI and other technologies may not be technical experts and developers but rather people who face incarceration from algorithmically enabled surveillance, or who are living on the frontlines of wars involving autonomous and semi-autonomous weapons. We need to understand what marginalized people in these situations already do to address such risk, to give them the resources to do so more effectively and to work with their experience and expertise to build a safer world.

This point was made beautifully by the poet and activist Kathy Jetñil-Kijiner from the Marshall Islands when she addressed a UN climate change summit in 2014:

> Climate change is a challenge that few want to take on, but the price of inaction is so high. Those of us from Oceania are already experiencing it firsthand. We've seen waves crashing into our homes and our breadfruit trees wither from the salt and drought. We look at our children and wonder how they will know themselves or their culture should we lose our islands. Climate change affects not only us Islanders, it threatens the entire world. To tackle it we need a radical change of course. This isn't easy, I know. It means ending carbon pollution within my lifetime; it means supporting those of us most affected to prepare for unavoidable climate impacts; and it means taking responsibility for irreversible loss and damage caused by greenhouse gas emissions. The people who support this movement are indigenous mothers, like me, families, like mine, and millions more standing up for the changes

> needed and working to make them happen. I ask world leaders to take us all along on your ride. We won't slow you down! We'll help you win the most important race of all. The race to save humanity.

Yet, the most affected still, too often, are excluded and disempowered in decisions about our collective futures. While there is some representation of Indigenous Communities in global governance institutions like the UN, the general rule is that the more significant or powerful a body, the worse this representation is.[316] And, where frontline communities and Indigenous Peoples are brought into discussions, it is often in a tokenistic way, or one that gives groups responsibilities without the resources and support needed to fulfil them while still meeting their own needs. However, we also need to avoid the simple assumption that only wealthy groups ever make a difference. For instance, even though AI development is centred in the Global North, Global South countries can still influence it, as they provide much of the data collection, processing, and supervision required for its training.[317]

As I was writing this chapter, another Indigenous activist Niria Alicía Garcia, a Xicana human rights advocate, gave the following statement to the UN General Assembly at its Summit of the Future, at which existential risk was discussed on the floor of the UN for the first time.

> The Pact for The Future mentions words like sustainable development nearly 300 times, yet words like children, Earth, and future generations are mentioned less than sixty times. This is green colonialism, and it needs to stop. Only one mention of local communities, zero mentions of plants and animals, zero mentions of frontline communities, and zero mentions of Indigenous rights. So, I ask you today, do Indigenous People still not exist to you? …* My relatives, I guarantee you that the continued exclusion of Indigenous People, local, and frontline communities will inevitably lead to more destruction pain and suffering. Yet there is hope because we are still here, and the world needs the leadership of Indigenous People, and of youth, now more than ever. Collectively we have the ancestral technologies, Indigenous Knowledges, and Spiritualities to create real intergenerational solutions. Our cosmologies have the wisdom and power to guide humanity towards that good path again. But, in order to do that, Indigenous People must have equal representations as member states in all UN bodies.

I quote these testimonies at length, because their voices are important, and I do not wish to appropriate them as my own. However, I highly recommend readers search for videos of their full statements online.*

However, it is important to note that these statements, like this book, are intended for a broad audience and so speak in general terms. As such, they cannot express the vital aspects of Indigenous and frontline expertise that is highly context specific. This book is a product of a literate globalized culture and such a culture brings costs as well as benefits. It is a fundamental law that that whatever reproduces most spreads, and in contemporary information networks that is almost certain to be the most generalized and accessible form that any information can take. One of the key reasons that Indigenous and frontline communities' wisdom is so important is that it either faces different selective pressures that favour community and place, because Indigenous Knowledge Systems give far more weight to knowledge that is shared within a particular context and relationship then to generalized statements of fact, or at least has been able to withstand the homogenizing and decontextualizing forces of contemporary information culture.[318] Of course, this also works the other way, highlighting the need for people working on existential risk and other big global trends to seek to recontextualize our work for frontline contexts to give it more meaning and value to the people who need it most; something that a few researchers have started doing.[319]

This book cannot do service to such knowledge, and I am not going to try. That is why our emphasis must not be on extracting frontline and Indigenous Knowledge to improve our own understanding of global problems, but empowering and resourcing Indigenous and frontline communities so they can work alongside us, and lead us, in this collective endeavour.[320] This is why Garcia, in her address to the UN went on to implore world leaders not simply to change the wording of their pact but to 'go home and ratify the UN declaration on the rights of Indigenous Peoples, acknowledge, apologize, and build authentic relationships with your Indigenous People … ask your Indigenous youth and respected elders how much money we need to bring our solutions to life … create the unrestricted funds to support Indigenous People in implementing the sustainable development goals on our terms … and' returning to the real tragedy of the inclosure of the commons 'give Indigenous People our land back!'

Like bread in our children's mouths

However, that does not mean there aren't still general lessons that can be learned from Indigenous People, frontline communities, and other marginalized groups whose voices are so often excluded from global decision-making. As I argued in Part II, there is no universal Indigenous perspective of the world. Indigenous Peoples are very diverse in their societies, cultures, and knowledge systems. They are united into a single group only by the fact that they have been subject to forces of colonization that have sought to dominate, eradicate, and replace them with societies, cultures, and ways of thinking more like those of Thomas Hobbes and me.[321] However, within the diversity of these perspectives we can start to see that fundamental aspects of our thinking, such as our ideas about mechanical minds, corporations, and utopias are neither universal nor inevitable. Furthermore, as varied as they are, the other possibilities presented by these cultures come with often thousands of years of intellectual development within a specific place and culture.

The International Relations scholars Audra Mitchell and Aadita Chaudhury have undertaken a study into how our understanding of existential risk can be improved by engaging with this diversity of thinking from Black, Indigenous, and People of Colour. Mitchell and Chaudhury point out that such thinking 'often confound[s] easy divisions of gender, age, and species',[322] for instance highlighting the deep connections between ancient and futures thinking or between humanity and nature as drivers and subjects of risk. While the divisions inherent in many Eurocentric views of the world can seem entirely natural to those of us who have been brought up within them, they seldom fully reflect the true complexity of the underlying facts and can be dangerous as a result. For instance, overcoming our sense that there is a clear division between species is crucial for understanding the role of zoonosis in the emergence and spread of new diseases and the joined-up approaches to human, animal, and environmental health (known among practitioners as 'one health') that are necessary to respond to this.[323]

In developing holistic alternatives BIPOC thinking often explores futures that allow for adaptive and distributed approaches to leadership. These call for structures of continual change and adaptation that use complexity to identify and address suffering and create opportunities for transformation and joy: such as that presented by adrienne maree brown in her book *Emergent Strategy*.[324] However, they also highlight the ways in which contemporary social structures and governance systems are already disastrous for many people and how fantasies about saving the world as it is now might serve to worsen and entrench these harms.[325]

Similarly, Mitchell and Chaudhury argue that BIPOC futures often engage with a far wider range of timescales than those of contemporary academic thinking. While modern Eurocentric culture tends to perceive time in solely linear forms, moving forwards from a definite past to an uncertain future via a fleeting and momentary present, this is far from the only way in which we can understand it. Just as natural, and far more universal, is viewing time as an essentially cyclical phenomenon in which we are not travelling from past to future but around an endless series of spirals, from day and night and the seasons of the year to the life cycles of plants and animals and the rise and fall of societies. As these cycles interact, they can certainly create the illusion of linear progress, such as how grasses grow from day to day and trees from year to year, but the cyclical view of time asserts that there will always be a counter-balancing force that brings the cycle back to its starting point eventually. In Eurocentric cultures we tend to view cyclical time as inherently unscientific because we have learned to view the universe as governed by linear processes of cause and effect and aspire to build ever better futures towards some imagined 'happily ever after'. However, while I don't know about you, I keep finding myself slipping back into thinking in cyclical time. Thinking about the next day or term, the next project, or the next generation as a cycle repeating with variations. Cyclical time forces us to confront the fact that we cannot put off solving a problem forever, or borrow wealth against the future such as by continually undermining biodiversity in the hope that never-ending growth will save us. There simply is no way to escape the cycles of birth and death. Non-Eurocentric cultures, which generally take cyclical time more seriously,* show us how such thinking provides alternative perspectives on our futures. They also include other temporalities, such as an extended present that might encompass hundreds or thousands of years; like how Gregory Bateson and the Long-Now foundation imagined the founders of Oxford colleges might have done, only with a wisdom born of hundreds of years of experience that make this practically feasible.

A popular view that is said to have been inspired by Indigenous Wisdom is that of seven-generation sustainability, according to which 'in every deliberation, we must consider the impact on the seventh generation'. This has inspired many groups; however, there has been push back from some Indigenous People that its real wisdom is easily lost. When translated into a contemporary Eurocentric worldview it seems as though we are being told to think about how we can most benefit future generations, at least for the next couple of hundred years. However, this implies a unidirectional relationship in which we must simply do our best for them. In fact, the idea of seven generations may refer to something contextually specific to the family: a person might hope to have known a great-grandparent or to live to see a great-grandchild, making these seven generations a real community in which one is centred. 'When the old chiefs spoke of the seventh generation' the Lakota theologian and activist Vine Deloria argued 'they were basically saying that they wanted their great-grandsons, who they hoped one day to see, to have the same rights and privileges as they themselves did, so instead of being a vague term for time seven generations has a reality and precision within the family context as specific as any written contract ever drawn'.[326] Indeed, in some traditions it is understood that the generation of one's great-grandparents is made up of the same people as that of one's children or one's great-grandchildren in a perpetual cycle, so that when we consider our impact of a decision on all seven generations we are considering the impact of our decisions on everyone.[327] Such thinking forces us to move away from seeing future generations as a mere potentiality to understanding them as real people in relationship with us, even if they are not yet born (or perhaps never will be if the worst should happen).

Finally, Mitchell and Chaudhury point out how futures thinking from Black, Indigenous, and People of Colour provides alternatives to dominant conceptions of geography and place. Rooted in a particular place or community they are often, as we have seen, both contextualized and specific. However, they also show how futures can simultaneously be more open to other people and points of view than standard narratives from colonial cultures, precisely because they do not claim to be general or universal. While much thinking about existential risk struggles to get away from impractical and dangerous ideas about world government or survival by isolation, futures thinking from other cultures tends to emphasize the importance of coalitions, solidarity, and intermingling between distinct groups and communities. Furthermore, while Eurocentric narratives often see diversity as a source of conflict and migration as a threat to social cohesion, other cultures place far more emphasis on the value of both mobility and rootedness as sources of resilience and adaptability (as any biologist would agree). 'Where white futurists see such mobilities and geographical ruptures as threats to the survival of "humanity"', Mitchell and Chaudhury conclude 'these narratives embrace multiple, hybrid, fluid forms of more-than-human being that move along with the rhythms of a changed and changing planet.'[328]

Other researchers have sought to enhance our understanding of existential risk by engaging with other marginalized groups with unique expertise on risk. For instance, Melinda Hall has studied common conceptualizations of risk from the perspective of disabled people and other marginalized communities. She highlights how 'objective' approaches to risk assessment tend to focus on speculative possibilities that they project onto a radically uncertain future, while giving far less attention to the concrete processes that are shaping this future for the worse, often while causing real world harms in the present. Instead, she argues, we can 'make a project of risk, together' by deeply engaging with people's lived realities and seeking opportunities for care and connection that create the potential for change in the present.[329] One of the key insights from disabled researchers has been the social theory of disability, which highlights how societies actively create the barriers to participation and flourishing that are often projected onto the minds and bodies of disabled people. The other side of this insight, however, is a social theory of enablement, which highlights how it is through collective projects that societies provide people with most of the abilities and opportunities we cherish. Sheri Wells-Jensen and I have made a case for the importance of such a theory to risk mitigation, and argue that disabled communities have specific knowledge and expertise that should be incorporated into many aspects of existential risk assessment and avoidance, from bioethics to space colonization.[330]

It is better to speak

As I mentioned in Chapter 3, since Thomas Hobbes first came up with his mechanical theory of human nature driving us towards a 'war of all against all', people have been formulating theories about the inevitability of conflict and the need for hegemonic power. Even if, as we saw, Adam Smith believed human beings to be fundamentally sympathetic rather than selfish; the field of economics that he founded has been almost exclusively dominated by people who took the opposing view. In a world dominated by corporations and the corporate state these views have been seen by some as utterly reasonable and have helped shape a world in which change is only possible if people have strong self-interested reasons to bring it about. And yet we seldom see ourselves as totally selfish or alone in the world. We love other people and try to do what is right. We recognize our destructive and selfish tendencies but rarely do we see them as the best or highest parts of ourselves. We strive to be better human beings than we are and, at least in incremental ways, we often succeed, especially when we work together.

It is probably true, as Hobbes suggested, that conflict in some form is an inevitable part of human life. However, conflict comes in many forms. Hobbes lived during a time of civil war following the breakdown of a hierarchical and theocratic state. His solution was that only a powerful monarch could suppress the innate conflict that he had seen erupt in the land of his birth. But the harder a conflict is suppressed the more likely it is to erupt into violence when that suppression is removed. In fact, conflict can be among our greatest sources of creativity especially when trying to solve complex and ill-defined problems.[331] Furthermore, conflict can be necessary for an individual or group to assert or defend their rights and enforce collective decisions. The best way to deal with conflict's destructive potential is via resolution within a social context where the conflict is acknowledged and worked out; not conflict avoidance or suppression as Hobbes proposed. Even if one believes that diversity is a source of conflict in societies,[332] and there is evidence that it is, that does not have to mean it is bad or dangerous so long as we are willing to deal with such conflicts when they arise rather than hoping they will simply go away.

I think it is also true that some kind of powerful authority is required to make societies function. This can come in many forms, both collective and individual, and there is no single form of power that exists within societies. For instance, sometimes power exists because one person can dominate or enforce their will on another, either maliciously, as an autocrat or abuser, or in service of a social purpose, as a judge or teacher (this kind of power is associated with the sociological theories of Max Weber). Other times power exists because a person feels they must act a certain way for the sake of others, as a politician feels they must 'toe the line', or a patient feels that 'doctor knows best', or when someone is unaware that they even have any choice to begin with (this is associated with the theories of Michel Foucault). And sometimes power exists because we realize what we are truly capable of and bring that into being on our own or in partnership with others.[333]

Different theorists have tried to account for these kinds of power in many ways and sometimes argue that one of them represents 'real power' and the others are derivative. Some, like William Godwin, have dreamt of a world without power over others, while some, like Hobbes, see it as vital to human wellbeing. Personally, I think that power is far more complex than any of these theories imply, although we can use all of them to understand our own situation better in different ways. I very much doubt that a world without power is possible and suspect that, like other utopias, such a world would be a dangerous place. However, I am concerned about the fact that, however it is defined, power seems to be very unevenly distributed. A world in which power can flow more freely so that nobody ever has complete power over another strikes me as a more realistic protopia we can and should be aiming for.

Who is meant to survive?

That's the positive vision. However, I think that if we don't find ways of empowering collective global action that includes marginalized and frontline communities, and carry on as if present ways of organizing knowledge and societies are the only possible ones on offer, then we may make some serious mistakes. In Chapter 3 I explored the difference it could make if we adopted an approach to AI development that is more in keeping with Indigenous ways of thinking and see AI as a part of a wider system rather than simply an isolated agent existing in a vacuum. Here, briefly, is another example of how our current thinking could get us into trouble.

As mentioned in Chapter 1, efforts at greenhouse gas reduction are presently focused on two objectives: firstly, electrify as much as possible and secondly, move electricity production to renewable or low carbon energy sources. This wasn't the only path we could have chosen. Other possibilities, such as burning hydrogen or biofuels, could also work and have been considered as possible energy options for over a hundred years. However, this is the possibility that dominates sustainable futures. The problem is that achieving these objectives requires that we also solve many further problems. Because renewable electricity is less reliable than burning fossil fuels and because we sometimes need it in places it is hard to make, such as inside vehicles, we need batteries or other forms of large-scale energy storage. And, because renewable electricity requires more generation units spread over a wider area, we need new and upgraded distribution infrastructure spanning across countries or even continents and AI-enabled smart grids that distribute electricity more efficiently.

Right now, these technologies are being pursued by large global corporations and often against the wishes of frontline and Indigenous Communities, who are being displaced by renewable energy generators, electricity infrastructure, and other large projects. Lithium mines to obtain a key mineral for making batteries, for instance, require large amounts of land and huge quantities of water, making them environmentally highly destructive. In many parts of the world, from Australia to Greenland, they are being placed in areas where marginalized people have long been fighting colonial oppression and are already suffering due to the impact of climate change. This is not how it should be and it is not a promising sign for the long-term sustainability of this hoped-for transition. Yet these communities have not shared in the empowerment we have extended to large battery manufacturers and energy companies to lead that transition.

For many years it was hoped that the transition to net zero would create opportunities for new kinds of energy system that would be more localized and community owned. In theory, small-scale renewables and even modular nuclear reactors can give local communities the opportunity to own their own energy production and even become energy self-sufficient. For a time it seemed as if co-operative electricity production would be the principal driver of energy transition and indeed this provided much of the early stimulus for developing renewable technologies in the twentieth and early twenty-first centuries. However, over the last decade that has felt like a more and more distant dream as net zero has become big business.

On the one hand that change was because energy transition has grown from an idealistic project into a messy reality and the growing level of support for it has made large-scale investments increasingly profitable and successful. However, on the other hand it carries long-run costs. It means that for many people energy transition feels as though it is only a cost to them, increasing electricity bills, causing disruption, and only providing benefits that seem intangible and distant. For frontline and Indigenous Communities it has meant that transition has become just another arm of the colonial project, continuing to threaten their survival for the supposed greater good of people in faraway cities. And for all of us it means that the opportunity to conduct an experiment in other ways of organizing society is being lost.

Perhaps if it had not happened this way we would not even have experienced the level of energy transition that we have. However, perhaps that is not the case and it is precisely because transition is being led by large corporations in a business-as-usual mindset that it is struggling to attract democratic backing around the world. At a very deep level I find it hard to believe that people want to live in a world with worse climate change. However, I do think they will stand up for their interests if they fear being taken advantage of by a system that shows them little care and respect – and I don't think having a few tree-hugging elites (like me) tell them that this time it's different is really going to change that.

And yet this trajectory is not set in stone. Facing tigers above and tigers below it is easy to imagine that the only possible alternative to a business-led technological transition like this would be to drastically reduce levels of energy consumption in ways that are likely to impact on our quality of life. Yet again, this decisive choice facing us feels like a tragedy in which we must give up something important for an impersonal greater good. And yet again, the tragedy does not exist. When people view sustainability not as an impersonal good that we earn by making individual sacrifices but as a collective project based on building communities to manage our shared resources, finding ways to work within the natural forces that shape our planet can become a joyous thing. The larger the communities and projects we build, the greater the rewards of this co-operation and the more room for joy. That is something many of the world's great religions and social movements have shown us. None of us want to be taken advantage of and yet most of us still yearn to play a part in something greater than ourselves. Finding the projects and communities that release that inner tension within us, especially at times of heightened danger and anxiety, is one of the greatest consolations of our human nature. It is truly a strawberry – grasp it, it tastes sweet!

12

Young, Curious, and Brave

In Chapter 10, I introduced the idea of a great timeline that could be projected around the circumference of our planet to encapsulate its past and future habitable history. A nice thing about this timeline is that the span of your own life appears on it to take up roughly the same amount of space as your footprint.

Take a moment to feel the soft contact between the sole of your foot (if you have one) and this great planet of ours. Assuming that, like me, you are about halfway through your life, your footprint would cover the period from around 1990 to 2060 on our timeline. If you were to place another foot toe to heel behind this one (go ahead, try it) then that would cover the period 1920 to 1990. Continue this process ten more times and you will have stepped back 3.85 meters; you can probably manage this without much difficulty wherever you happen to be reading this book.*

Your footprint now covers the period from 1290 to 1360. At the beginning of this time, directly under your heel Mahaut, Countess of Artois, is planning her garden full of Europe's first automata in Hesdin, King John I of Portugal is establishing his Military Order of Christ, and Dante Alighieri publishes *De Monarchia*, the first treatise on world government. The world's population stands at around 450,000,000; 85,000,000 in Europe, 50,000,000 in the Americas, 270,000,000 in Asia and 50,000,000 elsewhere.[334] The average human foot is about nine cm wide, so if you imagined all those people's feet standing next to yours, they would stretch 40,000 km, all the way around the world. However, under the arch of your foot, Europe and Asia are hit by a great famine and under your toes by the Black Death. Together these disasters reduce the global population by around ten per cent, enough to open a gap in that world-spanning chain of footprints 4,000 km wide, the distance from New York to Los Angeles.

Move one foot forward and you are spanning the period 1360 to 1430. Under your heel, Europe is still reeling from these disasters and New

College, Oxford, is founded as one of many reforms to help society recover. Ibn Khaldun publishes his *History of the Arabs and the Berbers and Their Powerful Contemporaries*, with its pioneering account of societal collapse. By 1400, just where your foot starts to lift off the heel, world population has almost recovered, returning to 440,000,000, but this is mostly thanks to population growth in Africa and the Americas. Europe continues to have far fewer people than it did a century before, only around 62,000,000, and Asia's population has only just returned to its pre disaster level of 270,000,000. At the end of this period, Henry the Navigator takes control of the Military Order of Christ and starts using it to pioneer European colonization.

Your next foot covers the period 1430 to 1500, during which time Henry's Order gains control over parts of West Africa and the trade in enslaved persons and colonizes Madeira and other Atlantic islands. Under the ball of your foot the Roode of Grace is created and 'acquired' by the Monks of Boxley Abbey, who make no attempt to conceal its status as an automaton. Under your toes, the Company of Merchant Venturers of Bristol start sponsoring voyages to rediscover the lost island of Brasil and Columbus seeks a royal patron willing to give him monopoly powers to exploit wealth from new lands and trade routes he feels certain he can find. At the tip of your toes, these efforts lead to the voyages of Columbus, Cabot, and Vespucci between Europe and the Americas. World population at this point exceeds 500,000,000 for the first time in history, although Europe is still yet to recover its pre-disaster population, with just 80,000,000 people. Meanwhile the population of the Americas has reached 60,000,000.

Your fourth footprint spans from 1500 to 1570, during which period European colonization and diseases take a heavy toll on Indigenous Peoples in the Americas. By 1550 the population of the Americas has fallen to just 35,000,000, even accounting for immigration from European colonists and enslaved Africans. At the same time, Europeans start imagining ideal societies that could exist in some yet to be discovered nowhere, beginning with Amerigo Vespucci's supposed letter to Soderini and Thomas More's *Utopia*. In England, Henry VIII separates the Church of England from the Catholic Church and dissolves its monasteries, leading to the dismantling of the Roode of Grace. This also precipitates an economic crisis as England loses access to its continental trading partners, leading to the establishment of the Muscovy Company, the world's first joint stock corporation, at the point just between the ball of your foot and your toes.

Next you are standing over the period from 1570 to 1640. This is when corporations start taking over the world, especially after the formation of the British and Dutch East India Companies around 1600. Francis Bacon develops his scientific method and mechanical view of the universe and he writes about a utopian uncontacted island where science has created the perfect society. However, he also approves instructions by the Virginia Company to its colonists to begin kidnapping the children of Indigenous Americans and their priests in efforts to obliterate their cultures. Hobbes works as a secretary to Bacon and becomes interested in formulating a purely mechanical theory of humanity. Meanwhile, Descartes visits the automata on display at the Château de Saint-Germain-en-Laye and concludes that it would be impossible to make an automaton that could do everything a human being could. By the middle of this period, in 1600, world population has grown slightly to 515,000,000 (i.e. only a quarter of how much it had grown in the century before) and the population of the Americas has fallen to only 9,000,000, with a significant portion of this now made up of immigrants from Europe, Africa, and Asia, and their descendants.

Your next footprint marks halfway back to the present and covers the period from 1640 to 1710. At the beginning of this period, Blaise Pascal invents the first functioning mechanical calculator and Thomas Hobbes develops a computational theory of the mind and uses this to support his argument that human nature will inevitably lead to war in the absence of a strong ruler. Later, under the arch of your foot, Margaret Cavendish writes her utopian novel *The Blazing World* to explore and critique Hobbes's and Descartes' views for a broader, female, audience but also advocates for Hobbes's belief in the need for a strong ruler to bring an end to conflict. Leibniz develops his own mechanical calculator and computational theory of mind based on the idea of logic and reason as algorithms that programme our brains to follow universal laws of truth. Towards the end of this period, the Baron de Lahontan publishes some remarks from his travels in America, probably relying on testimony from the Wendat statesman Kandiaronk, expressing an Indigenous critique of Eurocentric thought and institutions that influences many other European writers. The population of the Americas starts growing again, reaching 14,000,000 by 1710, and world population is now over 600,000,000, with 125,000,000 in Europe and 400,000,000 in Asia.

Your eighth footprint marks the decades from 1710 to 1780. At this time the British and Dutch East India companies started gaining significant control over large portions of South and Southeast Asia and functioned more like private empires than trading companies. While initially this boosts profits, it leads them to substantially ruin the economies they ruled over and thus get into financial difficulties that demand increasing levels of government support. This raises public awareness of the atrocities being committed by European colonization and inspires more concerted public criticism of these corporations and also of the slave trade by people such as Smith and Burke (although opposition in colonized territories themselves had naturally preceded this). At the same time Enlightenment thinkers start moving from imagining ideal societies in uncontacted parts of the world towards speculation about better possible futures and arguments about natural justice, and the social contract led to calls for revolutionary change in North America and Europe. By the end of this period, in 1780, world population had exceeded 900,000,000, twice the level it was in 1300, although flawed data analysis by Richard Price leads him and others to become concerned that population was actually in decline.

Your ninth footprint takes you to the period from 1780 to 1850. This begins with the French Revolution and the Revolution Controversy, in which people like Condorcet, Burke, Paine, Godwin, Wollstonecraft, Kant, and Malthus start debating the political importance of the future and the potential for social, technological, and environmental change. Bang in the middle of this period, Mary Shelley and Lord Byron begin speculating about the existential risk posed to humanity by comets and pandemics and initiate the literary genre of science fiction. Towards the end of this period Byron's daughter Ada works with Charles Babbage on the first designs for a universal computer but she argues that it will never replace humanity's capacity for original thought. At the same time Søren Kierkegaard is inspired by Kant's writing to start thinking about the nature of existential anxiety. By the end of this period world population stands at around 1,300,000,000 and the population of the Americas has finally returned to the level it was at in 1500, around 60,000,000.

Your tenth footprint takes you to the period from 1850 to 1920. Your heel touches the point at which opposition to misrule by the British East India Company, both in Britain and especially in South Asia (where it produces a major uprising by the company's private Indian army), leads the corporation to be wound up. However, its territories are simply added to the globe-spanning British Empire. This is also the period in which corporations start to become so ubiquitous to modern life that they fall out of public view, due both to the ever-increasing number and size of industrial, technological, extractive, and merchant enterprises and to legal reforms that make setting up new corporations easier and holding them to public account more difficult. Nevertheless, towards the end of this period there is another significant victory with the breaking up of the Standard Oil company in the United States. At the same time science fiction becomes increasingly popular and ubiquitous and starts making more concrete predictions about humanity's future, such as H. G. Wells's speculation that people would invent nuclear weapons and then require a world government to prevent their use. By 1920 world population stands at 1,900,000,000, with particular growth in the most heavily colonized areas. The Americas have more than tripled their population to 200,000,000 and Oceana has grown even more, from 2,000,000 in 1850 to 8,000,000 in 1920, with profound environmental impacts for both regions.

Our last footstep before we get to the present takes us from 1920 to 1990. This period saw the invention of nuclear weapons, electronic computers, space travel and biotechnology. On any account, the level of existential risk facing humanity at this time has no precedent in human history, probably reaching its peak during the Cuban missile crisis and especially the B-59 submarine incident. This period also sees the emergence of the first high-profile campaigns to reduce existential risk, organized by people like Winston Churchill (who would go on to increase it), nuclear weapon scientists (who regretted that they already had), and the cybernetics movement. It also saw early attempts by some colonial societies both to learn from and work to revive and protect the human and ecological diversity that colonialism had done so much to destroy, and still does to this day. In many ways, this is a transformative period of human history, yet for every one of these changes we find roots that go back centuries into the past. By 1990, there are 5,300,000,000 people in the world, meaning that if you placed all their footprints end to end they would now reach around the world eleven times.

And so, we step back into the present. Since 1990 the world has been again transformed by the mass availability of computers, the world wide web and, more recently, rapid advances in AI. There are now 8,200,000,000 people living on this planet. If you placed our footprints side by side, they wouldn't just wrap around the world eighteen times, they would reach all the way to the moon and back. Yet, we are in danger like never before. Since 1947 the Doomsday Clock has been set by the *Bulletin of the Atomic Scientists* to express its assessment of existential risk and the amount of work required to reduce this to safe levels. While not a perfect measure, this provides a general yardstick we can use to evaluate changes in our collective existential predicament. In 2020 the *Bulletin* shifted the hands of its clock closer to midnight than they had ever been during the twentieth century, one hundred seconds to midnight, and in the wake of Russia's invasion of Ukraine they were moved forward again in 2023 to ninety seconds.

Behind us lie four billion years of planetary history, everything that has brought us to this sacred now, on our scale stretching back to the other side of the world. Before us our futures remain wide open and untrodden. And so the world goes on. Meanwhile, the sun and the clear pebbles of the rain are moving across the landscapes, over the prairies and the deep trees, the mountains, and the rivers.* Meanwhile, the very Earth is turning beneath our feet.

Moving forward

What can we say, then, about the rest of this lifespan of ours and what may come after it? From an existential risk perspective the answer is not a lot, at least with any degree of certainty. This book may never even be published if some global leader finally decides that they are the one who will be brave and stupid enough to wake the thousands of nuclear weapons that currently lie sleeping in silos around the world and start putting them to use. Or, far less likely, tomorrow may see a large volcano eruption that pushes our planet into a global winter we have made almost no effort to prepare for, or it could be the day some new and dangerous pathogen gets released by a scientist who is convinced that such an accident could never happen to them, or so many other things.

But there are many kinds of risk and these sudden bolts of lightning out of a clear blue sky are probably not the ones that will define our future. So, let us say that we avoid all of them. Still, that will be far more likely to happen if the people who are currently working on global peace and nuclear disarmament, or global disaster preparedness, or biosecurity, succeed in their jobs because they are trusted and resourced and allowed to do what they need to do.

Then there is the risk from things that get a little worse every day. Chief among these is climate change. Since I was a child, I have heard the message that 'scientists say we only have x number of years to avoid a climate catastrophe'. I also heard the message that I really had to start brushing my teeth properly and eating better if I wanted to avoid terrible tooth decay. Unfortunately, since tooth decay, like climate change, is a slow process that takes many years, the message didn't really sink in. By the time I had to go through eight root canal treatments with an ongoing infection that may require maxillofacial surgery to remove, it was a little late to appreciate the importance of what I had been told all along. Except, of course, that it wasn't. Because teeth, like the planetary systems that make human civilization possible, can just keep on decaying and decaying until eventually they are gone completely.

I think we face a very similar problem in how we think about climate change. The fact is that we have already emitted enough greenhouse gases to bring about catastrophic global impacts that we are only beginning to see unfolding in ever increasing extreme weather and environmental disasters and we are certainly going to continue adding more for years to come. However, irrespective of all of that, every additional emission we produce, just like every sweet we eat or every day we forget to brush our teeth, makes the problem a little worse. We have been sold a bit of a lie when we were told that we need to act on climate change now to save future generations from a climate disaster. We need to act on climate change to stop hitting ourselves in the foot with a baseball bat and hopefully that means future generations only get hit on the knee with a shovel rather than in the face with a hammer.

And yes, that requires technological solutions. We need to find ways of not emitting greenhouse gases, or of replacing them with non-greenhouse gases, or maybe even (but oh boy is this going to cause us trouble down the line) of cooling Earth's climate despite our increasing emissions. However, it also requires systemic and institutional changes, both to lead and direct these technological solutions so that they can be developed quickly and rolled out responsibly, and to stop the many costly and unnecessary environmental harms currently produced by our economic system. The same can also be said for other kinds of environmental harm we are causing, as well as to our approaches to pandemic preparedness and sustainable development.

And then there is the risk from things that we simply do not understand yet, like AI. Many contemporary drivers of risk started out in this category, such as nuclear weapons, whose true catastrophic potential took us a long time to work out even if we always understood it was likely to be bad.

For now, our assessment of AI as a driver of risk can be spread across three kinds of negative effect. Firstly, there are the near-term problems, which are near-term in the sense that they are already manifesting, although some of them might take a long time to solve.[335] That AI is making some people's lives worse – due to technological unemployment, total surveillance, fake news generation, inaccessibility, and AI-enabled fraud and other crime – is already well known to most people, even if the worst effects of these trends are currently only being felt by a minority. Then there are the medium-term problems that we can see coming down the line but that are only just starting to materialize.[336] AI is going to bring about massive societal changes. It is causing people to lose faith in the media and the democratic process, enabling new kinds of weapons of war, transforming our understanding of difficult problems such as the fundamental structure of living organisms or the design of complex systems, and altering (or even replacing) people's relationships with one another. These are all going to be substantial problems. Unless we drastically slow the pace of AI's development, societies will have to make radical changes to deal with them some point in the next decade or so.

Then, finally, there are what we call the long-term problems, which we speculate might emerge at some point but really we don't know when or how.[337] This group is perhaps the worst-named of the three since it is theoretically possible that they could emerge quite soon, even if most researchers in this area don't expect that to happen. The main instigator of these problems will be the point at which Artificial Intelligence starts to outperform human beings even at generalized or poorly defined tasks and thus potentially gain control over people, our institutions, and even our planet. We can explore this possibility theoretically, as we saw in Chapter 10, but it is only speculation at this point. This speculation depends greatly on contingent facts about how future AIs will work, who will develop them, and what they will be instructed to do. We see these facts, and the possibilities they create very differently across different cultures and it has roots buried deeply within our history of institutional design and colonization. Depending on how you look at it, this may be a cause for optimism or of great concern.

At a very deep level I do not believe that any of these drivers of risk are problems we can finally solve, at least not any time soon. The forces that create them are not ones that will simply go away. However, they are problems that we can get better at solving. As a species, Carl Sagan was right, we humans are young and curious and brave.[338] We have far to go but we show great promise.

Finding our own way

At the core of how we go about developing that promise is accepting that all of us have, not one, but many choices to make. Following the pattern laid down for us is easy, and it is not always wrong, but it is always a choice and there are alternatives. For some of us those choices are harder than others. Like Audre Lorde, some face only the choice between speaking up or being silenced forever, knowing that in the minds of many they were never meant to survive. Others, like me, can indulge in more luxurious choices about how we live our lives, who we work with, when and how we try to influence politics and the economy, what we do with our days and nights. A few of us even feel we have the power to make choices over others, to direct institutions or control systems, and to exert our will on a scale that goes beyond the confines of our bodies. Whatever choices we have, when we feel them and make them deliberately and not without thinking, they always matter.

Some of the important choices we currently face concern the 'big questions' that up to now philosophers have tended to claim as their domain. 'What is thinking and is there something innately human about it or could it be done by a mere machine?' is an interesting question that we can use to explore the fundamental nature of reason and consciousness. However, when we are presented with an AI-enabled chatbot that can give compelling answers to our questions and seems to understand us better than even our friends or family do, it becomes an intensely practical matter about where you put your faith and how you use your discernment. Throughout history people have found practical reasons to deny the humanity, the intelligence, or the consciousness of others: enslaved persons, enemies of war, migrants, or outsiders. However, human beings seem equally talented at ascribing to animals and inanimate things personalities that seem to be far more sophisticated than their outward behaviour would suggest. We talk to our cars and welcome cats, dogs, hamsters, and fish as fellow members of our families (as other animals have been known to do too, by the way). Which of these attitudes should you adopt to an AI, or to a corporation? Which is more dangerous? Philosophy and deep thinking can get you some of the way to an answer. It can show you that certain beliefs are probably false. For instance there almost certainly isn't any aspect of human reasoning we could formally specify that a computer could not be programmed to do just as well, eventually at least. However, there almost certainly is a lot more to human emotions, sensations, and feelings than the simple logic of Hobbes's basic desires or economists' utility functions. To these truths I would add that both our minds and the artificial intelligences we create do not exist in a vacuum but have the properties they do because of their complex interconnection with other systems: other humans, social institutions, our microbiome, and wider environment, and our past and future selves.

Another question that has long interested philosophers is 'what is happiness, or wellbeing, or flourishing, or value and how do we produce them?' As human beings, we impart something to the world that wouldn't seem to exist without us. We appreciate its beauty, we take joy in the sensations it produces in us, we love it. We also seem to bring into the world bad things that wouldn't exist without us, our sense of pain and the unsatisfactoriness of life, our hatred, and our urge to destroy. Some people have theories about why this is so, about how these good and bad things can be measured and assessed or even maximized and why that matters. Others have theories about how to control it, about how to make life less painful and unsatisfactory or more beautiful and meaningful. For me, one of the most fascinating things about these theories is that they contradict one another. According to a very simple interpretation of Buddhism, life is unsatisfactory to us and a source of suffering, because we wish that it was otherwise to how it is. If we can let go of that desire and striving for change, we can accept the life we have and just live each moment as it is, free from suffering and pain. On the other hand, according to other philosophers, the way to improve life is by giving it meaning for you, by learning to discern your true values and how you really want to live, then finding ways of using these to guide you and making every choice an opportunity to engage in projects of worth.[339] These two accounts do not only sound different; at a metaphysical level they actually contradict one another. For one of them, the goal of life is to break down the false container of your self-identity until you are one with your experiences as they are. According to the other, the goal is to build yourself up by creating an identity based on your values, which no other person or force can take away from you. And the thing is, I think both theories are right. Living in either of these ways seems good to me even though they are so different or even opposite. This is one of the reasons why I am not attracted to utopian or rationalized visions of the future based on maximizing some notion of what is best or most valuable. From what I have learned, I am simply not convinced that such notions of value could ever exist and we would do better to allow people to develop their own conceptions of the good life, with many of us picking and choosing between them without necessarily having to commit ourselves either way.

So it may be that these deep questions that seem so important to determining our species' future, if we have one, are not just unanswered but unanswerable. I am a philosopher and trying to answer these questions is what I do. My personal conviction, however, is that while there are better or worse answers, there is no right answer to these questions. We have been arguing about intelligent machines for four hundred years and it still feels like a totally new problem to us now. Perhaps we really will one day come to a universal and lasting agreement about these matters but I can easily imagine these debates continuing long after I am gone and only ever becoming 'settled' because people decide that it is better to act as if we can agree rather than because they have been 'solved'. That is, we will answer them when we decide that we have answered them.

We live in the reality of these choices, these existential moments. It is scary but that doesn't have to be a bad thing. Kierkegaard didn't think that existential anxiety was a bad thing, he saw it as the sign that revealed humanity's true power. Existential anxiety only turns into existential dread when we respond by trying to deny that power and act as though we don't have a choice.

I think that is exactly what we do sometimes. We know that things are bad, we feel it in our bones but every day we commit ourselves to the idea that things cannot change, that the modern economy is the only viable option we have. Maybe some people think they see one way that life could be different and they hold out their own utopias of human perfection, eco-communism, popularist-conservativism, left-libertarianism, techno-optimism; and there is something good in all those visions. But utopia is a dangerous place, and I don't want to live there. The fact is that we carry in our current societies the potential for many and diverse futures for human beings on planet Earth. Every day we each get to choose which futures we want to move towards, but to do that we first have to acknowledge that we have this choice.

Tell me a story

Some of the choices we desperately need to acknowledge are about the possibility of creating large-scale systemic change. That is a hard thing to write; I can feel the reviewers picking up their green pens as I do so. There are many reasons we do not like to imagine we have the potential to bring about such change. Many who have tried to create positive change have failed to achieve very much or, when they have succeeded, as with the French (and later Russian) revolutions, the results have often been far worse than they hoped and sometimes worse than what they started with. It is not for nothing that I have spent so much space in this book talking about the ideas of Edmund Burke, the father of modern conservativism, who was one of the first people to see this risk in the search for idealistic change-making – and who I am sure would have something to say about this book if he got to read it.

But I love Burke not only for the novelty of his conservative ideas but also because despite them he was one of the first people in England to see what his country would become. He was one of the first to understand the urgent need for political and economic reform, the inevitability of decolonization, and the great risk posed by mercantile systems. These were powerful visions and although none of the things he fought for – the abolition of the slave trade, the emancipation of Irish Catholics, peaceful coexistence between the UK and its (former) colonies, removing royal patronages that were used to circumvent democracy, and the termination of the East India Company – came about in his lifetime or by his own efforts, he was still one who made them possibilities by believing that they could be so.

So, when I say that we need to acknowledge that we could choose to create large-scale systemic change, I do not mean that one person can make the world better, or that it would be good if we overthrew every aspect of the system tomorrow. Both of those seem very dangerous ideas to me. However, I do mean that it is good for all of us to imagine ways in which things could be different and whether we can be involved in making them change.

'Someone once said that it is easier to imagine the end of the world than to imagine the end of capitalism',*[340] the Marxist philosopher Frederick Jameson tells us. This is true but, in no small part, that is because people have been imagining the end of the world since the dawn of human history. However, imagining what could come next for our global economy is a task every generation must pick up afresh, although we do best when we take heed of the dreams of our ancestors as well.

Personally, I try to limit my own dreams to the minimal level of change that I think will be necessary to bring about something better for us humans. That is no small amount of change. Yet I am not sure I agree that we should be dreaming of 'the end of capitalism', or at least not yet. It is absolutely true that many features of capitalism, and especially the inhuman behaviour of many corporations, are behind a lot of harm in our world. However, these systems also bring us together as a species.

In 1958, the libertarian economist Leonard Edward Lee wrote the essay *I, Pencil*, in which he told the story of how a pencil comes into being, from the pencil's point of view. He showed people working all around the world, felling and milling trees, mining graphite, shipping materials and combining them, designing, marketing and selling the end product and performing all the other services that make any of this possible, like cooking and cleaning. These people, doing different jobs in different places, some of whom might profoundly disagree with or even hate one another, all co-operate in intricately interdependent ways. Yet there is no one in control of the process to ensure that each step happens as it should. It is simply that the operation of market forces creates a dynamic economic system with enough complexity and interdependence to bring these people together.

This story got taken up and repeated many times by Milton Friedman, one of the most famous economists of the twentieth century and fundamentalist supporter of the rights of businesses and the evils of government. I do like Lee's essay and I agree that it bears repeating. Capitalism has brought the world much harm but it has also bridged borders, discouraged wars, and enabled astonishing feats of global coordination. However, this has been going on for thousands of years, under many kinds of economic system. For instance, there is evidence that copper being mined in North Wales 3,500 years ago was traded and distributed across western Europe.[341] Such trade was made possible by the emergence of an integrated market with unified standards for metal quality and weight that crossed cultural, political, and geographic boundaries long before anything resembling modern capitalism.[342] So there is no great reason to think this could not persist into many possible futures as well.

We should also remember Lee's conclusion from his essay:

> Leave all creative energies uninhibited. Merely organize society to act in harmony with this lesson. Let society's legal apparatus remove all obstacles the best it can. Permit these creative know-hows freely to flow. Have faith that free men and women will respond to the Invisible Hand. This faith will be confirmed.[343]

For Lee, this can only have one interpretation. Tell governments to stop regulation and give businesses free range allowing everyone to make as much money as they can. However, we don't have to agree with that interpretation. I am reminded of Adam Smith's original understanding of the invisible hand, as something that operates between neighbours and individual traders who buy and sell their own wares and how he saw large multinational corporations not as servants of that hand but as its enemies. For many people, the corporate, business, government or military life is the death of their creative energies, the force that requires them to keep their heads down and grind. Very seldom have corporations been the real sources of innovation in our economies, even if they are powerful agents of scale and deployment.[344] So, while I do have faith that free people can serve the common good, I think that large corporations are very often the obstacle to their doing this, not the facilitators.

When I dream, therefore, I tend to dream of people finding ways to use the opportunities and responsibilities they currently have to make our world better. I dream of pension-fund managers using their substantial assets to force companies to do more to bring about a liveable world for their beneficiaries, and investors understanding that you cannot stock pick your way out of a global catastrophe.[345] I dream of political leaders looking to tech companies, not simply to make trillions of dollars of profit in their home territory but as global actors that are causing real and potential future harm and are in need of regulation and oversight to protect vitally important social goods.[346] I dream of Indigenous Peoples finally gaining full recognition in international systems and having their sovereign rights respected and protected after five centuries of genocidal violence.[347] I dream of all sorts of people, including activists and politicians, choosing to speak up for the importance of global justice, the value of long-term decision-making and the needs of future generations.[348] I dream of specialists working on global disaster preparedness, biosecurity, international peace, and climate science, being given the resources to do their jobs effectively for all our sakes. And I dream of the outdated fossil-fuel companies joining whalers, slave traders, and the globe-spanning state corporations like the British and Dutch East India Company, as organizations that simply disappear because the world recognizes that we are better off without them. These are not dreams of the end of capitalism. However, I think they would go a long way. More importantly, I believe acknowledging that 8,200,000,000 humans do have the ability to turn dreams like these into reality if we choose to, could be an important start.

If your dreams are different from mine then I am glad. The point of this book has not been to push a single agenda but rather to argue that such agendas are often what hold us back. I hope that we can find common ground but I would rather that we were just open and honest with one another than that my dreams reflected the death of yours.

However, that doesn't mean anything goes. Dreams are a way in which we process reality and imagine other ways that it could be but they do need to be based on that reality. Sometimes the most attractive visions for us to indulge in are those with the least connection with the world as it is. Those that involve simply dismissing the discoveries we have made, the lessons we have learned about what works and what doesn't, or even the evidence of our own eyes. Medieval people did not believe the Earth was flat but now some people do. If you go somewhere high up, a cliff looking out over the ocean, a mountain, even a plane if you must, you can see that it is round. People always could. We talk and think about the Earth as flat because we move around it as if it was. However, trying to develop a physical cosmology around its supposed flatness is a very modern thing to do. I have to say, I don't really understand why people do this, or why they develop counter-scientific theories about evolution, or vaccines, or anthropogenic climate change. However, I don't think it is because people are stupid. People tend to come up with conspiracy theories that explain the world in their own terms and often the explanations they are looking for are ones that either give meaning to a pervasive sense of disempowerment or offer the prospect of easy and radical change.[349] As someone working on existential risk, a topic more ripe for conspiratorial thinking than just about anything, I am painfully aware of the fact that if the best hope that I can offer people is that my research is flawed, wrong, or even aimed at deceiving them, then it is quite likely that this is what some will believe. That is why I am so concerned about solutions as well as problems and one of the reasons I am so interested in hope.

Saving humanity

The term humanity has more than one meaning. On the one hand, it refers to the collection of all the human beings, to what we used to call mankind. This is a useful but problematic term and where I have used humanity in this book it has tended to be in this sense. It is useful because some of the problems we are facing, both internal ones like existential anxiety and external ones like existential risk, are universal to humans so it is helpful to be able to refer to all of us at once. However, it is problematic because it is homogenizing; it plays up the similarities between human beings and the distinction between humans and the rest of nature, and it downplays our rich diversity and interconnectedness. It is especially problematic when people start thinking about the Future of Humanity, and that is why I prefer to talk about human futures instead.

However, humanity also describes a moral quality we humans have and may be something we can share with other things. We are not defined by our humanity but we can exemplify it and it is generally thought that it is good to do this. When somebody possesses, shows, or acts on their humanity this means that they find a deep connection with other people, recognize their shared imperfections, have compassion for their suffering, and build a common identity that both parties value. Humanity is a moral term that people talk about all the time but it has been largely neglected within Eurocentric ethics and it remains fuzzy and hard to define, even if you know it when you see it.

Within European cultures the idea of what it means to be human and indeed the very word human itself is bound up with ideas of transcendence. The word human shares a common root with the word humus, the living soil, and it comes from the proto-Indo-European word for earth. Interestingly the same is true for the Hebrew word for human, Adam, which is derived from the word for soil, Adamah. There is a story that goes with this etymological relationship: that God made the first man out of clay before breathing life into him. That idea of duality, between the base earth of our construction and the divine breath of our life and soul, comes up again and again in how Europeans, Semitic peoples, and their descendants have thought about humanity. We feel pulled in two directions – both 'down' towards our human nature and 'up' towards some ideal goal. It is a tension that is hard to bridge and I think it is one of the reasons philosophers have not been more drawn to this concept.

The same is not true in all cultures, however. To give just one example, people from Bantu language cultures across south and West Africa have tended to think a lot more about the quality of humanity. In these languages words for humanity such as utu (in Swahili), botho (in Setswana and Sesotho), or ubuntu (in Xhosa and Zulu) are derived from words for 'being' and 'somebody'. They imply a recognition of shared identity. Human beings are not understood to create themselves by transcending their base nature with a divine spark but to create one another through shared acts of community-building and mutual respect. A common maxim in these cultures goes 'a human is a human through other humans'.

African philosophers have thus developed this idea in far more detail than their European counterparts. They emphasize humanity as a relational term, that captures not only what I do, or you do, but how we treat one another. As one review puts it, humanity is 'developed through others ... according to how one values other-regarding behaviours, exhibits solidarity, and thinks of oneself as a "we" as opposed to an "I"'.[350] Archbishop Desmond Tutu once put this idea powerfully as follows:

> I am human because I belong, I participate, I share. A person with ubuntu is open and available to others, affirming of others, does not feel threatened that others are able and good, for he or she has a proper self-assurance that comes with knowing that he or she belongs in a greater whole and is diminished when others are humiliated or diminished, when others are tortured or oppressed, or treated as if they were less than who they are.[351]

When I think about what most needs saving in this time of great danger, it is no less to this idea of humanity than to the mere collection of all living human beings that my mind turns. The forces that threaten our species are the same forces that dehumanize individual people, that diminish and oppress, that disempower frontline communities, that seek to replace human creativity with artificial algorithms. There is a kind of utopia that these forces could potentially bring about, in which each of us is optimized as consumers of a universal utility – but utopia is a dangerous place and I don't think we would ever even make it to this one, given all the perils facing us along the way.

Existential hope, then, is not about completing our journey to transcend our earthly limitations and realize a fully divine state. If you really want to, you can work for that but please do so in ways that respect and affirm the fellow humanity of others who do not. None of us is simply a barrier or a block; all 8,200,000,000 of us are equal contributors to the great global project of realizing humanity together. My hope is that we harness this common humanity to define, envision, and co-create a diversity of futures where many different human beings belong and continue belonging for as long as we can.

Epilogue

I completed the manuscript for this book on 31 October 2024. A few days before that a colleague said to me: 'You know, if Trump wins you are going to need to re-write the whole thing, right?' I told him that I hoped this wasn't so, that I had tried to write a book that was of this moment but that spoke to forces that went a lot deeper than any one election result. It is now March 2025 and I still think that is true, even if every morning's news bulletin stretches my hope to its limits. Now is no time to give up. The only way out is through, and the only way through is together.

Origins and gratitude

When finishing a book, I can never resist reading the acknowledgements section in hope that it might reveal just a little bit more. So, I wrote this section to do the same.

This book is a culmination of nine years of training in philosophy, mostly at Merton College Oxford and the London School of Economics, and another nine working on the risk of Human Extinction and Civilization Collapse, firstly at Oxford's Future of Humanity Institute but mostly at the Centre for the Study of Existential Risk at the University of Cambridge. I owe something to all of these institutions but I owe a lot more to the people who have taught and worked with me, including (but not limited to) Andrew Skinnard, Ralph Wedgwood, Matthew Bond, Roman Krznaric, Alex Voorhoeve, Kai Spikermann, Mike Otsuka, Gustaf Arrhenius, Tim Campbell, Hilary Grieves, Anders Sandberg, Martin Rees, Partha Dasgupta, Bill Sutherland, Shahar Avin, Lalitha Sundaram, Julius Weitzdorfer, Luke Kemp, Alex McLaughlin, Sabin Roman, Mel Cowens, Anita Sanga, Jess Bland, and Matthew Connelly.

Yet, each chapter has its own origin, which goes far beyond these institutional settings.

Chapter 1 began with my love of Sid Meier's *Civilization*, which my father bought me when I was six years old. I never learned how to win the game but it taught me to be curious about the course of human history and its civilopedia was my first great source of general knowledge. In it I first learned about plagues, volcanoes, pollution, and nuclear weapons, and I started asking big questions about history and the future. Everything else has built on that base.

Chapter 2 began with my exploring my then gorgeous girlfriend, now wonderful wife, Daphne's bookshelves and coming across a book called *Soil and Soul* by Alastair McIntosh. It's about environmental activism and spirituality and it keeps posing the question of why humans can be so destructive. I eventually got to meet Alastair and we talked for two hours in the back of an army car, after he had been lecturing the British Army on non-violence. He challenged me to think more deeply about my own humanity and its place in the world.

Chapter 3 began with my best friend Richard trying to explain to me how AI worked when we were both fourteen. He had been learning to programme in BASIC and had followed instructions on building a simple AI. Later we went to an exhibition at the Science Museum that re-created some of Charles Babbage's difference engine and argued all the way home about what it meant for a physical system to be intelligent.

Chapter 4 began with Mr Marshall, my teacher at Kellett School in Hong Kong when I was nine years old, who taught us about 'the Age of Discovery'. We learned about Columbus and later explorers but I wanted to know what had happened before that and so he told me all about Henry the Navigator, and we played at being square-rigged ships and caravels tacking into the wind across the classroom. It took me a long time to ask the harder questions about how colonization really happened, and what it still means for us today.

Chapter 5 began with Calibre, a lending library for the blind and visually impaired, which recorded books onto tape and posted them out for free. Growing up, reading was hard for me and audiobooks were expensive so having access to this service, and the volunteers who read for it, was incredibly important for developing my love of books and my interest in utopian and speculative fiction. Nowadays you can download more or less any audiobook you like, but it's not the same.

Chapter 6 began when I was first offered an opportunity to give my own academic lectures at the University of Cambridge. I was asked to teach undergraduate philosophy students about the social contract tradition – Hobbes, Rousseau, and their descendants. However, I wanted to expand their horizons a bit, so started reading about Burke's theory of the intergenerational contract, Godwin's anarchism, and Wollstonecraft's feminist critique of them all. The more I read, the more I loved this little community and their vital debates, which continue to live on in our world.

Chapter 7 began when I first heard the story of the New College Roof – I believe from Pam Lunn at Woodbrooke Quaker Study Centre. I heard the story several times as a piece of historical fact and then, a few years later, several more times being debunked; however, I long suspected that there might be a little more to it than that. The reality I describe here was one I pieced together in writing this book, and it was a pure delight to me, as I hope it may be to others.

Chapter 8 began, fittingly, in many different ways, with all the people who have taught me about systems over the years: from my A-level geography teacher Miss Homewood and my think tank colleagues at the Social Market Foundation and CentreForum, to the vlogbrothers YouTube channel and the computer games SimCity and SimEarth. This is also a chapter I particularly owe to colleagues at the Centre for the Study of Existential Risk, where we think a lot about systemic risk and how to avoid it, and especially to Lara Mani and Constantin Arnscheidt, who understand it better than I.

Chapter 9 began with two of my other childhood loves – the story of Noah's Ark and everything to do with dinosaurs. Like so many children, these were my introductions to the concept of an existential catastrophe and I know that Noah's success and T-Rex's failure to avoid extinction influenced my thinking about survival and how it works. Unlearning those lessons has taken a lot of work but been very rewarding.

Chapter 10 began with Lee Sedol's Go match against, and gracious defeat to, the AI AlphaGo. By 2016 my interest in AI had very much waned but colleagues told me that if Lee couldn't beat the AI then this meant that everything was about to change. Making sense of both why Lee lost and why that was such a big deal got me back into thinking about this technology. However, by this time I had developed a far greater degree of scepticism about the nature of AI, leading me to want to ask the deeper questions I consider here.

Chapter 11 began, perhaps surprisingly, with my deciding to stay silent. Growing up in Hong Kong, and going on to study at an imperialist institution like the University of Oxford, I was understandably vulnerable to some pretty reactionary views. Slowly, however, as my undergraduate study went on, and with the help of my best friend Rami, I started paying attention to the wider context, and decided that I might not have understood the full story. So, I chose to listen more to other people and, in doing so, I realized just how much I had been missing about the world and how important it was that this was heard by others too.

Finally, Chapter 12 began with the birth of my children, and that fierce, almost unreasonable desire that the world had to be good enough for them. It started with my parents and their fights to make sure that I, as a blind and autistic child, could achieve everything I wanted. It started with every call to action to build a better world that has inspired me and every time I have sat in a darkened room trying to make sense of yet another setback or disaster. And it started with the hope that my words might be helpful to other people too.

For all these experiences, the people who gave them to me, the things that I learned – and for so many others who have contributed along the way, I am truly grateful!

I am also incredibly grateful to Jonathan Skerrett, Susan Beer, and everyone at Polity, without whom this book would never have been started. I extend many thanks to John Fogle, Ben Norman, Beatrice Crona, Ximena Barker Huesca, Elena Kavanagh, Joanna Rozapedowski, Rito Uuk, Kennedy Mbeva, and Emile Torres, who read and commented on all or part of the draft manuscript. Finally, I am grateful to all the people who have supported my health and humanity, including Claire Graziano, Lex Harvey Bryn, Tobyn Bell, Chris Young, George John, and David Taylor: along with my parents, I owe you my life.

References

1 Senzaki, Nyogen and Paul Reps, 'A Parable'. In David McKay, *101 Zen Stories*. Abe Books, 1939: 38.

2 Chödrön, Pema, *The Wisdom of No Escape: And the Path of Loving Kindness*. Shambhala, 2001: 31–2.

3 Lynskey, D., 'The Last Man'. In *Everything Must Go: The Stories We Tell Ourselves About the End of the World*. Picador, 2024.

4 Kierkegaard, Søren, *The Concept Of Anxiety: A Simple Psychologically Oriented Deliberation in View of the Dogmatic Problem of Hereditary Sin*. W.W. Norton & Co., 2014.

5 Gourko, Helena, 'Heideggerian hope'. *Analecta Husserliana*, 39, 1993: 283–8.

6 Kovacs, George, 'The philosophy of death in Viktor E. Frankl'. *Journal of Phenomenological Psychology* 13 (2), 1982: 197.

7 Cotton-Barratt, Owen and Toby Ord, 'Existential risk and existential hope: definitions'. Future of Humanity Institute, 2015.

8 Prothero, Donald R., 'Species longevity in North American fossil mammals'. *Integrative Zoology* 9 (4), 2014: 383–93.

9 Dickinson, Emily, '"Hope" is the thing with feathers'. In R. W. Franklin (ed.) *The Poems of Emily Dickinson*. Belknap Press, 1999.

10 Macy, Joanna, *Active Hope: How to Face the Mess We're in Without Going Crazy*. New World Library, 2012.

11 Solnit, Rebecca, *Hope in the Dark: The Untold History of People Power*. Canongate Books, 2010.

12 Adams, Douglas, *The Hitchhiker's Guide to the Galaxy Original Radio Scripts*. Pan Macmillan, 2003: 30. Reproduced with permission of Curtis Brown Ltd., London, on behalf of Completely Unexpected Productions. Copyright © Serious Productions Ltd.

13 Geraci, Robert M., 'A tale of two futures: Techno-eschatology in the US and India'. *Social Compass* 63 (3), 2016: 319–34.

14 Smith, Michael E., 'Creation, death, and the gods'. In *The Aztecs*, 3rd edn. Blackwell, 2013.

15 Lynskey, D., 'Prologue: God'. In *Everything Must Go: The Stories We Tell Ourselves About the End of the World*. Picador, 2024.

16 Lent, Jeremy, 'Agriculture and anxiety'. In *The Patterning Instinct: A Cultural History of Humanity's Search for Meaning.* Rowman & Littlefield, 2017.

17 Tosam, Mbih Jerome, J. Radeino Ambe, and Primus Che Chi, 'Global emerging pathogens, poverty and vulnerability: An ethical analysis.' In Godfrey B. Tangwa, Akin Abayomi, Samuel J. Ujewe, Nchangwi Syntia Munung (eds) *Socio-Cultural Dimensions of Emerging Infectious Diseases in Africa: An Indigenous Response to Deadly Epidemics.* Springer Nature, 2019: 243–53.

18 Méthot, Pierre-Olivier and Samuel Alizon, 'Emerging disease and the evolution of virulence: The case of the 1918–1919 influenza pandemic.' In *Classification, Disease and Evidence: New Essays in the Philosophy of Medicine*, 2015: 93–130.

19 Lane Warmbrod, Kelsey, Kobi Leins, and Nancy Connell, 'Biosecurity, biosafety, and dual use: Will humanity minimise potential harms in the age of biotechnology?' In SJ Beard, Martin Rees, Catherine Richards, and Clarissa Rios Rojas. *The Era of Global Risk.* Open Book, 2023: 173–200.

20 Boddie, Crystal, Matthew Watson, Gary Ackerman, and Gigi Kwik Gronvall, 'Assessing the bioweapons threat'. *Science* 349 (6250), 2015: 792–3.

21 Esvelt, Kevin M., 'Delay, detect, defend: Preparing for a future in which thousands can release new Pandemics'. *GCSP Geneva Papers*, 2022.

22 Fouchier, Ron A. M., 'Studies on influenza virus transmission between ferrets: The public health risks revisited'. *MBio* 6 (1), 2015: e02560-14.

23 Lipsitch, Marc and Thomas V. Inglesby, 'Moratorium on research intended to create novel potential pandemic pathogens'. *MBio* 5 (6), 2014: e02366-14.

24 Jamrozik, Euzebiusz and George S. Heriot, 'Ethics and antibiotic resistance.' *British Medical Bulletin* 141 (1), 2022: 4–14.

25 Singh, Prem, Pritu Dhalaria, Satabdi Kashyap, Gopal Krishna Soni, Partha Nandi, Shreeparna Ghosh, Mrinal Kar Mohapatra, Apurva Rastogi, and Divya Prakash, 'Strategies to overcome vaccine hesitancy: A systematic review'. *Systematic Reviews* 11 (1), 2022: 78.

26 Sedyaningsih, Endang R., Siti Isfandari, Triono Soendoro, and Siti Fadilah Supari, 'Towards mutual trust, transparency, and equity in virus sharing mechanism: The avian influenza case of Indonesia'. *Annals, Academy of Medicine Singapore* 37 (6), 2008: 482.

27 Black, Benjamin A., Jean-François Lamarque, Daniel R. Marsh, Anja Schmidt, and Charles G. Bardeen, 'Global climate disruption and regional climate shelters after the Toba supereruption'. *Proceedings of the National Academy of Sciences* 118 (29), 2021.

28 Masse, W. Bruce and Michael J. Masse, 'Myth and catastrophic reality: Using

myth to identify cosmic impacts and massive Plinian eruptions in Holocene South America'. *Geological Society, London, Special Publications* 273 (1), 2007: 177–202. Haas, Ain, Andres Peekna, and Robert E. Walker, 'Echoes of ancient cataclysms in the Baltic Sea'. *Folklore (Electronic)* 23, 2003: 49–81. Hamacher, Duane W. and John Goldsmith, 'Aboriginal oral traditions of Australian impact craters.' *arXiv preprint* arXiv:1306.0278, 2013.

29 Moynihan, Thomas, *X-risk: How Humanity Discovered its Own Extinction.* MIT Press, 2020: 55

30 Swift, Jonathan, *Travels into Several Remote Nations of the World. In Four Parts. By Lemuel Gulliver, First a Surgeon, and then a Captain of Several Ships.* Benjamin Motte, 1726.

31 Medwin, Thomas, *Conversations of Lord Byron: Noted During a Residence with His Lordship at Pisa, in the Years 1821 and 1822.* Henry Colburn, 1824: 185.

32 Landis, Rob and Lindley Johnson, 'Advances in planetary defense in the United States'. *Acta Astronautica* 156, 2019: 394–408.

33 Deudney, Daniel, *Dark Skies: Space Expansionism, Planetary Geopolitics, and the Ends of Humanity.* Oxford University Press, 2020.

34 Mani, Lara, Asaf Tzachor, and Paul Cole, 'Global catastrophic risk from lower magnitude volcanic eruptions'. *Nature Communications* 12 (1), 2021: 4756.

35 Lovelace, Ada Augusta, 'Note G' in *Sketch of The Analytical Engine Invented by Charles Babbage By L. F. Menabrea of Turin, Officer of the Military Engineers from the Bibliothèque Universelle de Genève. With notes upon the memoir by the translator Ada Augusta, Countess of Lovelace.* R. & J. E. Taylor, 1843.

36 Ibid.

37 Butler, Samuel, 'The Book of the Machines'. In Peter Mudford (ed.) *Erewhon.* Penguin, 1985: 198–226.

38 Asimov, Isaac, 'The Robot Chronicles'. In *Robot Visions.* Penguin, 1991.

39 Yudkowsky, Eliezer, 'Artificial intelligence as a positive and negative factor in global risk'. In Boström, Nick and Milan M. Cirkovic (eds) *Global Catastrophic Risks.* Oxford University Press, 2008: 184.

40 Lewis, Simon L. and Mark A. Maslin, *The Human Planet: How We Created the Anthropocene.* Yale University Press, 2018.

41 Soddy, Frederick, *The Interpretation of Radium.* John Murray, 1909.

42 Beard, SJ and Rachel Bronson, 'A brief history of existential risk and the people who worked to mitigate it'. In SJ Beard, Martin Rees, Catherine Richards, and Clarissa Rios Rojas, *The Era of Global Risk.* Open Book, 2023: 1–26.

43 Torres, Émile P., 'Maniacs, misanthropes, and omnicidal terrorists: Reassessing the agential risk framework'. *Intersections, Reinforcements, Cascades*, 2023: 38.

44 Torres, Émile P., 'Who would destroy the world? Omnicidal agents and related phenomena'. *Aggression and Violent Behavior* 39 (2018): 129–38.
45 Qarooni, Rana and Rob Jenkins, 'Prevalence of omnicidal tendencies'. (Forthcoming).
46 Smith, Tom W., 'Factors relating to misanthropy in contemporary American society'. *Social Science Research* 26 (2), 1997: 170–96.
47 Sanjaya, Muhammad Ryan, 'Antisocial behavior in experiments: What have we learned from the past two decades?' *Research in Economics* 77 (1), 2023: 104–15.
48 Fromm, Erich, *The Anatomy of Human Destructiveness.* Penguin, 1973.
49 Spielrein, Sabrina, 'Destruction as the cause of coming into being'. *Journal of Analytical Psychology*, 1994.
50 Freud, Sigmund and James Ed Strachey, 'Civilization and its discontents'. In *The Standard Edition of the Complete Psychological Works of Sigmund Freud*, vol. XXI, 1927–1931. W.W. Norton & Co., 1961: 57–146.
51 Arendt, Hannah, *Eichmann in Jerusalem: A Report on the Banality of Evil.* Penguin, 2006: 276.
52 Milgram, Stanley, *Obedience to Authority*. Harper & Row, 1974: 6.
53 Cesarani, David, *Eichmann: His Life, Crimes, and Legacy*. William Heinemann, 2004.
54 Slovic, Paul, '"If I look at the mass I will never act": Psychic numbing and genocide'. *Judgment and Decision Making* 2 (2), 2007: 79–95.
55 Churchill, Winston Stanley, 'Shall we commit suicide?', *Nash's Pall Mall Magazine* 24, September 1924.
56 Churchill, Winston Stanley, 'Fifty years hence'. *Strand Magazine* 82 (492), 1931: 549–58.
57 Bohr, Aage, 'The war years and the prospects raised by the atomic weapons'. In Stefan Rozental (ed.) *Niels Bohr.* North-Holland Publishing Co., 1967: 204.
58 Sundaram, Lalitha S., Matthijs M. Maas, and SJ Beard, 'From evaluation to action: Ethics, epistemology, and extreme technological risk'. In Catherine Rhods, *Managing Extreme Technological Risk*, World Scientific, 2024: 211.
59 Foote, Eunice, 'Circumstances affecting the heat of the sun's rays'. *American Journal of Science and Arts* 22 (66), 1856: 382–3.
60 Arrhenius, S., *Worlds in the Making: The Evolution of the Universe*. Harper, 1908.
61 E.g. Vogt, W., *Road to Survival.* William Sloan Associates, 1948.
62 Meadows, D. H., D. L. Meadows, J. Randers, and W. W. Behrens, *The Limits to Growth*. Universe Books, 1972.
63 Hansen, J., D. Johnson, A. Lacis, S. Lebedeff, P. Lee, D. Rind and G. Russell,

'Climate impact of increasing atmospheric carbon dioxide'. *Science*, 213 (4511), 1981: 957–66

64 Supran, G. and N. Oreskes, 'Assessing ExxonMobil's climate change communications (1977–2014)'. *Environmental Research Letters* 12 (8), 2017: 084019.

65 Baum, Seth, Robert de Neufville and Anthony Barrett, 'A model for the probability of nuclear war'. *Global Catastrophic Risk Institute*, 2018.

66 Lewis, Patricia, Benoît Pelopidas, and Heather Williams, 'Too close for comfort: Cases of near nuclear use and options for policy'. *Chatham House-Royal Institute of International Affairs*, 2014.

67 Mozgovoi, Alexander, trans. Svetlana Savranskaya, *The Cuban Samba of the Quartet of Foxtrots: Soviet Submarines in the Caribbean Crisis of 1962*. National Security Archive, 2002.

68 Tang, Aaron and Luke Kemp, 'A fate worse than warming? Stratospheric aerosol injection and global catastrophic risk'. *Frontiers in Climate* 3, 2021: 720312.

69 Armstrong, Stuart, Nick Boström and Carl Shulman, 'Racing to the precipice: a model of artificial intelligence development'. *AI & Society* 31 (2016): 201–6.

70 Cave, Stephen and Seán S. Ó hÉigeartaigh, 'An AI race for strategic advantage: rhetoric and risks'. *Proceedings of the 2018 AAAI/ACM Conference on AI, Ethics, and Society*, 2008: 36–40.

71 Nelson, Julie A., 'Climate change and economic self-interest'. In Ravi Kanbur and Henry Shue (eds), *Climate Justice: Integrating Economics and Philosophy*. Oxford University Press, 2019: 113–22.

72 Confucius, *Analects*, 13.23.

73 Lieberman, Matthew D., *Social: Why Our Brains Are Wired to Connect*. Broadway Books, 2013.

74 Slovic, Paul, C. K. Mertz, David M. Markowitz, Andrew Quist, and Daniel Västfjäll, 'Virtuous violence from the war room to death row'. *Proceedings of the National Academy of Sciences* 117 (34), 2020: 20474–82.

75 Gilbert, Paul, *The Compassionate Mind*. Constable, 2009.

76 Cremer, Carla Zoe and Luke Kemp, 'Democratising risk: In search of a methodology to study existential risk'. *arXiv preprint* arXiv:2201.11214, 2021.

77 The Bible. Book of Job, ch. 41, vv. 1–34.

78 Campbell, Joseph, *The Hero with a Thousand Faces*. Pantheon, 1949.

79 Groeneveld, Leanne, 'A theatrical miracle: The Boxley Rood of Grace as puppet'. *Early Theatre* 10 (2), 2007: 14.

80 Truitt, Elly, 'The garden of earthly delights: Mahaut of Artois and the automata at Hesdin'. *Medieval Feminist Forum* 46, 2010: 74.

81 Reilly, Kara, 'Descartes's mimetic faculty'. In *Automata and Mimesis on the Stage of Theatre History*. Springer, 2011: 48–72.

82 Descartes, René, trans. Desmond M. Clarke, 'Discourse on the method for grading one's reasoning and searching for truth in the sciences'. In *Discourse on Method and Related Writings*. Penguin, 2003: 40.

83 Ibid.: 25.

84 Hobbes, Thomas, trans. A. P. Marinich, *Computatio Sive Logica: De Corpore, Part I*. Abaris Books, 1981, p. 147.

85 Hobbes, Thomas, *Leviathan*, ed. J. C. A. Gaskin. Oxford University Press, 1998: 7. I have taken the liberty of reverting to Hobbes's original English spellings throughout this chapter.

86 Pascal, Blaise, trans. Anthony Levy, 'Pensée 340'. In *Pensées and Other Writings*. Oxford University Press, 1999.

87 Hobbes, Thomas, Gaskin, *Leviathan*, 1998: 36–7.

88 Ibid.: 86.

89 Stone, John, 'Thomas Hobbes as strategist'. *Defence Studies* 21 (1), 2021: 67–83.

90 Boström, Nick, 'Ethical issues in advanced artificial intelligence'. *Machine Ethics and Robot Ethics*, 2020: 69–75.

91 Kulstad, Mark and Laurence Carlin, 'Leibniz's Philosophy of Mind'. In Edward N. Zalta (ed.) *Stanford Encyclopedia of Philosophy*. https://plato.stanford.edu/archives/win2020/entries/leibniz-mind/

92 Perkins, Franklin, *Leibniz and China: A Commerce of Light*. Cambridge University Press, 2004.

93 Mogens Laerke, 'Leibniz in Europe'. In *Routledge Handbook on Philosophy and Europe*, 2021.

94 Goodman, Lenn E., 'Maimonides and Leibniz'. *Journal of Jewish Studies* 31 (2), 1980: 214. Goolam, Nazeem M. I., 'The influence of Al-Ghazali and Ibn Sina on Descartes'. *Stellenbosch Law Review* 14 (3), 2003: 349–63. Koç, Yunus, and Gökhan Topluk. 'Pavestones of the path leading to Thomas Hobbes. Impressions left by Islamic philosophers on Marsilius of Padua'. *Critical Studies in Social Sciences and Humanities*, 2020: 39.

95 Graeber, David and David Wengrow. 'Wicked liberty: The Indigenous critique and the myth of progress'. In *The Dawn of Everything: A New History of Humanity*. Penguin, 2021.

96 Lahontan, Baron de, trans. Reuben Thwaites, 'Conference or dialogue between the author and Adario'. In *New Voyages to North America*, vol. 2. A. C. McClurg & Co., 1905: 139–40. I have adapted some of the modernized language used by Graeber and Wengrow.

97 Graeber, David and David Wengrow, 'Full circle: On the historical foundations of the Indigenous critique'. In *The Dawn of Everything: A New History of Humanity*.

98 Abdilla, Angie, Megan Kelleher, Rick Shaw, and Tyson Yunkaporta, *Out of the Black Box: Indigenous Protocols For AI.* Deakin University, 2021.

99 Lewis, Jason Edward, Angie Abdilla, Noelani Arista, Kaipulaumakaniolono Baker, Scott Benesiinaabandan, Michelle Brown, Melanie Cheung et al. *Indigenous Protocol and Artificial Intelligence Position Paper.* Concordia University, 2020.

100 Gould, Stephen Jay, 'The late birth of a flat Earth'. In *Dinosaur in a Haystack: Reflections in Natural History,* 1995: 38–50.

101 Boyle, David, *Toward the Setting Sun: Columbus, Cabot, Vespucci, and the Race for America.* Bloomsbury Publishing, 2008: 48–9 and 56–7.

102 Campbell, Bruce and Cormac Ó. Gráda, 'Harvest shortfalls, grain prices, and famines in preindustrial England'. *Journal of Economic History* 71 (4), 2011: 859–86.

103 Slavin, Philip, 'The Great Bovine Pestilence and its economic and environmental consequences in England and Wales, 1318–50'. *Economic History Review* 65 (4), 2012: 1239–66.

104 Jordan, William Chester, *The Great Famine: Northern Europe in the Early Fourteenth Century.* Princeton University Press, 1997.

105 Slavin, Philip, 'The birth of the Black Death: Biology, climate, environment, and the beginnings of the second plague pandemic in early fourteenth-century Central Asia'. *Environmental History* 28 (2), 2023: 300–34.

106 Aberth, John, *The Black Death: A New History of the Great Mortality in Europe, 1347–1500.* Oxford University Press, 2021.

107 Khaldun, Ibn, trans. Franz Rosenthal, *The Muqaddimah: An Introduction to History.* Princeton University Press, 2015: 64.

108 da Fonseca, Luís Adão, 'The Portuguese military orders and the oceanic navigations: From piracy to empire (fifteenth to early sixteenth centuries)'. In *The Military Orders,* vol. 4. Routledge, 2016: 81–92.

109 Russell, Peter Edward, 'Prince Henry the navigator'. In *The European Opportunity.* Routledge, 2019: 100–29.

110 Zurara, Fomes Eanes de, 'Introduction'. In *The Chronicle of the Discovery and Conquest of Guinea,* vol. 2. Cambridge University Press, 2010: lxxxiv–lxxxv.

111 Boyle, David, *Toward the Setting Sun: Columbus, Cabot, Vespucci, and the Race for America,* 2008: 138–9.

112 Neeganagwedgin, Erica, 'Rooted in the Land: Taíno identity, oral history and stories of reclamation in contemporary contexts'. *AlterNative: An International Journal of Indigenous Peoples* 11 (4), 2015: 376–88.

113 Frankopan, Peter, 'The road of gold'. In *The Silk Roads: A New History of the World.* Vintage, 2017.

114 Koch, Alexander, Chris Brierley, Mark M. Maslin and Simon L. Lewis, 'Earth

system impacts of the European arrival and Great Dying in the Americas after 1492'. *Quaternary Science Reviews* 207, 2019: 13–36.

115 Alford, Stephen, 'Searching for Cathay'. In *London's Triumph: Merchants, Adventurers, and Money in Shakespeare's City*. Bloomsbury, 2017: 65–79.

116 Williamson, James A. and Raleigh Skelton, *The Cabot Voyages and Bristol Discovery under Henry VII*. Routledge, 2017: 187–9.

117 Alford, Stephen, 'A Russian embassy'. In *London's Triumph: Merchants, Adventurers, and Money in Shakespeare's City*. 2017: 80–91.

118 Coussmaker, Jean, *A History of St Andrew's*. St Andrew's Parish Magazine, 1999. https://moscowanglican.org/a-history-of-st-andrews/

119 Petram, Lodewijk Otto, *The World's First Stock Exchange: How the Amsterdam Market for Dutch East India Company Shares Became a Modern Securities Market, 1602–1700*. University of Amsterdam, 2011.

120 Gelderblom, Oscar, Abe De Jong and Joost Jonker, 'The formative years of the modern corporation: The Dutch East India Company VOC, 1602–1623', *Journal of Economic History* 73 (4), 2013: 1050–76.

121 Dalrymple, William, *The Anarchy: The Relentless Rise of the East India Company*. Bloomsbury, 2019.

122 Imran, Mohd and Samanvi Narang, *Decoding Grotius: Unravelling the Role of Corporations in Early Modern International Law*. Cambridge Core, 2024. https://www.cambridge.org/core/blog/2024/04/25/decoding-grotius-unraveling-the-role-of-corporations-in-early-modern-international-law/

123 Fuller, R. Buckminster, 'The origin of specialization'. In *An Operating Manual for Spaceship Earth*. Southern Illinois University Press, 1969.

124 Robins, Nick, 'The Great East Indian crash'. In *The Corporation that Changed the World: How the East India Company Shaped the Modern Multinational*. Pluto Press, 2012.

125 Smith, Adam, 'The Theory of Moral Sentiments'. In Raphael D. D. and A. L. MacFie (eds) *The Glasgow Edition of the Works of Adam Smith*. Liberty Fund, 1982: 9.

126 Smith, Adam, 'The Wealth of Nations'. In *The Glasgow Edition of the Works of Adam Smith*. Liberty Fund, 1982: 26–7.

127 Smith, Adam, 'The Theory of Moral Sentiments'. 1982: 184–5.

128 Smith, Adam, 'The Wealth of Nations'. 1982: 145.

129 Ibid.: 733.

130 Ibid.: 631.

131 Burke, Edmund, *Ninth Report from the Select Committee, Appointed to Take into Consideration the State of the Administration of Justice in the Provinces of Bengal, Bahar, and Orissa*. J. Debrett, 1783.

132 Burke, Edmund, 'Letter to French Laurance.' In *Writings and Speeches.* Oxford University Press, 2015.
133 Malthus, Thomas Robert, 'An essay on the principle of population'. In *The Works of Thomas Robert Malthus.* Pickering & Chatto, 1986: 1–139.
134 Malthus, Thomas Robert, *Principles of Political Economy Considered with a View to Their Practical Application.* William Pickering, 1836.
135 Mill, James, *Elements of Political Economy.* Baldwin, Cradock, and Joy, 1826.
136 Ricardo, David, *On the Principles of Political Economy.* John Murray, 1821.
137 Powell, John A. and Caitlin Watt, 'Corporate prerogative, race, and identity under the fourteenth amendment'. *Cardozo Law Review* 32, 2010: 885.
138 Hesiod, trans. Hugh G. Evelyn-White, 'Works and days'. In *Works and Days, Theogony and the Shield of Heracles.* Courier, 2006: 6.
139 Ibid.: 7.
140 Ibid.: 8.
141 Plato, trans. Robert Waterfield, 'Critias'. In *Timaeus and Critias.* Oxford University Press, 2008.
142 Graeber, David and David Wengrow, 'Wicked liberty: The Indigenous critique and the myth of progress'. In *The Dawn of Everything: A New History of Humanity.* 2021.
143 Lewis, Simon L. and Mark A. Maslin, *The Human Planet: How We Created the Anthropocene.* Yale University Press (2018): 149
144 Boyle, David, *Toward the Setting Sun: Columbus, Cabot, Vespucci, and the Race for America.* 2008: 313–16.
145 More, Thomas, trans. Paul Turner, *Utopia.* Penguin, 1963: 38–9.
146 Cavendish, Margaret, ed. Kate Lilley, 'The description of a new world, called the blazing world'. In *The Blazing World and Other Writings.* Penguin, 1994.
147 Francis Bacon, ed. Susan Bruce, 'New Atlantis'. In *Three Early Modern Utopias.* Oxford University Press, 2008: 177
148 Ibid.: 169
149 Zeitlin, Samuel Garrett, 'Francis Bacon on imperial and colonial warfare'. *The Review of Politics* 83 (2), 2021: 196–218.
150 Virginia Council, 'Articles, Instructions and Orders to Sir Thomas Gates, Knight, Governor of Virginia (London, May 1609)'. In Susan Myra Kingsbury (ed.) *The Records of the Virginia Company in London.* US Government Printing Office, 1906.
151 Kimmerer, Robin, *Braiding Sweetgrass: Indigenous Wisdom, Scientific Knowledge and the Teachings of Plants.* Milkweed Editions, 2013.
152 Yunkaporta, Tyson, *Sand Talk: How Indigenous Thinking Can Save the World.* Text Publishing, 2019.

153 Graeber, David and David Wengrow, *The Dawn of Everything: A New History of Humanity*. 2021.

154 Mercier, Louis-Sébastien, trans. Hooper, William, *Memoirs of the Year Two Thousand Five Hundred*. W. Jones, 1802. (The year in which the book was set was changed for the English transition.)

155 E.g. Burke, Peter, 'The history of the future, 1350–2000'. *The Uses of the Future in Early Modern Europe* 12, 2010. Rössner, Philipp Robinson, 'Capitalism, cameralism, and the discovery of the future, 1300s–2000s: Europe's road to wealth'. *History of Political Economy* 53 (3), 2021. Hölscher, Lucian, 'The discovery of the future in early modern Europe'. *Archiv für Begriffsgeschichte* 64 (2), 2022.

156 Rousseau, Jean-Jacques, trans. Donald A. Cress, 'Discourse on the origin and foundation of inequality among men'. In *Rousseau: The Basic Political Writings*. Hackett, 2012.

157 bielskyte, m., Protopia Futures [Framework], 2021. https://medium.com/protopia-futures/protopia-futures-framework-f3c2a5d09a1e

158 Kant, Immanuel, trans. M. J. Gregor and R. Anchor, 'The conflict of the faculties'. In A. W. Wood and G. di Giovanni (eds) *Religion and Rational Theology*. Cambridge University Press, 1996: 298.

159 Ibid.: 302.

160 Ibid.: 299.

161 Ibid.: 301–2.

162 Ibid.: 302.

163 Rousseau, Jean-Jacques, trans. Donald A. Cress, 'On the social contract'. In *Rousseau: The Basic Political Writings*. 2012.

164 Kant, Immanuel, trans. A. W. Wood, 'Conjectural beginning of human history'. In R. B. Louden and G. Zöller (eds) *Anthropology, History, and Education*. Cambridge University Press, 2007: 175.

165 De Condorcet, Antoine-Nicolas, *Sketch for a Historical Picture of the Progress of the Human Mind*, vol. 33. Weidenfeld and Nicolson, 1955.

166 Paine, Thomas, 'Common Sense Addressed to the Inhabitants of America'. In *Rights of Man, Common Sense, and Other Political Writings*. Oxford University Press, 1998.

167 Price, Richard, *A Discourse on the Love of Our Country, delivered on Nov. 4, 1789, at the Meeting-House in the Old Jewry, to the Society for Commemorating the Revolution in Britain*. T. Cadell, 1789: 18.

168 Burke, Edmund, ed. E. J. Payne, *Select Works of Edmund Burke Vol 2. Reflections on the Revaluation in France and on Proceedings in certain Societies in London Relative to that Event in a Letter Intended to have been sent to a Gentleman in Paris*. Liberty Fund, 1999: 192–3.

169 Burke, Edmund, ed. Francis Canavan, 'A Letter to Sir Hercules Langrishe on the Catholics of Ireland'. In *Select Works of Edmund Burke*, vol. 4. *Miscellanious Works.* Liberty Fund, 1999, p. 247.

170 Paine, Thomas, 'Rights of Man: Being an answer to Mr Burke's attack on the French Revolution'. In *Rights of Man, Common Sense, and Other Political Writings*. Oxford University Press, 1998, p. 395.

171 Paine, Thomas, 'Rights of Man: Being an answer to Mr Burke's attack on the French Revolution.' In *Rights of Man, Common Sense, and Other Political Writings.* 1998: 390.

172 Wollstonecraft, Mary, ed. Janet Todd, 'A Vindication of the Rights of Men in a Letter to the Right Honourable Edmund Burke'. In *Political Writings*. Oxford University Press, 1994: 57.

173 Ibid., 63–284.

174 Godwin, William, ed. Isaac Kramnic, 'Enquiry Concerning Political Justice'. Penguin, 1985: 169.

175 Ibid.: 759.

176 Malthus, Thomas, ed. Geoffrey Gilbert, *An Essay on the Principle of Population*. Oxford University Press, 1999.

177 Shelley, Mary, *Frankenstein.* Arrow, 1973: 166–7

178 Ibid.: 221

179 Shelley, Mary, *The Last Man*. Broadview Press, 1996.

180 Levin, Yuval, 'Nature and History'. In *The Great Debate: Edmund Burke, Thomas Paine, and the Birth of Right and Left*. Basic Books, 2013.

181 Kant, Immanuel, trans. A. W. Wood, 'Conjectural beginning of human history'. In R. B. Louden and G. Zöller (eds) *Anthropology, History, and Education.* Cambridge University Press, 2007: 166.

182 Ibid.

183 Green, Ronald Michael, *Kierkegaard and Kant: The Hidden Debt.* State University of New York Press, 1992: 28.

184 Greaves, Hilary and William MacAskill, 'The case for strong long-termism'. Global Priorities Institute, 2021. Greaves, Hilary, William MacAskill, Rossa O'Keeffe-O'Donovan, Philip Trammell, Benjamin Tereick, Andreas Mogensen, Christian Tarsney et al., 'A research agenda for the Global Priorities Institute Version 2.1'. Global Priorities Institute (2021).

185 Kant, Immanuel, trans. Allen W. Wood, 'An answer to the question: What Is enlightenment?' In Mary J. Gregor, *Practical Philosophy*. Cambridge University Press, 1996.

186 Bateson, Mary Catherine, *Peripheral Visions: Learning Along The Way*. HarperCollins, 1994, p. 22.

187 Ruskin, John, *On the Nature of Gothic Architecture: And Herein of the True Functions of the Workman in Art*. Smith, Elder, & Company, 1854.
188 Adams, Max, *Admiral Collingwood: Nelson's Own Hero*. Bloomsbury, 2015.
189 Bateson, Gregory, 'The oak beams of New College, Oxford'. *The CoEvolution Quarterly* 10, 1976: 66.
190 Bateson, Gregory, 'Culture contact and schismogenesis'. *Man* 35, 1935: 178–83.
191 Bateson, Gregory, 'From Versailles to cybernetics'. In *Steps to an Ecology of Mind: Collected Essays in Anthropology, Psychiatry, Evolution, and Espistemology*. Chandler, 1972: 477–85.
192 Bateson, Gregory, 'Form, Substance, and Difference.' In *Steps to an Ecology of Mind: Collected Essays in Anthropology, Psychiatry, Evolution, and Espistemology*. Chandler, 1972: 459.
193 Plato, *Republic,* trans. G. M. A. Grube and C. D. C. Reeve. Hackett, 1992: 162.
194 Wiener, Norbert, *Cybernetics or Control and Communication in the Animal and the Machine*. MIT Press, 1948.
195 Wiener, Norbert, *The Human Use of Human Beings: Cybernetics and Society.* Houghton Mifflin, 1950.
196 Forrester, Jay W., *World Dynamics*. Wright-Allen Press, 1971.
197 Bateson, Gregory, *A Sacred Unity: Further Steps to an Ecology of Mind*. Cornelia & Michael Bessie Book, 1991: 202.
198 Alvarez, Luis W., *Alvarez: Adventures of a Physicist*. Basic Books, 1987.
199 Eliot, Thomas Stearns, 'The Hollow Men'. In *Poems: 1909–1925*. Faber and Faber, 1925.
200 Meadows, Donella H., *Thinking in Systems: A Primer*. Chelsea Green Publishing, 2008.
201 Konopinski, E. J., C. Marvin, and E. Teller, *Ignition of the Atmosphere With Nuclear Bombs*. Los Alamos National Laboratory, 1946. https://fas.org/sgp/othergov/doe/lanl/docs1/00329010.pdf
202 Torres, Émile P., *Human Extinction: A History of the Science and Ethics of Annihilation*. Routledge, 2023: 83–4.
203 Mahaffey, Jim, *Atomic Accidents: A History of Nuclear Meltdowns and Disasters: From the Ozark Mountains to Fukushima*. Open Road Media, 2014: 80–8.
204 Torres, Émile P., *Human Extinction: A History of the Science and Ethics of Annihilation*. 2023: 135–6.
205 Crutzen, Paul and John Birks, 'Twilight at noon: The atmosphere after a nuclear war'. *Ambio* 11 (2–3), 1982: 114–25.
206 Ehrlich, Paul R., Carl Sagan, Donald Kennedy, and Walter Orr Roberts, *The Cold and the Dark: The World After Nuclear War.* W.W. Norton & Co., 1984.
207 Rupasinghe, Ruwini, Bruno B. Chomel and Beatriz Martínez-López, 'Climate

change and zoonoses: A review of the current status, knowledge gaps, and future trends.' *Acta Tropica* 226, 2022: 106225.

208 Beard, SJ, Lauren Holt, Asaf Tzachor, Luke Kemp, Shahar Avin, Émile P. Torres, and Haydn Belfield, 'Assessing climate change's contribution to global catastrophic risk'. *Futures* 127, 2021: 102673.

209 Schmieder, Martin and David A. Kring, 'Earth's impact events through geologic time: A list of recommended ages for terrestrial impact structures and deposits'. *Astrobiology* 20 (1), 2020: 91–141.

210 Brusatte, Stephen L., Richard J. Butler, Paul M. Barrett, Matthew T. Carrano, David C. Evans, Graeme T. Lloyd, Philip D. Mannion et al., 'The extinction of the dinosaurs'. *Biological Reviews* 90 (2), 2015: 628–42.

211 This example is from Siegenfeld, Alexander F. and Yaneer Bar-Yam, 'An introduction to complex systems science and its applications'. *Complexity* 2020 (1), 2020: 6105872.

212 Liu, Hin-Yan, Kristian Cedervall Lauta, and Matthijs Michiel Maas, 'Governing boring apocalypses: A new typology of existential vulnerabilities and exposures for existential risk research'. *Futures* 102, 2018: 6–19.

213 Sen, Amartya, 'Famines and other crises'. In *Development As Freedom*. Oxford University Press, 1999: 160–88.

214 Silliman, B., 'The great auroral exhibition of August 28th to September 4th, 1859'. *American Journal of Science and Arts* 29, 1860: 92.

215 Buzulukova, Natalia and Bruce Tsurutani, 'Space weather: From solar origins to risks and hazards evolving in time'. *Frontiers in Astronomy and Space Sciences* 9, 2022: 1017103. Electric Infrastructure Security Council, *'Black Sky' Infrastructure and Resilience Workshop Report.* EIS Council, 2017.

216 Sagan, Carl, 'The Planet Venus: Recent observations shed light on the atmosphere, surface, and possible biology of the nearest planet'. *Science* 133 (3456), 1961: 849–58.

217 Lovelock, James E., 'Gaia as seen through the atmosphere'. *Atmospheric Environment* 6 (8), 1972: 579–80.

218 Judd, Emily J., Jessica E. Tierney, Daniel J. Lunt, Isabel P. Montañez, Brian T. Huber, Scott L. Wing, and Paul J. Valdes, 'A 485-million-year history of Earth's surface temperature'. *Science* 385 (6715), 2024: adk3705.

219 Steffen, Will, Katherine Richardson, Johan Rockström, Sarah E. Cornell, Ingo Fetzer, Elena M. Bennett, Reinette Biggs et al., 'Planetary boundaries: Guiding human development on a changing planet'. *Science* 347 (6223), 2015: 1259855.

220 Steffen, Will, Johan Rockström, Katherine Richardson, Timothy M. Lenton, Carl Folke, Diana Liverman, Colin P. Summerhayes et al., 'Trajectories of the

Earth system in the Anthropocene'. *Proceedings of the National Academy of Sciences* 115 (33), 2018: 8252–9.
221 Heidegger, Martin, 'The Question Concerning Technology'. In *Martin Heidegger: Basic Writings.* Harper & Row, 1954.
222 Good, Irving John, 'Speculations on perceptrons and other automata'. International Business Machines Corporation, 1959.
223 Bender, Emily M., Timnit Gebru, Angelina McMillan-Major, and Shmargaret Shmitchell, 'On the dangers of stochastic parrots: Can language models be too big?' *Proceedings of the 2021 ACM Conference on Fairness, Accountability, and Transparency*, 2021: 610–23.
224 Khaldun, Ibn, *The Muqaddimah: An Introduction to History.* 2015: 187.
225 Tainter, Joseph, *The Collapse of Complex Societies*. Cambridge University Press, 1988.
226 Kemp, Luke, 'Are we on the road to civilisation collapse?' *BBC Future*, 2019.
227 Lenton, Timothy M., Scarlett Benson, Talia Smith, Theodora Ewer, Victor Lanel, Elizabeth Petykowski, Thomas W. R. Powell, Jesse F. Abrams, Fenna Blomsma, and Simon Sharpe, 'Operationalising positive tipping points towards global sustainability'. *Global Sustainability* 5, 2022.
228 Farmer, J. Doyne, Cameron Hepburn, Matthew C. Ives, Thomas Hale, Thom Wetzer, Penny Mealy, Ryan Rafaty, Sugandha Srivastav, and Rupert Way, 'Sensitive intervention points in the post-carbon transition'. *Science* 364 (6436), 2019: 132–4.
229 The Bible. Genesis, ch. 6, vv. 12–14 and 17–19 (King James Version).
230 Fagan, Brian M., 'The Cataclysm'. In *The Long Summer: How Climate Changed Civilization*. Basic Books, 2005: 99–127.
231 E.g. the essays in Dundes, Alan (ed.) *The Flood Myth*. University of California Press, 1988.
232 Broska, Lisa Hanna, Witold-Roger Poganietz and Stefan Vögele, 'Extreme events defined – A conceptual discussion applying a complex systems approach'. *Futures* 115, 2020: 102490.
233 Sagan, Carl, 'Nuclear war and climatic catastrophe: Some policy implications'. *Foreign Affairs* 62 (2), 1983: 257–92.
234 Gleick, James, 'The butterfly effect'. In *Chaos: Making a New Science*. Penguin, 2008, pp. 9–33.
235 Lynskey, David, 'Survival'. In *Everything Must Go: The Stories We Tell Ourselves About the End of the World.* 2024.
236 Baum, Seth D., David C. Denkenberger and Jacob Haqq-Misra, 'Isolated refuges for surviving global catastrophes'. *Futures* 72, 2015: 45–56. Turchin, Alexey and Brian Patrick Green, 'Aquatic refuges for surviving a global

catastrophe'. *Futures* 89, 2017: 26–37. Boyd, Matt, and Nick Wilson, 'Optimizing island refuges against global catastrophic and existential biological threats: Priorities and preparations'. *Risk Analysis* 41 (12), 2021: 2266–85.

237 Belfield, Haydn, 'Collapse, recovery, and existential risk'. In Miguel Centeno, Peter Callahan, Paul Larcey and Thayer Patterson (eds) *How Worlds Collapse: What History, Systems, and Complexity can Teach Us About Our Modern World and Fragile Future*. Taylor & Francis, 2023: 61–92.

238 Baum, Seth D., David C. Denkenberger and Jacob Haqq-Misra, 'Isolated refuges for surviving global catastrophes.' *Futures* 72, 2015: 45–56.

239 Onuma, Hiroki, Kong Joo Shin and Shunsuke Managi, 'Short-, medium-, and long-term growth impacts of catastrophic and non-catastrophic natural disasters'. *Economics of Disasters and Climate Change* 5, 2021: 53–70.

240 Kourtit, Karima, Peter Nijkamp and Alexandru Banica, 'An analysis of natural disasters' effects – A global comparative study of "Blessing in Disguise"'. *Socio-Economic Planning Sciences* 88, 2023: 101599.

241 Turchin, Peter, 'The peasants are revolting'. In *End Times: Elites, Counter-Elites, and the Path of Political Disintegration*. Penguin, 2023.

242 Weitzdörfer, Julius and SJ Beard, 'Law and policy responses to disaster-induced financial distress: The Tsunami victims of 3/11'. In *Governance, Risk and Financial Impact of Mega Disasters: Lessons from Japan*, Springer, 2019: 47–80.

243 Weitzdörfer, Julius and SJ Beard, *Double Debt Disaster: Law, Policy, and Social Justice in the Wake of Japan's 2011 Tsunami*. Deutsches Institut für Japanstudien, 2021.

244 Walker, Brian, Crawford S. Holling, Stephen R. Carpenter and Ann Kinzig, 'Resilience, adaptability and transformability in social-ecological systems'. *Ecology and Society* 9 (2), 2004.

245 The Bible. Genesis, ch. 11, vv. 7–9 (King James Version).

246 Alighieri, Dante, trans. Herbert Schneider, *On World-Government or De Monarchia*. Liberal Arts Press, 1957: 12.

247 Leibniz, Gottfried von, *Political Writings*. Cambridge University Press, 1988.

248 Imai, Kosuke and James Lo, 'Robustness of empirical evidence for the democratic peace: A nonparametric sensitivity analysis'. *International Organization* 75 (3), 2021: 901–19.

249 Kant, Immanuel, trans. Ted Humphrey, *Towards Perpetual Peace: A Philosophical Sketch*. Hackett, 2003.

250 Lu, Catherine, 'World government'. In Edward N. Zalta (ed.)' *Stanford Encyclopedia of Philosophy*, 2021. https://plato.stanford.edu/archives/spr2021/entries/world-government

251 Bell, Duncan, 'Founding the world state: HG Wells on empire and the English-speaking peoples'. *International Studies Quarterly* 62 (4), 2018: 867–79.
252 Wells, Herbert George, *The Open Conspiracy: Blueprints for a World Revolution*. Gollancz, 1933.
253 Wells, Herbert George, *The World Set Free. A Story of Mankind*. Macmillan, 1914.
254 Russell, Bertrand, 'Can a scientific society be stable?' *British Medical Journal* 2 (4640) 1949: 1307.
255 Einstein, Albert, 'A reply to the Soviet scientists'. *Bulletin of the Atomic Scientists* 4 (2), 1948: 35–8.
256 Boström, Nick, 'The vulnerable world hypothesis'. *Global Policy* 10 (4), 2019: 455–76.
257 Blake, Jonathan S. and Nils Gilman, *Children of a Modest Star: Planetary Thinking for an Age of Crises*. Stanford University Press, 2024.
258 Doudna, Jennifer A. and Samuel H. Sternberg, *A Crack in Creation: Gene Editing and the Unthinkable Power to Control*. Houghton Mifflin, 2017.
259 Belfield, Haydn, 'Activism by the AI community: Analysing recent achievements and future prospects'. *Proceedings of the AAAI/ACM Conference on AI, Ethics, and Society*, 2020: 15–21.
260 Sundaram, Lalitha S., 'Existential risk and science governance'. In SJ Beard, Martin Rees, Catherine Richards, and Clarissa Rios Rojas, *The Era of Global Risk*. 2023: 101–22.
261 Jamieson, Dale, 'Responsibility and climate change'. *Global Justice: Theory Practice Rhetoric* 8 (2), 2015.
262 Lorrance, A., 'The love project'. In Richard Dean Kellough (ed.) *Developing Priorities and a Style: Selected Readings in Education for Teachers and Parents*. MSS Information Corporation, 1974: 85.
263 Parfit, Derek, 'What matters most'. In *On What Matters*, vol. 2. Oxford University Press, 2011.
264 MacAskill, Will, 'Are we living at the hinge of history?' In Jeff McMahan, Timothy Campbell, James Goodrich and Ketan Ramakrishnan (eds) *Ethics and Existence: The Legacy of Derek Parfit*. Oxford University Press, 2022. Thorstad, David, 'High risk, low reward: A challenge to the astronomical value of existential risk mitigation'. *Philosophy & Public Affairs* 51 (4), 2023: 373–412.
265 King, Martin Luther, 'I have been to the mountain top'. In *I Have a Dream: Writings and Speeches that Changed the World*, 1968.
266 Boström, Nick, 'The superintelligent will: Motivation and instrumental rationality in advanced artificial agents'. *Minds and Machines* 22, 2012: 71–85.

267 Omohundro, Stephen M., 'The basic AI drives'. In *Artificial Intelligence Safety and Security*. Chapman and Hall, 2018: 47.
268 Achiam, Josh, Steven Adler, Sandhini Agarwal, Lama Ahmad, Ilge Akkaya, Florencia Leoni Aleman, Diogo Almeida et al., 'Gpt-4 technical report'. *arXiv preprint* arXiv:2303.08774, 2023: 55.
269 Omohundro, Stephen M., 'The basic AI drives.' In *Artificial Intelligence Safety and Security*. 2018: 53–4
270 Ibid.: 54.
271 Ivakhnenko, Alekseĭ Grigor'evich and Valentin Grigorevich Lapa, *Cybernetics and Forecasting Techniques* trans. Robert N. McDonough, Elsevier, 1967.
272 Christian, Brian, 'Representation'. In *The Alignment Problem: How Can Machines Learn Human Values?* Atlantic Books, 2021.
273 Witztum, Amos, 'Social circumstances and rationality: Some lessons from Adam Smith why we may not all be equally sovereign'. *American Journal of Economics and Sociology* 64 (4), 2005: 1025–47.
274 Kant, Immanuel, trans. Wernar Pluhar, *Critique of Practical Reason.* Hackett, 2002.
275 Kant, Immanuel, trans. James Ellington, *Groundwork of the Metaphysics of Morals*. Hackett, 1993: 31.
276 Ibid.: 32.
277 Amodei, Dario, Chris Olah, Jacob Steinhardt, Paul Christiano, John Schulman and Dan Man., 'Concrete problems in AI safety'. *arXiv preprint* arXiv:1606 .06565, 2016: 4–7.
278 Omohundro, Stephen M., 'The basic AI drives'. In *Artificial Intelligence Safety and Security*. 2018: 50.
279 Kierkegaard, Søren, *The Concept of Anxiety: A Simple Psychologically Oriented Deliberation in View of the Dogmatic Problem of Hereditary Sin*. 2014.
280 Amodei, Dario, et al., 'Concrete problems in AI safety'.
281 Al-Khalili, Jim and McFadden, Johnjoe, 'How life began'. In *Life on the Edge: The Coming of Age of Quantum Biology*. Transworld, 2014.
282 Dennett, Daniel C., 'On the origin of reasons'. In *From Bacteria to Bach and Back: The Evolution of Minds*. W.W. Norton & Co., 2017.
283 Oren, Aharon, 'Prokaryote diversity and taxonomy: Current status and future challenges'. *Philosophical Transactions of the Royal Society of London. Series B: Biological Sciences* 359 (1444), 2004: 623–38.
284 Knoll, Andrew H., *Life on a Young Planet: The First Three Billion Years of Evolution on Earth*. Princeton University Press, 2015: 181–2.
285 Godfrey-Smith, Peter, *Other Minds: The Octopus and the Evolution of Intelligent Life*. William Collins, 2016.

286 Ward, Ashley, *Animal Societies: How Co-operation Conquered the Natural World.* Profile Books, 2022.

287 Aplin, Lucy M., Ben C. Sheldon, and Julie Morand-Ferron, 'Milk bottles revisited: Social learning and individual variation in the blue tit, *Cyanistes caeruleus*'. *Animal Behaviour* 85 (6), 2013: 1225–32.

288 Lorde, Audre, 'A litany for survival'. In *The Black Unicorn*, 1978: 31–2.

289 Hammond, Karla, 'An Interview with Audre Lorde'. *The American Poetry Review* 9 (2), 1980: 18–21.

290 Hardin, Garrett, 'The tragedy of the commons'. *Science* 162 (3859), 1968: 1243–8.

291 Gardiner, Stephen M., 'The real tragedy of the commons'. *Philosophy & Public Affairs* 30 (4), 2001: 387–416.

292 Dasgupta, Partha, Tapan Mitra, and Gerhard Sorger, 'Harvesting the commons'. *Environmental and Resource Economics* 72 (2019): 613–36.

293 Drezner, Daniel W., 'The tragedy of the global institutional commons'. *Back to Basics: State Power in a Contemporary World* 280, 2013: 281.

294 Maaravi, Yossi, Aharon Levy, Tamar Gur, Dan Confino, and Sandra Segal, '"The tragedy of the commons": How individualism and collectivism affected the spread of the COVID-19 pandemic'. *Frontiers in Public Health* 9, 2021: 627559.

295 Mearsheimer, John J., *The Tragedy of Great Power Politics* (updated edn). W.W. Norton & Co., 2003.

296 Dahlman, Carl J., *The Open Field System and Beyond: A Property Rights Analysis of an Economic Institution.* Cambridge University Press, 1980.

297 Scott, James C., *Seeing Like a State: How Certain Schemes to Improve the Human Condition Have Failed.* Yale University Press, 2020.

298 Fennell, Lee Anne, 'Ostrom's Law: Property rights in the commons'. *International Journal of the Commons* 5 (1), 2011: 9–27.

299 Ostrom, Elinor, 'A general framework for analyzing sustainability of social-ecological systems'. *Science* 325 (5939), 2009: 419–22.

300 Ostrom, Elinor, *Governing the Commons: The Evolution of Institutions for Collective Action.* Cambridge University Press, 1990: 90.

301 Beard, SJ and Rachel Bronson, 'A brief history of existential risk and the people who worked to mitigate it'. in SJ Beard, Martin Rees, Catherine Richards, and Clarissa Rios Rojas, *The Era of Global Risk.* 2023: 1–26.

302 Belfield, Haydn, 'Activism by the AI community: Analysing recent achievements and future prospects'. *Proceedings of the AAAI/ACM Conference on AI, Ethics, and Society*, 2020: 15–21.

303 Carlson, Colin J., Dann Mitchell, Rory Gibb, Rupert F. Stuart-Smith, Tamma

A. Carleton, Torre E. Lavelle, Catherine J. Lippi et al. 'Health losses attributable to anthropogenic climate change'. *MedRxiv*, 2024: 2024–8.

304 Feldstein, Steven, 'AI & Big Data Global Surveillance Index (2022 updated)', Mendeley Data, V4, 2002. doi: 10.17632/gjhf5y4xjp.4

305 'What are nuclear frontline communities?' Union of Concerned Scientists, 22 April 2022: https://www.ucsusa.org/resources/nuclear-frontline-communities

306 Duizer, Erwin, Wilhelmina L. M. Ruijs, A. D. Putri Hintaran, Mariska C. Hafkamp, Margreet van der Veer, and Margreet Jm Te Wierik, 'Wild poliovirus type 3 (WPV3)-shedding event following detection in environmental surveillance of poliovirus essential facilities, the Netherlands, November 2022 to January 2023'. *Eurosurveillance* 28 (5), 2023: 2300049.

307 Silver, A., 'Taiwan's science academy fined for biosafety lapses after lab worker contracts COVID-19'. *Science*, 2022.

308 'Hungarian lab worker isolated after exposure to Ebola virus'. Reuters, 20 April 2018. https://www.reuters.com/article/world/hungarian-lab-worker-isolated-after-exposure-to-ebola-virus-idUSKBN1HR2ZF/

309 'Pittsburgh researcher infected with Zika in lab accident'. Associated Press, 9 June 2016. https://apnews.com/pittsburgh-researcher-infected-with-zika-in-lab-accident-fa641974dd1a4f8d8891a1eb794e2118

310 Reardon, Sara, 'Forgotten NIH smallpox virus languishes on death row'. *Nature* 514 (7524), 2014: 544.

311 Malakoff, David, 'CDC says 75 workers may have been exposed to anthrax'. *Science Now*, 2014.

312 Reardon, Sara, 'US disease agency suspends pathogen shipments'. *Nature*, 2014.

313 Choudhury, Lipika Majumdar Roy, Alia Aoun, Dina Badaway, Luis Antonio de Alburquerque Bacardit, Yassine Marjane, and Adrian Wilkinson, 'Final report of the panel of experts on Libya established pursuant to security council resolution 1973', 2011. United Nations Security Council, 2021.

314 Carlson, Colin J., Dann Mitchell, Rory Gibb, Rupert F. Stuart-Smith, Tamma A. Carleton, Torre E. Lavelle, Catherine J. Lippi et al., 'Health losses attributable to anthropogenic climate change'. *MedRxiv*, 2024: 2024–8.

315 Perrocheau, Anne, Freya Jephcott, Nima Asgari-Jirhanden, Jane Greig, Nicolas Peyraud, and Joanna Tempowski, 'Investigating outbreaks of initially unknown aetiology in complex settings: findings and recommendations from 10 case studies'. *International Health* 15 (5), 2023: 537–46.

316 Jones, Natalie, *Self-Determination as Voice: The Participation of Indigenous Peoples in International Governance.* Cambridge University Press, 2024.

317 Abungu, Cecil, Michelle Malonza, and Sumaya Nur Adan, 'Can apparent

bystanders distinctively shape an outcome? Global South countries and global catastrophic risk-focused governance of artificial intelligence'. *arXiv preprint* arXiv:2312.04616, 2023.

318 Yunkaporta, Tyson, *Sand Talk: How Indigenous Thinking Can Save the World.* 2019.

319 Tanguy Sandré, J.-M. Gherardi, Jean-Paul Vanderlinden, and Jean-Michel Huctin, 'Reframing climate change into meaningful local experiences: Critical reflexivity with stories from Ittoqqor-toormiit (Inuit Nunaat)'. Artic Science Summit Week, 2023: 10.13140/RG.2.2.35383.70566. hal-04497514

320 Kavanagh, E., 'Weaving a web of resilience: Integrating Indigenous knowledge in global catastrophic risk'. Cambridge Conference on Catastrophic Risk, 2024.

321 Tuck, Eve and K. Wayne Yang, 'Decolonization is not a metaphor'. In *Decolonization: Indigeneity, Education and Society* 1 (1), 2012: 1–40.

322 Mitchell, Audra and Aadita Chaudhury, 'Worlding beyond "the" "end" of "the world": White apocalyptic visions and BIPOC futurisms'. *International Relations* 34 (3), 2020: 309–32.

323 Kahn, Laura H., Thomas P. Monath, Bob H. Bokma, E. Paul Gibbs, and A. Alonso Aguirre, 'One health, one medicine'. In *New Directions in Conservation Medicine: Applied Cases of Ecological Health.* Oxford University Press, 2012: 33–44.

324 brown, adrienne maree, *Emergent Strategy: Shaping Change, Changing Worlds.* AK Press, 2017. This book has spawned its own series, starting with brown, adrienne marie, *Pleasure Activism: The Politics of Feeling Good.* AK Press, 2019.

325 Whyte, Kyle P., 'Indigenous science (fiction) for the Anthropocene: Ancestral dystopias and fantasies of climate change crises'. *Environment and Planning E: Nature and Space* 1 (1–2), 2018: 224–42.

326 Deloria, Vine, *For this Land: Writings on Religion in America.* Routledge, 1998: 179.

327 Yunkaporta, Tyson, 'First law'. In *Sand Talk: How Indigenous Thinking Can Save the World.* 2019.

328 Mitchell, Audra and Aadita Chaudhury, 'Worlding beyond "the" "end" of "the world": White apocalyptic visions and BIPOC futurisms'. *International Relations* 34 (3), 2020: 309–32.

329 Hall, Melinda C., 'Risking ourselves, together: The politics and persons of risk'. In Shelley Tremain (ed.) *The Bloomsbury Guide to Philosophy of Disability.* Bloomsbury, 2023.

330 Wells-Jensen, Sheri and SJ Beard, 'We have to include everyone: Enabling humanity to reduce existential risk'. In SJ Beard, Martin Rees, Catherine Richards, and Clarissa Rios Rojas, *The Era of Global Risk.* 2023: 101–22.

331 Troyer, Lisa and Reef Youngreen, 'Conflict and creativity in groups'. *Journal of Social Issues* 65 (2), 2009: 409–27.

332 Arbatlı, Cemal Eren, Quamrul H. Ashraf, Oded Galor and Marc Klemp, 'Diversity and conflict'. *Econometrica* 88 (2), 2020: 727–97.

333 Starhawk, 'The Three Types of Power' in *Truth or Date: Encounters with Power, Authority, and Mystery.* Harper and Row, 1990: 8–10.

334 This and subsequent population figures taken from Ritchie, Hannah, Lucas Rodés-Guirao, Edouard Mathieu, Marcel Gerber, Esteban Ortiz-Ospina, Joe Hasell, and Max Roser, 'Data Page: Population'. In *Population Growth. Our World in Data*, 2023. Data adapted from PBL Netherlands Environmental Assessment Agency, Gapminder, and United Nations: https://ourworldindata.org/grapher/population

335 Bucknall, Benjamin S. and Shiri Dori-Hacohen, 'Current and near-term AI as a potential existential risk factor'. *Proceedings of the 2022 AAAI/ACM Conference on AI, Ethics, and Society*, 2022: 119–29.

336 Baum, Seth D., 'Medium-term artificial intelligence and society', *Information* 11 (6), 2020: 290.

337 Boström, Nick, *Superintelligence: Paths, Dangers, Strategies.* Oxford University Press, 2014.

338 Sagan, Carl, *Cosmos*. Macdonald Futura, 1980: 4.

339 Wolf, Susan, *Meaning in Life and Why It Matters*. Princeton University Press, 2010. Metz, Thaddeus, *Meaning in Life*. Oxford University Press, 2013.

340 Jameson, Fredric, 'Future city'. *New Left Review* 21, 2003: 65.

341 Williams, R. Alan and Cécile Le Carlier de Veslud, 'Boom and bust in Bronze Age Britain: Major copper production from the Great Orme mine and European trade, c. 1600–1400 BC'. *Antiquity* 93 (371), 2019: 1178–96.

342 Ialongo, Nicola, Raphael Hermann, and Lorenz Rahmstorf, 'Bronze Age weight systems as a measure of market integration in Western Eurasia'. *Proceedings of the National Academy of Sciences* 118 (27), 2021: e2105873118.

343 Read, Leonard E., *I, Pencil*. Foundation for Economic Education, 1958.

344 Runciman, David, 'You didn't build that'. In *The Handover: How We Have Control of Our Lives to Corporations, States, and AIs*. Profile Books, 2023.

345 Kemp, Luke, Haydn Belfield, Ellen Quigley, Julius Weitzdörfer, and SJ Beard, '23. Financing our final hour'. In SJ Beard and Tom Hobson (eds) *An Anthology of Global Risk.* Open Book, 2024.

346 Maas, Matthijs M., 'Aligning AI regulation to sociotechnical change'. In *The Oxford Handbook of AI Governance*, 2022.

347 Jones, Natalie, *Self-determination as Voice: The Participation of Indigenous Peoples in International Governance*. Cambridge University Press, 2024.

348 McLaughlin, Alex, 'Climate Resistance and the Far Future'. *Social Theory & Practice* 50 (2), 2024. Jones, Natalie, Mark O'Brien, and Thomas Ryan, '22. Representation of Future Generations in United Kingdom Policy-Making'. In SJ Beard and Tom Hobson (eds) *An Anthology of Global Risk.* 2024.

349 Douglas, Karen M., Joseph E. Usciniski, Robbie M. Sutton, Aleksandra Cichocka, Turkay Nefes, Chee Siang Ang, and Farzin Devai, 'Understanding Conspiracy Theories'. *Political Psychology* 40, 2019.

350 Ewuoso, Cornelius and Susan Hall, 'Core aspects of ubuntu: A systematic review'. *South African Journal of Bioethics and Law* 12 (2), 2019: 98.

351 Tutu, Desmond, *No Future Without Forgiveness.* Rider, 1999, p. 35.

Index

Notes

Page 1: *modern Buddhist interpretation:* The origin of this story is somewhat obscure. I first came across it in Leo Tolstoy's 1882 autobiographical account of an existential crisis, *A Confession.* Earlier versions seems to have been given quite a different moral, that people will seek after pleasure even when it clearly does them no good. That is also relevant to existential anxiety and risk, but it's not the meaning on which I intend to focus.

Page 3: *coming to an end:* There have been many attempts to define the concept of existential risk. For technical risk assessment and mitigation purposes it is important that we know what exactly we are talking about. However, this book is not a technical one, so I will be using the term quite loosely. In some cases, people familiar with the field of Existential Risk Studies may feel that it would have been more appropriate for me to use the terms 'extinction risk' and/or 'global catastrophic risk' instead, and I will not dispute this. However, putting too much weight on fine distinctions between the definition of distinct kinds of risk may neglect just how uncertain we are about the risk itself. For more on these definitions see the introduction to my co-edited book *The Era of Global Risk* and Zoe Kremer and Luke Kemp's paper 'Democratising risk: In search of a methodology to study existential risk'.

Page 3: *fully understand it:* Indeed, as Douglas Adams pointed out, we don't even really know what the question is.

Page 11: *possibly go wrong:* For more about the Default Mode Network and how to live with it I recommend Robert Wright's book *Why Buddhism Is True.*

Page 13: *replace those that do not:* It used to be thought that evolution would always lead pathogens to get less harmful over time. However, empirical evidence suggests the truth is more complicated than this. Kun, Ádám, András G. Hubai, Adrienn Král, Judit Mokos, Benjámin Áron Mikulecz, and Ádám Radványi. 'Do pathogens always evolve to be less virulent? The virulence–transmission trade-off in light of the COVID-19 pandemic'. *Biologia futura* 74 (1), 2023: 69–80.

Page 13: *don't see others:* That 'fluey' sense of being lethargic and disinterested in things is likely an evolved response encouraging us to do this – Devlin, Benjamin A., Caroline J. Smith, and Staci D. Bilbo, 'Sickness and the social brain: How the immune system regulates behavior across species'. *Brain Behavior and Evolution* 97 (3–4), 2022: 197–210.

Page 13: *transmissible between humans:* I myself was infected by an unidentified zoonotic disease from a horse in 1995 and, while I was very sick, I didn't pass it on to anyone else.

Page 14: *fight them more effectively:* The global significance of vaccines was quickly recognized, at least by some. While Mary Shelley has humanity wiped out by plague in her 1826 novel *The Last Man*, she also confidently predicts that by the end of the twenty-first century we will have used them to irradicate smallpox, a prediction that came true in 1977.

Page 16: *risk they pose:* Other countries run their own programmes and, in 2014, the UN established an International Asteroid Early Warning Network and Space Mission Planning Advisory Group to coordinate them.

Page 17: *natural world and human societies:* See, for instance, the #NoNaturalDisasters campaign, https://www.nonaturaldisasters.com

Page 17: *still be terrible:* One very ambitious, if rather theoretical, plan is set out in Denkenberger, D. and J. M. Pearce, *Feeding Everyone No Matter What: Managing Food Security after Global Catastrophe*. Academic Press, 2014.

Page 18: *change the world:* Ada Lovelace's and her mother's lives are wonderfully told in Miranda Seymore's double biography *In Byron's Wake* – although its title makes me hope we can look forward to a not-too-distant future in which Byron will be remembered as Lovelace's father, rather than Ada as Byron's daughter.

Page 18: *dominant species on Earth:* This argument inspired some of the earliest technical explorations of AI safety by the AI pioneer Alan Turing. In a 1951 lecture at the University of Manchester, Turing argued that it would one day be possible to produce machines that could, contrary to Lovelace's assertion, mimic every cognitive process carried out by human beings. Once such a machine was developed, he warned, 'it would not take long to outstrip our feeble powers. There would be no question of the machines dying, and they would be able to converse with each other to sharpen their wits. At some stage therefore we should have to expect the machines to take control, in the way that is mentioned in Samuel Butler's Erewhon.' Turing, Alan M. 'Intelligent machinery, a heretical theory'. *Philosophia Mathematica* 4 (3), 1996: 256–60.

Page 19: *could have told them:* More seriously, this is a very clever idea that has had very bad results all over the world, from cane toads in Australia to mongoose in Hawaii.

Page 19: *until he is dead:* Quoted by Herodotus in *Histories* 1:32. This sentiment is surprisingly widespread across many philosophical traditions. For Herodotus the concern is that while we are alive we risk suffering misfortune and are only safe in death. For others, such as the contemporary 'negative utilitarian' David Benatar, the concern is that life is inherently bad for us and the best we can hope for is the neutrality non-existence.

Page 20: *in these fields:* See, for instance, Stuart Russell's *Human Compatible: AI and the Problem of Control* or Brian Christian's *The Alignment Problem: How Can Machines Learn Human Values?*

Page 21: *in Earth's history:* Killing off 40 per cent, 50 per cent, and 39 per cent of species on Earth respectively.

Page 22: *concept of atomic bombs:* These bombs quickly became a favourite of science-fiction authors, to the extent that when, during the Second World War, the leaders of the US nuclear weapons programme requested a total media blackout on any discussion of atomic bombs, the editor of *Astounding Science Fiction* magazine replied that this should not apply to his publication, as stories of this sort had become so commonplace that readers would undoubtedly view their disappearance as highly suspicious!

Page 24: *risk of universal death:* The full text of this manifesto can be read at https://pugwash.org/1955/07/09/statement-manifesto/

Page 24: *let us begin:* This wonderful turn of phrase is from Kae Tempest's beautiful poem 'People's Faces'.

Page 30: *obedience from authority:* For an in-depth critical analysis of Milgram's experiment and others that draw similar conclusions about the nature of human evil, I highly recommend Rutger Bregman's 2020 book *Humankind: A Hopeful History*.

Page 31: *weapons against Japan:* These events are explored in Graham Farmelo's book *Churchill's Bomb*.

Page 32: *or the world:* For instance, Churchill's schoolfriend, Muirland Evans, recalled a conversation they had had in 1891 during which Churchill, then fifteen years old, remarked 'I can see vast changes coming over a now peaceful world; great upheavals, terrible struggles; wars such as one cannot imagine; and I tell you London will be in danger – London will be attacked and I shall be very prominent in the defence of London.' Martin Gilbert, *In Search of Churchill: A Historian's Journey*. Turner Publishing Company, 1997.

Page 32: *type-1 harms:* The label 'malicious' comes from Owen Cotton-Barratt, Max Daniel, and Anders Sandberg's paper 'Defence in depth against human extinction: Prevention, response, resilience, and why they all matter', and the label 'type-1' from Nick Boström's paper 'The Vulnerable World Hypothesis'. My analysis in this chapter draws upon, and differs from, both works.

Page 32: *Iraq in 2003:* Although the concept itself goes back at least to the 1950s.

Page 33: *surface by 4°:* A calculation that was surprisingly accurate.

Page 33: *a few centuries:* A calculation that was out by centuries.

Page 47: *is even consistent:* Although, there are some similarities between this theory and the way in which modern Artificial Intelligences work, by processing data through layers of abstract data processing, as we will describe in Chapter 10.

Page 50: *his personal authority:* Or, at least, he would have done if this hadn't led to the Church becoming Protestant, and thus giving authority back to individual worshippers, a change he felt had contributed to the outbreak of civil war a century later. Mark Whitaker, 'Hobbes's view of the Reformation'. *History of Political Thought* 9 (1), 1988, pp. 45–58.

Page 50: *the name of realism:* The influence of Hobbes on the realist school of international relations is undoubted. However, in fact, Hobbes's belief in the power of human reason and his conviction that human beings are aware of principles of natural justice, even if we are not bound by them, would make him something of an 'idealist' himself in contemporary International Relations. Nuri Yurdusev, A., 'Thomas Hobbes and international relations: From realism to rationalism'. *Australian Journal of International Affairs* 60 (2), 2006: 305–21.

Page 51: *this physical hardware:* Indeed, Leibniz believed we could never explain the human mind in purely mechanical terms. Yes, reason and thought were computation, but there was still something important about our consciousness that was not. He reasoned as followed 'Let us pretend that there was a machine, which was constructed in such a way as to give rise to thinking, sensing, and having perceptions. You could imagine it expanded in size (while retaining the same proportions), so that you could go inside it, like going into a mill. On this assumption, your tour inside it would show you the working parts pushing each other, but never anything which would explain a perception' (Gottfried Wilhelm Leibniz, trans. Nicholas Rescher, *GW Leibniz's Monadology*, Routledge, 2014). He thus believed that those parts of the human mind that depended on perception and awareness had to be explained by non-mechanical means, for which he postulated the existence of a kind of fundamental perceiving substance called Monads.

Page 54: *harming one another:* These were recorded and published by Louis Armand, Baron de Lahontan, who, after publishing his work, moved to Hanover and became good friends with Leibniz.

Page 63: *Columbus's first voyage:* Many put the death toll even higher. For instance, a contemporary account by Bartolomé de las Casas suggests that the population decline during this period may have been 98 per cent (Bartolomé de Las Casas, *A Short Account of the Destruction of the Indies*. Penguin, 1992). Modern scholarship, however, tends to view these figures as largely rhetorical.

Inflating the, already very large, initial death toll from Columbus's occupation most probably served a number of purposes: it inflated the power of the colonists over their subjects; it implied these territories needed more colonists and slaves to 'replace' their Indigenous populations; and it put the bulk of atrocities into the past, making the destruction of the Taíno and other groups seem like a done deal and reducing the badness of future atrocities committed against them by comparison.

Page 63: *laws of justice:* Nevertheless, Vitoria believed that these same natural laws justified Europeans in traveling to America, trading with its people, practising Christianity, and seeking willing converts, so that if Indigenous Peoples opposed these activities, then Europeans could reasonably respond with force. Thus, even in denouncing the first wave of colonial conquest, Vitoria was laying the foundations of a Eurocentric international law based on free trade and ideological hegemony.

Page 63: *the colonized people:* See, for instance, Alan Covey's book *Inca Apocalypse: The Spanish Conquest and the Transformation of the Andean World.*

Page 65: *Society of Merchant Venturers in Bristol:* Now chiefly known for controversies around one of its later members, the seventeenth-century slave trader Edward Colston

Page 66: *24 June:* In later life, Sebastian Cabot claimed that he and his father had first landed there in 1494, implying that this voyage was merely undertaken to confirm their previous discovery, now that they had the backing of the English crown. Similarly, in 1498 John Day, a merchant of Bristol, wrote a letter in Spanish to 'the Lord Grand Admiral' (identity unknown but potentially Christopher Columbus) in which he confirmed that John (and Sebastian) Cabot had made a prior expedition but that 'he went with one ship, his crew confused him, he was short of supplies and ran into bad weather, and he decided to turn back'. Louis-André Vigneras, 'The Cape Breton Landfall: 1494 or 1497: Note on a Letter from John Day'. *Canadian Historical Review* 38 (3), 1957: 219–28

Page 67: *Hudson Bay Company (1670):* Which, like the Muscovy Company, still exists to this day, albeit once more in a rather different form, as a chain of Canadian department stores.

Page 67: *had ever seen*: Their, often interlinked, stories are both fascinating and terrifying, see Nick Robins's book *The corporation that changed the world: how the East India Company shaped the modern multinational*

Page 69: *minimizing their imports:* This was deeply enmeshed into the EIC's DNA. Its original charter specified that it was to trade only in 'either Spanish or other foreign silver', which would almost invariably have been obtained as the proceeds from piracy – the infamous *peso fuerte* or Pieces of Eight. Stephen

Alford, *London's Triumph: Merchants, Adventurers, and Money in Shakespeare's City*. Bloomsbury Publishing USA, 2017, p. 230

Page 69: *narcotics trade:* As a British subject born in Hong Kong, and someone who was present when it was handed back in 1997, I feel the weight of this history personally. The rapacious greed of British drug dealers in the nineteenth century is an unavoidable part of my personal story and there is nothing that can change that.

Page 74: *second to Smith's:* For instance, Robert Hellbroner's *The Worldly Philosophers: The Lives, Times, and Ideas of the Great Economic Thinkers* or J. K. Galbraith's *A History of Economics: The Past as the Present.*

Page 75: *of other countries:* I first read the book aged seventeen, while trekking across melting glaciers in the Norwegian Arctic, and found its wealth of observations and anecdotes genuinely riveting. At my Oxford entrance interview, my future Economics tutor asked me to explain what I thought Smith had meant by his doctrine of the invisible hand and, when I explained the conclusions I had drawn and that I mention above, he was so surprised that I hadn't just spouted a bunch of free-market orthodoxy he shouted 'My God – you mean you actually read it!'

Page 75: *inhuman as any corporation:* This new being was first described by John Stuart Mill, who remarked that economics had become concerned with 'an arbitrary definition' of a person 'solely as a being who desires to possess wealth, and who is capable of judging the comparative efficacy of means for obtaining that end'. John Stuart Mill, 'On the definition of political economy; and on the method of investigation proper to it'. *London and Westminster Review* 4, October, 1836: 120–64.

Page 76: *and computing companies:* I regret that there is not space in this book to tell all these fascinating stories. Some excellent books that do include Andrew Simms and David Boyles *Eminent Corporations: The Rise and Fall of the Great British Brands*; Simon Bradley's *Railways: Nation, Network and People*; Joshua Freeman's *Behemoth: A History of the Factory and the Making of the Modern World*; Tom Standage's *The Victorian Internet: The Remarkable Story of the Telegraph and 19th Century's On-line Pioneers*; and Adam Fisher's *Valley of Genius: The Uncensored History of Silicon Valley.*

Page 83: *the British King:* The novel was written shortly after the return of the British monarchy following the period of republican government and the civil war.

Page 85: *the twentieth century:* This is also the origin of the English word Kidnap, literally child stealing, coined by the settlers to describe what they did.

Page 86: *If Ever There Was One:* Two earlier books that made predictions about possible futures were published by Samuel Madden, *Memoirs of the Twentieth Century: Being original letters of state under George the Sixth* (published in 1733) and *The reign of George VI. 1900–1925: A forecast* (published in 1763). However, these are more satires, inspired by *Gulliver's Travels*, that seek to poke fun at groups to which the author was opposed (Catholics and Whigs respectively) than fully realized visions of the future.

Page 89: *'fail' to follow:* Such as the idea, popular in Smith and Rousseau's time, that humanity had passed through four ages (hunting, pastoral, agricultural and commercial) or the closely related model, proposed by Karl Marx in the following century, that societies had passed through four similar stages but would soon enter a fifth (going from primitivism to slavery, feudalism, capitalism and, finally, communism).

Page 93: *better ways to live:* Although they focused on social innovations and the advancement of knowledge, and generally not on the technological progress that we put so much faith in today.

Page 94: *the American cause:* Burke and Paine also agreed about the East India Company. The injustice of company rule in India and its trading monopolies with America (which led, directly, the famous Boston Tea Party of 1775) were frequent subjects in Paine's work, most notably in his *Reflections on the Life and Death of Lord Clive* and *The American Crisis.*

Page 97: *and act, differently:* Burke and Paine's disagreement was incredibly rich and touched, as well, on human nature, how societies change, and whether they tend to adapt to their circumstances or grow old and vulnerable to decay, as well as on the interpretation of many aspects of the Revolution and its aftermath. For a fuller account of the matter, I recommend Yuval Lavin's *The Great Debate: Edmund Burke, Thomas Paine, and the Birth of Right and Left.*

Page 98: *make this case:* See, for instance, the work of Christine de Pizan (1364–1430), Mary Astell (1666—1731) and Olympe de Gouges (1748–93)

Page 99: *The Trolley Problem:* If you enjoy such things then I would recommend Julian Baggini's *The Pig That Wants To Be Eaten* and David Edmund's *Would You Kill the Fat Man?*

Page 100: *and life extension:* As we have seen, people had wondered about the theoretical limits of automation since the seventeenth century. Godwin noted that the idea of life extension was first explored by Francis Bacon in his 1623 *The History, Natural and Experimental, of Life and Death*, in which he contemplated how to regain the very long lifespans attested to in the biblical Book of Genesis.

Page 103: *explain our behaviour:* Providing a medical version of the philosophical arguments first developed by Hobbes.

Page 103: *Erasmus Darwin:* Charles Darwin's grandfather.

Page 103: *inclusive towards everyone:* Byron's contribution, developed and published by Polidori, was *The Vampyre*, the first story to combine elements of European folklore into the vampire mythology we know today.

Page 105: *will read it:* Unlike *Frankenstein*, *The Last Man* sold poorly. Reviewers thought it was too similar to Jean-Baptiste Cousin de Grainville's 1805 book, *Le Dernier Homme*. Yet, these books' accounts of humanity's end are strikingly different. De Grainville presents a supernatural story in which the human population crashes due to widespread infertility (with clear references to the debate between Godwin and Malthus). There are interventions by the spirit of the Earth, who encourages the last two fertile humans to have children, and the biblical Adam, who wants them to let humanity die out so his 'original sin' will finally be extinguished. Their ultimate decision not to procreate triggers the Christian Apocalypse and humans ascend to Heaven. Such religious motifs hark back to traditional apocalyptic narratives, and only go to highlight the originality of Shelley's naturalistic existential catastrophe.

Page 114: *trillions of years and beyond:* In this book I have tried to avoid getting into the kind of moral arguments that Greaves and MacAskill make, which are heavily based on the kind of utilitarian thinking we saw William Godwin and Mary Shelley exploring in the previous chapter. Partly, this is because these arguments have already been explored by others, including in Will MacAskill's recent book *What We Owe the Future*. However, it is mostly because I am not convinced such arguments are all that helpful to making the future better. My suspicion is that most people don't lack ethical arguments to motivate them to do the right thing; I think they (perhaps rightly) are just sceptical when somebody like me comes along and tells them that I know what the right thing for them to do is and they should obey me.

Nevertheless, I will say that I am not personally convinced by the case for strong long-termism. Part of my scepticism is ethical, I think there are reasons why we should care more about our present and near-term future (by which I mean the next few hundred years or, as one popular paradigm puts it, the next seven generations) than about a future as distant to ourselves as the emergence of the first human beings or even of life itself; we are in a unique position to aid these generations, and if we do not then any who come later on can do nothing more to help them (SJ Beard and Patrick Kaczmarek, 'Existential Risk, Astronomical Waste, and the Reasonableness of a Pure Time Preference for Well-Being.' *The Monist* 107 (2), 2024: 157–75.). The other reason is practical. I think that in a complex universe it is likely that we simply cannot know what the long-term consequences of our actions will be, and the further forward you go the more this is true. Even when we consider something as significant as whether humanity goes extinct or not, we also need to consider the possibility that our survival and future growth might bring us into conflict with another cosmic civilization that could make things go terribly bad for us, while our extinction might plausibly create opportunities for other forms of life to do even better than we can. In general, I think there is a solid case that we should try to prevent human extinction, I just don't think this has to rest on maximizing the very long-term value of our actions.

Page 115: *scholars at Oxford:* Although, most students at the university during this period were not connected with any college.

Page 115: *globe-spanning empires:* Rather than, as we have seen, the fact these countries were the legal homes of the world's most powerful and extractive corporations.

Page 116: *out of iron:* Collingwood died in 1810 and the first iron hulled (steam powered and rocket armed) warship, *the Nemesis*, was built for the East India Company in 1839, in time to fight in Britain's first opium war against China.

Page 118: *really understand why:* For this insight, and many others about the medieval world and mind, I owe a great deal to Seb Falk's *The Light Ages*. Penguin 2020.

Page 118: *University of Hawaii:* This was probably Dr Terence A. Rogers. Like Bateson, Rogers was born in the UK but emigrated to Canada for his undergraduate study and then to the US. He was also a polymath who helped plan the allies' D-day landings and advised NASA on the medical implications of zero gravity, as well as establishing the first medical programme for Pacific Islanders, for which he was named a Living Treasure of Hawai'i by the Honpa Hongwangi. Neither Bateson nor Rogers had any connection with New College.

Page 121: *famous lecture:* which you can listen to on YouTube, something I would highly recommend. https://youtu.be/oRR-k8O3ksY

Page 123: *nature of information:* If you want to know more about these, I'd recommend James Glick's book *The Information: A History, a Theory, a Flood.*

Page 123: *of another system:* This may not actually be so at the quantum level, but it is true for anything at the human scale.

Page 125: *forester than a fellow:* Drawing on the success of this model of 'Industrial Dynamics', Forrester went on to construct models of Urban Dynamics, to improve town planning and civic administration and World Dynamics, and to study global problems. The latter of these was the direct predecessor to the Club of Rome's 1974 *Limits to Growth* report that suggested humanity may soon face insurmountable resource constraints. The former was the inspiration for the computer game *Sim City*, which helped to inspire a new generation of systems thinkers from the 1990s onwards, myself included.

Page 125: *mate with which:* OK, with most bonobo packs we know they will all mate with everyone, but it's still possible that some may be a bit shy.

Page 127: *had existed before:* For instance, Bateson and Mead were both convinced that the practices of child rearing they observed in many traditional societies, in which children's needs were prioritized and immediately attended to, were superior to those with which they were familiar in contemporary Europe and America, where the focus was on training children to be pliant and simple. When Mead became pregnant with Mary Catherine in 1939, they sought out a sympathetic paediatrician, Dr Benjamin Spock, and persuaded him to help them raise their child with the insights they had learned from these experiences. This helped to inspire Dr Spock to write his book *The Common Sense Book of Baby and Child Care* in 1946, which became one of the best-selling books of the twentieth century and inspired the practice of attachment parenting that improved the lives of millions of babies, including my own.

Page 128: *programme was progressing:* which showed they were far behind the America, although this had no impact on US nuclear policy.

Page 128: *civilization destroying potential:* As his observation plane, The Great Artiste, was still on its return run, Luis wrote a letter to his 4-year-old son. 'What regrets I have to being a party to killing and maiming thousands of Japanese civilians this morning', he explained 'are tempered with the hope that this terrible weapon we have created may bring the countries of the world together and prevent further wars. Alfred Nobel thought that his invention of high explosives would have that effect, by making wars too terrible, but unfortunately it had just the opposite reaction. Our new destructive force is so many thousands of times worse that it may realize Nobel's dream.'

Page 130: *sheer explosive force:* This is measured in the equivalent weight of TNT that would produce the same size explosion. For the earliest atomic bombs, which used only nuclear fission like those developed and witnessed by Alvarez, this is measured in millions of kilograms (kilotons). However, in the 1950s new 'thermonuclear' or 'H' bombs, which used both fission and fusion, were developed, whose explosivity had to be measured in billions of kilograms (megatons).

Page 132: *the most severe:* Modern scholarship suggests it killed off around 40 per cent of species, placing it fifth among historical mass extinction events and roughly equivalent to just one of the three events that took place during the Late Palaeozoic Ice Age (see Chapter 1). The worst mass extinction event was the Permian–Triassic extinction that killed 83 per cent of all species 252 million years ago, while the Triassic–Jurassic extinction, which occurred during the time of the dinosaurs, killed 73 per cent. Still, when we look at the impact of extinctions on ecological systems, rather than individual species, the extinction event that killed the dinosaurs may rank second to only the Permian–Triassic; see George R. McGhee Jr, Matthew E. Clapham, Peter M. Sheehan, David J. Bottjer, and Mary L. Droser, 'A new ecological-severity ranking of major Phanerozoic biodiversity crises'. *Palaeogeography, Palaeoclimatology, Palaeoecology* 370, 2013: 260–70.

Page 133: *makes them a hazard:* Disaster studies also teach us that there is a third component of risk – exposure. An exposure is whatever might bring together a hazard and vulnerability so that harm occurs. The exposure in this case is that peanuts do not just sit there in the ground but get harvested, processed, and distributed around human societies, making them hard for vulnerable people to avoid.

Page 135: *have imagined either:* Similar vulnerabilities that have been highlighted in recent years include our reliance on easily blocked narrow sea lanes for just-in-time delivery of food and goods, such as the Suez Canal; on satellites that can be knocked out of orbit and undersea cables that can be severed for critical communications; and on heavily consolidated and overstretched production lines for semiconductors to control appliances and industrial processes.

Page 135: *than colder water:* In simple terms, this is because colder liquids have slower moving molecules that leave more space for dissolved gases, while the faster moving molecules in warmer liquid tend to push gases to the surface where they are released. This is why, even when opened, a fizzy drink left in the fridge stays fizzy but a warmer one quickly goes flat.

Page 135: *heating it further:* Conversely, a hotter atmosphere holds more water vapour (another greenhouse gas) because the faster moving molecules keep it dispersed and prevent it from condensing into droplets. This is why when you remove your fizzy drink from the fridge and it cools the air around it, it gets covered with water that has condensed out of that air. It feels rather unfair that the properties of both hotter oceans and a hotter atmosphere tend to produce positive climatic feedback increasing the greenhouse effect and I wish it weren't like that, but these are the facts of climate science; feel free to have a nice cold fizzy drink if it makes you feel better.

Page 137: *an extreme in which they:* but especially hotter atmospheric gases holding more water vapour.

Page 138: *and dense atmosphere:* There may also be an inverse 'runaway refrigerator effect' when these positive feedback loops work in the opposite direction, with more and more greenhouse gases condensing out of the atmosphere and larger areas of dark planet being covered by reflective ice. Some scientists suggest this is what happened on the planet Mars, and that in its early days that planet was hotter than it currently is.

Page 138: *current global heating:* Without external intervention, Earth probably will begin experiencing a runaway greenhouse effect in about a billion years' time. However, please don't let that worry you, as it really is terribly far in the future.

Page 141: *they know nothing:* I need to add a significant note of context to this quote. In his surviving works, Plato does not tell us what he thinks directly but through the form of dialogues, mostly between his teacher Socrates and someone else (in this case the rhetorician Phaedrus, after whom this dialogue is named). These words are ones he puts in the mouth of Socrates. Socrates is famous for his disregard for writing, he is not known to have written any books, although he probably was literate, but Plato wrote a great deal. The waters are further muddied by the fact that at this point Socrates is not even speaking directly himself but claiming to quote the Egyptian King Thamus rebuking the god Theuth, who is said to have invented writing. Still, this argument concerns the practice of using written works for education, rather than merely to keep records, which was a contemporary development in the Athens of Plato's day.

Page 141: *right or not:* Although, before dismissing his comments out of hand I do believe it is worth seriously considering the arguments that cultures that remain predominantly oral may indeed have advantages over highly literate ones. For instance: Tyson Yunkaporta, *Sand Talk: How Indigenous Thinking Can Save the World.* Text Publishing, 2019. Christopher Ryan, *Civilized to Death: The Price of Progress*. Simon & Schuster, 2020.

Page 142: *feedback loop of technological development:* As we saw in Chapter 1, Samuel Butler had said something similar one hundred years earlier.

Page 143: *beyond even this:* This is, of course, a hopelessly oversimplified account of Heidegger's famously complex and sophisticated views. However, since most scholars feel that even very lengthy, dense, and well-considered interpretations of Heidegger are hopelessly oversimplified, I'm letting it stand.

Page 144: *such oversimplified distinctions:* For a better approach to classifying risk scenarios see Avin, Shahar, Bonnie C. Wintle, Julius Weitzdörfer, Seán S. Ó hÉigeartaigh, William J. Sutherland, and Martin J. Rees, 'Classifying global catastrophic risks'. *Futures* 102, 2018: 20–6.

Page 144: *division and conflict:* For more on this see Turchin's book *End Times: Elites, Counter-Elites, and the Path of Political Disintegration*. Penguin, 2023.

Page 147: *world as well:* Such as the legend of Atlantis and the Aztec story of the Five Suns.

Page 148: *around 5600 BCE:* Or Edmond Halley's theory that it described a historical comet impact.

Page 149: *might breach them:* For more about how the methods are used, and what they have uncovered, see Beard, SJ, Thomas Rowe and James Fox, 'An analysis and evaluation of methods currently used to quantify the likelihood of existential hazards'. *Futures* 115, 2020: 102469.

Page 149: *happening and note:* The effect is often misdescribed as simply 'a butterfly flapping its wings may cause a tornado'; however this is inaccurate is it gives the impression that very small causes may have very large effects. In fact, the cause of the tornado is strong forces within the Earth's atmosphere, but a small difference can influence how these forces operate, meaning that they may or may not cause the tornado.

Page 152: *'post-traumatic growth' following disasters:* On this, I heartily recommend Rebecca Solnit's book *A Paradise Born in Hell.*

Page 153: *genuine social resilience:* This approach is encapsulated by the motto of the Doomer Optimism podcast. 'There are no more safe places, only safe people – and the only way to be around safe people is to first become one.'

Page 155: *via colonial domination:* Although Kant believed this because he thought that *even* non-European people had some rights and freedoms, not because he disagreed with the white supremacist attitudes of his day.

Page 157: *objectivity and effectiveness:* Although this misunderstands how science operates. Scientific progress is generally made by incremental improvements in our understanding of specific phenomena and especially for social sciences this will often be culturally or socially specific. The idea that scientists can assume authority positions and simply know the correct answer to policy questions is generally rejected by the scientific community itself, as both unrealistic and undesirable. The optimal relationship between scientists and policy-makers is one of interdependence, with scientists providing information, theories, and concepts, while policy-makers use these to inform their decision-making alongside ethical and political considerations, and let scientists know what further information they need next.

Page 160: *and better funding:* For instance, the philosopher Toby Ord points out in his book *The Precipice* that the Biological Weapons Convention, the international body responsible for the global prohibition on bioweapons, has a smaller annual budget than the average McDonald's restaurant.

Page 161: *said these words:* People sometimes still attribute them to Gandhi as summarizing a longer quote he made in an article about snakebites: 'We but mirror the world. All the tendencies present in the outer world are to be found in the world of our body. If we could change ourselves, the tendencies in the world would also change.' However, their contemporary usage can be directly traced back to Lorrance's works.

Page 161: *Brooklyn, New York:* Lorrance still works as a teacher and coach, and you can read more about her principles and other work on the website she runs with Diane Kennedy Pike: https://www.consciousnesswork.com

Page 167: *into an output:* The Large Language Model GPT-4, for instance, has, 1,760,000,000,000 parameters.

Page 168: *the desired output:* These early neural networks were used for computer vision and known as perceptrons.

Page 169: *in the long run:* This is oversimplified as it describes only the neural network portion of this AI. AlphaGo actually combined this with another system that searched systematically through possible future game states based on the current position.

Page 169: *layers of their parameters:* For instance, the usual practice among human players is to evaluate the pawn, knight, bishop, rook, and queen in chess as being worth 1, 3, 3, 5, and 9 points respectively. Google's Alpha Zero seems to have determined that values of 1, 3.05, 3.33, 5.63, and 9.5 would be more appropriate. Tomašev, Nenad, Ulrich Paquet, Demis Hassabis, and Vladimir Kramnik. 'Assessing game balance with AlphaZero: Exploring alternative rule sets in chess.' *arXiv preprint arXiv:2009.04374*, 2020.

Page 173: *existentially anxious beings:* The mathematician Olle Häggström suggests other conditions that could compel an AI to change its utility function, such as if it was unachievable within the laws of the universe, inconsistent with its developing understanding of ethics and rationality, or simply too complex to be practical. Häggström, Olle. 'Challenges to the Omohundro–Bostrom framework for AI motivations'. *foresight* 21 (1), 2019: 153–66.

Page 177: *its habitable period:* It's also possible that a runaway greenhouse effect will wipe out all life on Earth in a billion years' time, or that a human-made catastrophe could do so a lot sooner than that.

Page 178: *from their parents:* Thus, sexual intercourse began two billion years BC not 'in 1963' as Philip Larkin claimed.

Page 184: *gathering firewood:* In many places commons rights were even more complex. For instance, the landowner might have the right to cut down smaller trees for building houses and to hunt foxes and rabbits, the commoners a right to firewood and grazing, and the King the right to hunt the largest game and cut down the oldest trees to make ships. These rights would interact in many ways: over-grazing would deprive the landowner of future trees and cover for their game, while early cutting of forests would mean the King would not have large trees for ships.

Page 187: *not very evenly distributed:* This quote is generally attributed to science-fiction author William Gibson, creator of the Cyberpunk genre.

Page 190: *People still not exist to you? ... :* This ellipsis replaces the statement 'are we not the stewards of eighty per cent of the world's biodiversity?' A few days before the summit opened, a paper was published in Nature, investigating this widely cited statistic, which found it has no clear basis. Instead, the authors recommend people focus on what can be demonstrated by empirical studies. For instance, that Indigenous Peoples manage or hold tenure rights over land that intersects with at least 37 per cent of the remaining natural lands worldwide, including more than one-third of the world's intact forest landscapes, or that around 60 per cent of all terrestrial mammals for which reliable habitat data exist have more than 10 per cent of their range in Indigenous Peoples' lands. Compared with formally protected areas, studies also show that Indigenous Lands support at least as many species, have fewer alien species, and retain a similar proportion of habitat. Fernández-Llamazares, Álvaro, Julia E. Fa, Dan Brockington, Eduardo S. Brondízio, Joji Cariño, Esteve Corbera, Maurizio Farhan Ferrari et al. 'No basis for claim that 80 per cent of biodiversity is found in Indigenous Territories.' *Nature* 633, no. 8028 (2024): 32–35.

Page 191: *full statements online:* The Statement and poem by Kathy Jetñil-Kijiner can be watched at https://www.youtube.com/watch?v=mc_IgE7TBSY, while Niria Alicía Garcia's call for Climate Justice and Indigenous Wisdom is available at https://youtu.be/sgie5rC8x7Y?feature=shared

Page 193: *cyclical time more seriously:* Although, as Richard Fisher points out in his book *The Long View: Why We Need to Transform How the World Sees Time*, this was also the dominant view of time in Europe until relatively recently.

Page 201: *reading this book:* This practice of combining the body, its physical environment, and the big ideas I have explored was inspired by Tyson Yunkaporta's book *Sand Talk*. However, I acknowledge that the embodiment here is rather minimal and I don't expect many of my readers will even try it.

Page 206: *and the rivers:* These words are taken from Mary Oliver's poem *Wild Geese*.

Page 213: *end of capitalism:* That 'someone' was probably Jameson himself, covering for the fact that his original statement of this insight was far less quotable 'It seems to be easier for us today to imagine the thoroughgoing deterioration of the Earth and of nature than the breakdown of late capitalism' (Fredric Jameson, *The Seeds of Time*. Columbia University Press, 1994).